JUST CALL ME MICKEY

ALSO BY WINT CAPEL

A Recent History of Thomasville 1952-1991
and
Thomasville 1852-2002, A History of City Government

On the Square: A Biography of Distinguished Thomasville Citizen George L. Hundley

Dethronement of Reason

The Good Doctor's Downfall:
Documentation of the 1921 Murder of Thomasville Police Chief by Dr. J. W. Peacock

The Wit and Wisdom of O.J. (Skipper) Coffin,
First Dean of UNC School of Journalism

Fiery Fastballer:
The Life of World Series Pitcher Johnny Allen.

In Words and Pictures: Thomasville in the Nineteen-Twenties

JUST CALL ME MICKEY

From Mill Village to Mills Home,
The Journey of Michael C. Blackwell

by Wint Capel

Jim Edminson
Coordinating Editor

2006
Parkway Publishers, Inc
Boone, North Carolina

Parkway Publishers, Inc.
P.O. Box 3678
Boone, North Carolina 28607

Library of Congress Cataloging-in-Publication Data

Capel, Wint.
  Just call me Mickey : from mill village to Mills
Home, the journey of Michael C. Blackwell / by Wint Capel.

     p. cm.

  Includes index.

  ISBN 1-933251-18-2
    1. Blackwell, Michael C. 2. Southern Baptist Convention--North Carolina--Clergy--Biography. 3.
Baptist Children's Homes of North Carolina, Inc.--Presidents--Biography. I. Title.

  BX6495.B59C37 2005
  286'.1'092--dc22   2005020500

Jacket and book design:
Jim Edminson/BCH Communications

DEDICATION

To Kathy Kanipe Blackwell

CONTENTS

Acknowledgments

Introduction

About the Author

Index

ACKNOWLEDGMENTS

A book is the sum of those who make it happen. Thus, a heartfelt thanks is offered in memory
to Wint Capel for his determination to see the project to completion despite the onset of cancer while he was writing.
He completed the manuscript before his death in 2005. His tenacity with interviews and research is evident on every page.
Wint would want to thank the subject of the book — Michael C. (Mickey) Blackwell — for the many hours he spent
opening his life and his archives to the author.

Earl T. Groves of Gastonia, N.C. deserves special thanks for the many hours he spent writing —
exclusively for this book — a history of the local textile industry, in which his family played a prominent role.

Two of Michael Blackwell's college classmates offered insights and valuable assistance. Jim Wallace, who chronicled
the Chapel Hill civil rights movement in photographs, graciously permitted use of several of his copyrighted pictures. Karen Parker,
the first African-American woman to receive an undergraduate degree from UNC-Chapel Hill, not only shared her friendship
with Mickey, but, as a professional journalist, assisted in editing and proofreading the book.

Michael's intrepid brother-in-law, Bob Denham, also assisted with the copy-editing.

To all who gave time to Wint Capel when he called for verification or clarification,
is hereby expressed sincere gratitude.

The Broyhill Family Foundation of Lenoir, N.C., awarded a grant to support the wider distribution of the book.

It was my privilege to lead in producing the book. I know the subject of the book
as "Dr. Blackwell" or "Boss," but most of all as "Friend."

— Jim Edminson
Coordinating Editor

INTRODUCTION
by Norman Jameson

Your first thought upon meeting Michael C. Blackwell won't be to call him Mickey. Not that there's anything wrong with it.

A little boy's moniker, however, simply does not fit a man as physically and professionally imposing as Michael C. Blackwell. When he offers his hand and speaks his introduction, you believe you hear the voice that dictated to Moses on Mt. Sinai.

I first heard "the pipes of God" from halfway across the continent when Michael called to see if I had interest in becoming his director of communications. I was associate editor of a very large weekly Baptist newspaper in Oklahoma and doubted a "children's home" in North Carolina would hold much professional challenge.

He asked me at least to "come take a look." I was so impressed with the scope of the work and the depth of the man that I moved my young family to North Carolina to embrace the challenge. We worked together 12 of Michael's first 17 years at the helm.

No journalist — including me — is easily impressed with "personalities." I've met presidents, interviewed governors, photographed international disasters, asked for support from multi-millionaires, and been to three county fairs and a hog killin', so it takes a lot to impress. Similarly, Wint Capel spent his career sorting the wheat from the chaff as a journalist, retiring as editor of the daily *Thomasville Times*. I was surprised — and pleased — to learn Wint was writing a biography of a Thomasville "outsider." I'm also grateful he finished the manuscript before his death in February, 2005.

Between the two of us, we have enough professional skepticism to keep from being enamored of anyone short of Mother Teresa. That said, Michael Blackwell's is a life worth examining.

His life is testament to the power of influence — the influence of a loving family, interested teachers, committed church staff. With the help of those influences, and his own drive, Michael grew from a boy on "mill hill" to a man whose opinions and endorsements are sought

by North Carolina's most influential people.

From a textile townie to president of an institution with national reputation, to a bank board, to leadership of a regional political organization. to becoming a name on every list for certain government positions where leadership, strength, presence, and vision are requirements, Blackwell has grown beyond his early environment.

Just Call Me Mickey reveals many details about the man that were pleasant surprises to me, although I've spent many hours with Michael. This is not a warts-and-all biography. But neither is it a sycophantic paean.

It was a pleasure to see revealed from Wint's extensive interviews parts of Michael's private character that make his public presence all the more impressive.

Michael has always been "hard-wired for work," as must be presidents of major institutions. That wiring was soldered early as Michael worked from the time he was a child. While he did not grow up hungry, he did grow up poor. He carried his weight early, selling papers, spinning records. He was so successful working his way through college that he started to repay his parents for their meager help before he finished.

Additionally, something in his character took shape early that said artificial barriers between races are wrong. He tried to raise attention to the issue by drinking from a "colored" fountain and sitting in the "colored" section in the movie theater. In college, he befriended a classmate who might have been one of the loneliest persons on campus — the first black woman to graduate from UNC.

The pinnacle of time affords a long view of how seemingly unrelated elements of life fall together to become the essential building blocks for a particular task. Michael Blackwell's early studies, hobbies, jobs, and career choices never seemed, in the midst of them, the bricks for his foundation.

Those wondering how to choose a life path that will lead to

a responsible, important, satisfying career should note that Blackwell's early choices did not obviously lead to his current destination. Their common denominator though, is that each resulted from following his rabid interests and passion.

His parents encouraged him to pursue his interests, and his loving father was his severest radio critic. Michael and rock 'n' roll music burst into community consciousness at the same time. In the same way, he burst onto North Carolina Baptist institutional life just when times were changing in the way communities cared for abused and neglected children. He seems always to have found a way to bring his talents to bear at the fulcrum of new opportunity.

Two and a half decades after "Mickey's Record Shop" made him the most popular radio personality in Gastonia — at the age of 16 — the experiences of his life melded with passion and opportunity just when Baptist Children's Homes of North Carolina needed a strong hand at the helm.

Only the momentum built in the past century continued to move the venerable institution forward. Few of even its most ardent supporters realized the ship was slowing in the water and could soon start to list.

Baptist Children's Homes needed a man who could become the face of the institution, who could carry the banner for children into every church and community and department of social services in the state, who could raise the profile of an institution growing hoary and make it young and vibrant again.

It would never be challenge enough for a Michael Blackwell to ride out a cresting wave. So immediately, he put new challenges before the staff and supporters. Instead of nursing the institution, he kicked it out of bed and made it run. Today Baptist Children's Homes is not "that grand old institution" but that "leading-edge child and family care environment" that is innovating for its peers.

Michael nurses his own demons. His weight rides up and down more than an amusement park roller coaster. Food is comfort during stress and, while he is a calm duck on the surface, he's paddling a lot

harder than people realize. And his confidence needs regular boosting because he measures his achievements not in what he has accomplished, but in the enormity of what remains.

It is telling that on his last visit to the boyhood pastor who led him to Christian faith — at a time when he already was president of BCH — Blackwell asked this personal hero, "How am I doing?" Like all of us, he needs to hear it.

I've never called Michael "Mickey" and never will. I was one of the few staff members who did not normally call him Dr. Blackwell. "Michael" seemed to me a nice balance of professional respect and personal familiarity.

But, as you will read in the pages following, Michael C., the pastor; or C. Michael, the radio personality, or Michael the friend, or Dr. Michael C. Blackwell, the national forum professional, is Mickey — by any other name.

Norman Jameson is the Executive Leader of Public Relations and Resource Development for the Baptist State Convention of North Carolina.

JUST CALL
ME MICKEY

"He had a good voice, a good radio presence.
He handled himself well. He played popular records
that would appeal to the kids of the time. I remember
people liked him, and he got a lot of mail."

CHAPTER ONE – *A Rockin' Debut*

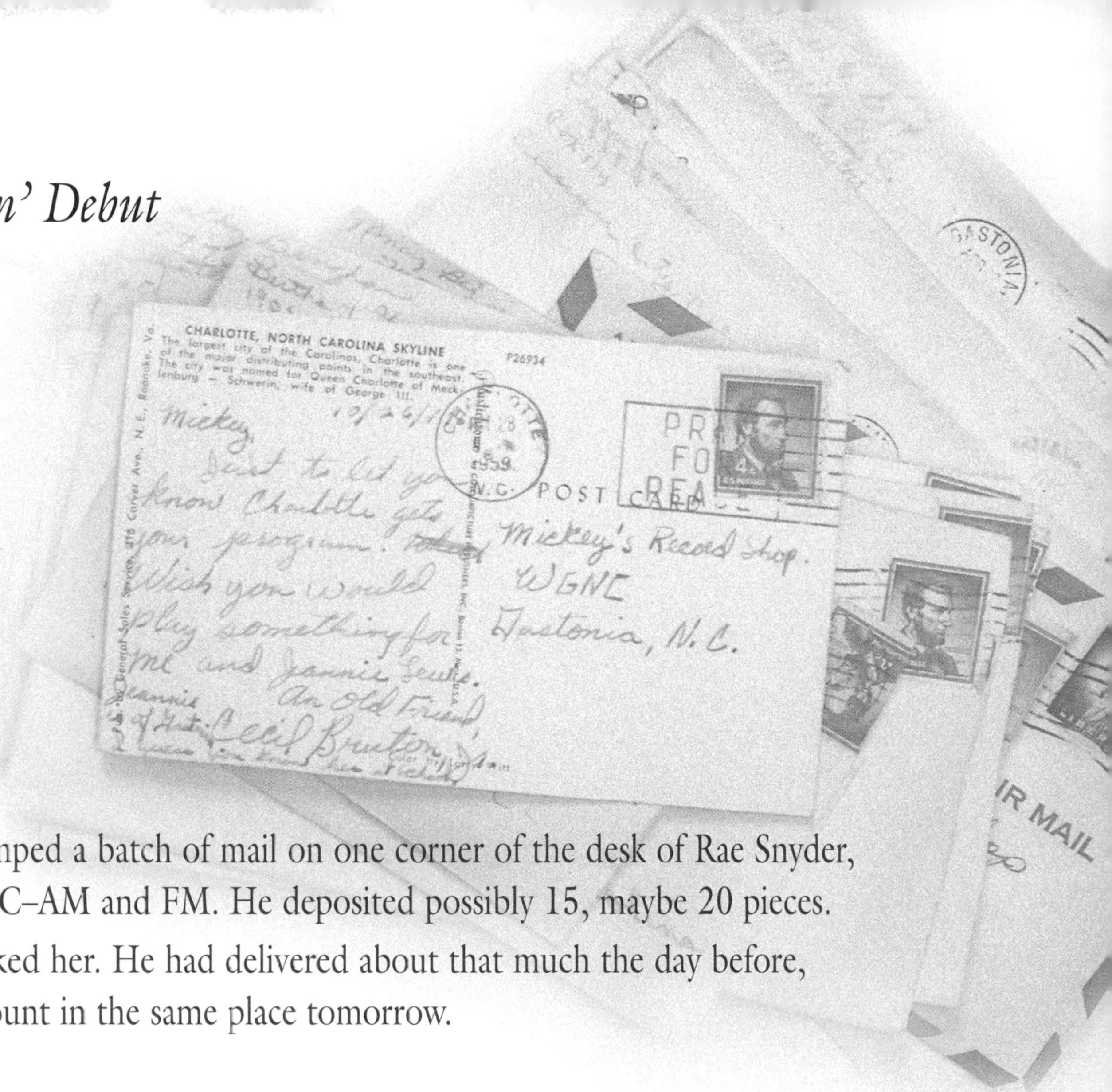

The postman trudged in and dumped a batch of mail on one corner of the desk of Rae Snyder, the secretary at Radio Station WGNC–AM and FM. He deposited possibly 15, maybe 20 pieces.

"What is all that, anyway?" he asked her. He had delivered about that much the day before, and probably would leave a like amount in the same place tomorrow.

"What it is, Sam, is fan mail."

"Well, in that case, I'd say y'all must be doing something right."

"Not us. Him," she corrected. "Him," she pointed out, was the kid over at the high school. "Mickey."

Mickey Blackwell, prodigy disc jockey.

Sixteen-year-old disc jockey Mickey Blackwell at WGNC AM-FM, Gastonia, N.C.

It was all quite predictable, the volume of mail and what the senders had in mind. Sometimes they wrote on a three-cent postcard but usually in the envelopes with a four-cent stamp were sheets of paper of many descriptions, usually written in pencil, and in longhand not always easy to decipher — letters that invariably began, "Dear Mickey, will you please play . . . "

Mickey was only 16 and was already the most popular radio personality in Gastonia, a textiles stronghold in the Piedmont of North Carolina. A feature story in Gastonia's daily newspaper noted that he had started out as possibly the youngest disc jockey in the country. His fan mail was pouring in at the rate of 50 cards and letters a week. Mickey relished every one, read every one, and did his best to comply with the request in every one.

Each weekday afternoon at the end of his last class at Gastonia's Ashley High, where he was a junior, he would double-time it to the station, scoop up his mail, and promptly

begin preparations for yet another broadcast. At 4:30 on the dot, he would take to the airways with, "Hey everybody, welcome to Mickey's Record Shop." For the next hour and a half, he would read a letter and then spin a record, usually the one the letter-writer wanted to hear. It was an all-request show. No phone calls, please. Requests-by-mail only.

WGNC-AM was only 250 watts, but its FM mate, or Mickey's outlet, projected a powerful signal at 11,100 watts. Mickey's missives arrived from as far away as Durham, 175 miles to the east. Some were from adults, but the vast majority were mailed by listeners who spoke Mickey's language and were crazy about his kind of music — the teenagers in Gaston County. His listeners couldn't see that he was tall, rather handsome, stylish, with flashing eyes, a bundle of energy,

1959
CHRISTMAS
MERCHANDISE SECTION
Begins on page 57

The Billboard

PRICE: 50 CENTS

LEADING NEWSWEEKLY (ABC)

nent Exhibits

but they loved his glib patter, his rich, warm, authoritative baritone. He sounded grown-up, not like a kid.

His kind of music was one with a decidedly different sound. Loud and sassy. A driving beat. With an odd name, rock and roll. It began

Downtown Gastonia

breaking into radio across the South about the time Mickey debuted at WGNC. He rode its intoxicating spiral upward in popularity. Young people celebrated how it made them want to dance. They were drawn to it no less than their elders were driven from it.

Mickey was at WGNC from the fall of 1957 until the summer of 1960, or until making ready to leave for college. The birth of rock and roll occurred July 5, 1954, when Elvis Presley recorded "That's All Right" at Sun Records in Memphis. Rock and roll was the dominant strain of American popular music throughout the '60s. It began to hit its stride when Bill Haley and his Comets came up with "Rock Around the Clock," the first legitimate rock and roll recording to make it to the top of the national pop music charts. Then, of course, there appeared Elvis Presley, Chuck Berry, Jerry Lee Lewis, Little Richard, and others, whose music held sway until the emergence of the Beatles in the mid-1960s. Along with Bob Dylan, the Beatles ushered in a form of music (some called it simply "rock") oriented more toward concerts than dance and linguistically and thematically sophisticated and complex.

Each week, Mickey would read *Billboard* magazine, the

bible of popular music, to help him make sure the station had every record on the *Billboard* Top 100 list in stock in order to cover almost any request, including those that were written in pig Latin. "Hello to Emily," he would say into the microphone, after having disposed of another commercial. "Hope you're listening. Got your letter, and I'm tickled I can play the record you asked for, 'Rave On,' by Buddy Holly, which you want dedicated to that special guy who's caught your eye . . ." And so it went.

Sometimes he had a guest. In September 1959, one was an Ashley High schoolmate, a foreign exchange student, Grethe Bisgaard from Randers, Denmark. She described how her native land was different

WEDNESDAY, SEPTEMBER 16, 1959

GRETHE ON THE AIR

Grethe Bisgaard, the foreign exchange student from Randers, Denmark, was a guest on Mickey Blackwell's radio program Tuesday, Mickey's Record Shop" over Station WGNC. Grethe talked with her fellow students and discussed her native land, how it differs from Gastonia, and other things of interest. Only one question stumped her—"How is the Danish pastry?" She had never heard of it.

from Gastonia. Only one of Mickey's questions stumped her: "How is the Danish pastry over there?" She had never heard of such a thing.

If he came across as a pro, it was because he was one. He was making a dollar an hour and had been spinning records on the air since age 14. Even before that, he had occasionally indulged his dream of breaking into broadcasting. A Charlotte station, WBTV, began television broadcasts in July 1949. A brand-new Truetone TV set at the Blackwell residence picked them up. Some afternoons, Mickey, while the set was on, would plant himself in the semblance of a broadcasting booth he had fashioned from a box, a chair, and a card table. As a telecast came to an end, he would turn down the set's volume and say into a make-believe microphone, "This is station WBTV, Channel 3, Charlotte. The time is 4:30." Then he would turn up the volume and watch what came next. His father, a part-time choir director who knew

Mickey with his father on 1959 vacation in Miami Beach

a thing or two about voices, could clearly see that his son was blessed with one that might help him succeed in any number of areas. So he would sit down with Mickey and have him read from a book or newspaper into the microphone of

a Wallensack tape recorder. After that he would play the tape and suggest how and where Mickey might improve on his elocution. Mickey considered his dad "my severest critic" but a great teacher. His dad hoped that he was training an offspring to be a senator or a judge. He couldn't imagine his son becoming a radio announcer enamored

Blackwell and co-thespian practice for the play "Seventeen."

of rock and roll.

When only 14, Mickey wrote the winning answer to a contest question, "Why I want to be a guest deejay on WLTC." That entitled him to appear one afternoon with Frank Thomas to help play records on the Thomas Show, a daily feature on WLTC, the other Gastonia station (1,000 watts, daytime only). What he experienced was exhilarating. It made him more certain that a career in broadcasting was what he should be working toward.

He biked the two miles back to the station several times to watch how a program was produced, to see what was expected of an announcer, and to study the dials on "the board." Station personnel were tolerant of a youngster whose potential was so obvious. When there seemed no end to his hanging around, he was surprised with an offer, his own show — with no pay — which he snapped up. So in December 1956, "Platter Party," with ninth-grader Mickey Blackwell as host, became

5

part of WLTC's regular programming. Mickey played records virtually unassisted from 2 to 4 o'clock each Saturday afternoon. The very first record he put on the air was "Ka Ding Dong" by the Hilltoppers. He made a go of it. He clicked. His performance was rewarded with more airtime. "Platter Party" also was allotted an identical time slot on Sunday afternoons. This went on through his ninth-grade year at school. All the time without a payday.

When word got around in June of 1957 that an announcer was leaving the station across town, WGNC, Mickey, hoping to improve his lot, knocked on the door there. Pat McSwain owned the station and its sister, WGNC-FM. Mickey "came out to the radio station and asked for a job," McSwain recalled years later. "I talked to him, gave him something to read, and talked to him so he had to give long answers to see how he would talk without a script, and he impressed me. He was quite

Blackwell, sitting on steps, practices for a community theater production of "Seventeen."

a success [at WGNC], considering his lack of experience and youth at the time."

McSwain added: "He had a good voice, a good radio presence. He handled himself well. He played popular records that would appeal to the kids of the time. I remember people liked him, and he got a lot of mail."

Would he work for a dollar an hour? You bet. His duty at first was to assist staff announcers and run errands. Several months went by before he was offered his own show.

The cards and letters kept piling up as long as "Mickey's Record Shop" was open. Its record-spinner didn't close it down until he needed time to complete arrangements to depart for college, where

Mickey Blackwell, 1960

he hoped to find new adventures in the field of communications. With a heavy heart, he bade his faithful listeners goodbye, leaving the title of Gastonia's top radio personality for someone else to claim. On that last day, he tuned himself out by playing, in its entirety, the Record Shop theme: "Rudy's Rock" by Bill Haley and the Comets.

He had saved all his listeners' requests and had them with him when he left the station for the last time. In his two-and-a-half years at WGNC, he had received one raise — to $1.10 an hour.

There were more tears and hugs at his church, Flint-Groves Baptist, where he had been active and an inspiration to many of its members. His pastor, the Rev. Wilburn Hendrix, advised him to consider studying to become a minister. Mickey replied, "No. Pastor Hendrix, my career is in radio."

* * *

Mickey carried his boxes of fan mail home. He wasn't sure why or what to do with them. He stored them away, then lost track of them.

In 1998, during Thanksgiving holidays, he was in Charlotte briefly. One thing he did while there was to clean out the attic of his in-laws' old house. In a corner, to his great surprise and delight, he found the boxes of fan mail. Then he remembered. They had been in a shed at the back of the family home in Gastonia for years. They had been moved to Charlotte and tucked away again after he got married.

The night of the day of discovery, he spent several hours reading one letter after another. It was great fun. Many memories came roaring back. He could remember some of the senders: "I mean, you just go back. I could see myself behind the microphone opening them. It was such a good time." He has yet to forsake rock and roll music.

Also included in what he uncovered were copies of *The Gastonia Gazette* and *Billboard* with dates of 1958 and 1959. He re-read some of those.

Nothing was thrown away. He still has all of it in storage where he lives now. He doesn't know why he still hangs on to it. Maybe it will be of some use should he ever decide to write about a period in his life that is unquestionably among the happiest.

TWO

Here's the cast of the senior class play. "Mountain
to right, Sandra Hatcher, Marshall Turner, Mickey Blackw
Further, Seated, Jane Francum and Donna Bradshaw.

CURTAI

**SENIOR PLAY
OPENS TONIGHT**

—BY MARCIA HOLLAND—
(High School Reporter)
"Mountain Gal," a three-act
comedy about hillbillies, is being
presented three times Thursday
and Friday by the Ashley High
School senior class.

AN ART CRAFT PLAY

Mickey Blackwell

Mountain Gal

A HILLBILLY COMEDY IN THREE ACTS

✦ ✦ ✦

By

B. E. MITCHELL
AND
LE ROMA GRETH

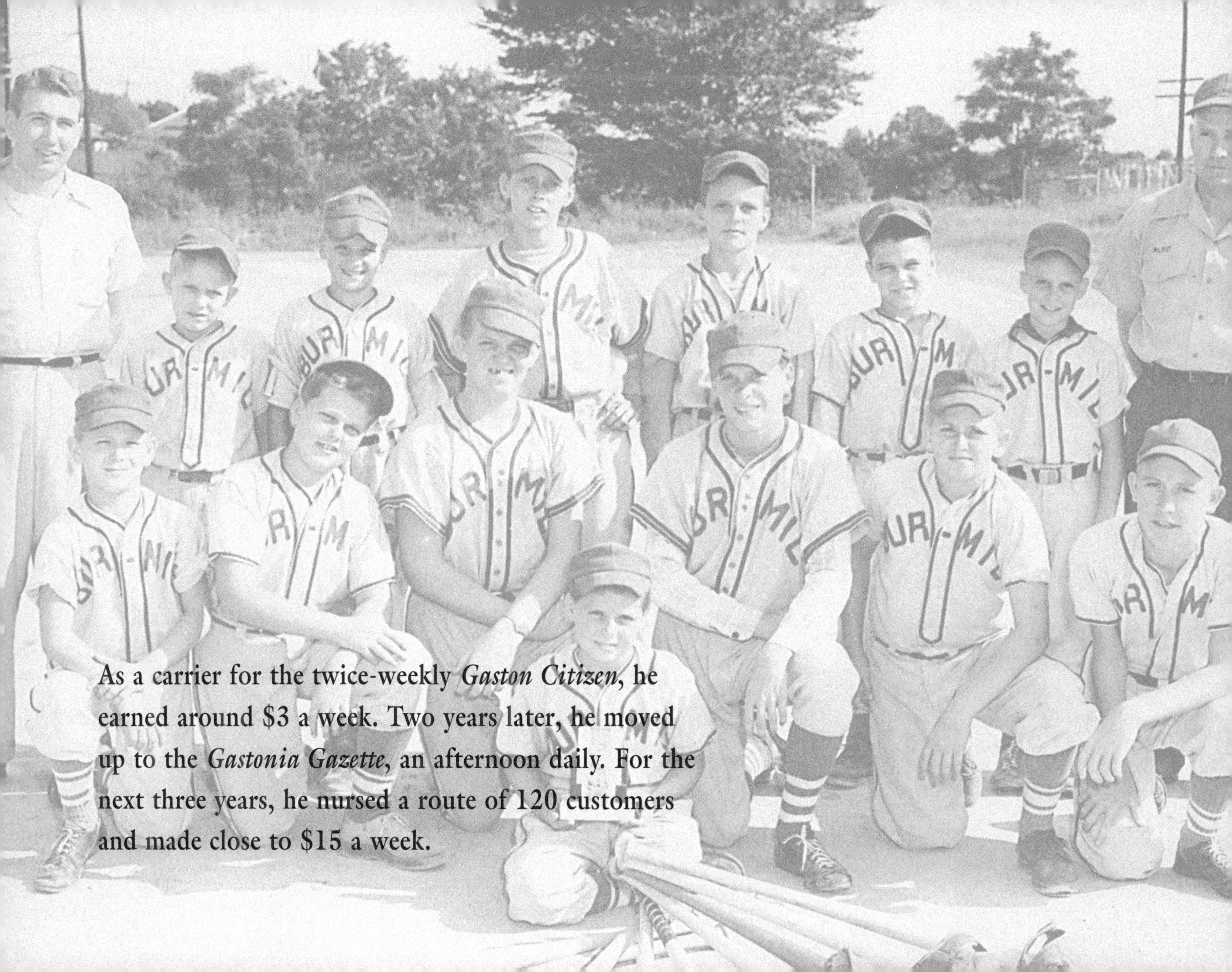

As a carrier for the twice-weekly *Gaston Citizen*, he earned around $3 a week. Two years later, he moved up to the *Gastonia Gazette*, an afternoon daily. For the next three years, he nursed a route of 120 customers and made close to $15 a week.

CHAPTER TWO – *Their Only Child*

Snapshots filled the table, telling the short version of the story of the arrival of the long-awaited son. Healthy baby, thankful mother, beaming father looking out from timeworn photos.

"Yessir, a big, fine male child — weight eight pounds, length 22 inches, chest 13 inches." Clitus shared his news with friends and well-wishers in Kings Mountain. Pictures passed around showed the newest Blackwell starring in every one of the hundred snaps — icing on the cake of a family montage.

The longer version of the tale began when the mother left home for her own mother's home to benefit from the comfort and assistance available there from her family doctor, Charles Sanders. Father saw his wife off to Gaffney, less than an hour's drive across the North Carolina/South Carolina line.

"Just think, when you come home, we'll be a whole new family," Clitus smiled, encouraging his tearful wife. His words were prophetic. A week later, new baby and new mom checked out of the Cherokee County Hospital to reunite with father-husband.

So Mickey was, very briefly, a South Carolinian. He was born in the Palmetto State on Sunday, May 3, 1942, at 11:55 p.m.

The family also lived, for a brief time, in Belmont, then moved to Gastonia, the last stop for the parents and where Mickey lived until he went off to college.

(Left to right) Clitus and Viola met at a party in Gaffney, S.C., and it was love at first sight. Six years after they were married in 1936, Mickey was born. The bond between father and son was lifelong.

The full title of the new baby was Michael Clitus Blackwell. His father was named Clitus (often misspelled as the more popular Cletus), Clitus Shelly Blackwell, that is. Mickey's mother was Edith Viola Maness.

Mickey would be their only child. Viola's experience with the birthing process discouraged her from having other children. Before Mickey's arrival, she had vomited every single morning for nine months.

Both Clitus and Viola had humble beginnings. Both were born in South Carolina. Clitus started out in Campobello on March 15, 1909, the ninth of the 13 children of Marion Belton Blackwell (1870-1937) and Hester Dockery Blackwell (1876-1946). He was the only one of the 13 to obtain a high school diploma, and he didn't get his until he was 21 years old.

The Blackwell forefathers were Britons.

Clitus met Viola, four years his junior, at a party one night. Clitus was smitten immediately! "You're the girl I'm going to marry," he announced; and he did, May 23, 1936, in Gaffney, the bride's hometown. He was 27. She was 23.

Her birth occurred in Winnsboro on February 9, 1913, a daughter of Roland Samuel Maness (1881-1928) and Katie Estelle Ramsey Maness (1886-1959). She had three brothers and one sister. When in the eighth grade, her father died. She then dropped out of school, to help her mother, and did not go back.

Mickey had made his appearance soon after this country had been drawn into devastating, far-flung warfare. His father, having passed his 32nd birthday, was not draft-eligible and, therefore, was spared military duty.

Clitus was employed as a line worker on the third shift at Margrace Textile Mill in Kings Mountain. After getting married, Viola did not do "public work," as the saying went. She was content to be a homemaker the rest of her life.

Mickey was only six weeks old when the family packed up and moved halfway

With Grandma Kate Maness and cousins in Gaffney

to Charlotte — to Belmont, exchanging one modest rented dwelling for another. Clitus went to work as a life insurance salesman. Imperial Life (to become Western-Southern Life) assigned him to a territory where, in making frequent door-to-door rounds, he sold policies and collected premium payments.

The relocation to Gastonia took place in 1946. Clitus's employment remained with Imperial Life Insurance. He was a valued agent and staff manager with that company until he retired after 32 years.

In adopting Gastonia, little more than a stone's throw from Belmont, Clitus had decided to buy rather than rent. For $2,500 he purchased a four-room frame house at 2106 Lander Avenue, Lander being a short dirt street in a mill village in East Gastonia, an area well beyond the reach of most vital municipal services. It was one of only two

Birthday number three (1945) in Belmont, N.C.

houses on Lander. They were much like the other abodes in the village. All appeared to have come from the same cookie-cutter. A big difference was that the Blackwell address had been blessed with an outside covering of white asbestos shingles. It rested on several brick pillars. Until the additions later on, there were two rooms down one side of the house, two down the other, and a hallway in between.

Since purchased by Clitus Blackwell, the home's owner always has been a Blackwell. Today 'tis Mickey, who is owner and landlord. (It's the only place he has ever lived in Gastonia.) The irises his mother planted around the brick pillars still bloom in the spring.

But it was a move with grave consequences. The houses rented by the family in Kings Mountain and Belmont had indoor plumbing. Alas, the one on Lander had only

11

Major snowfall...tricycle...galoshes... and short pants?!

a vintage outhouse.

Mickey has not been able to erase from memory those pre-flush adversities on Lander Avenue. Before old enough to sashay down a path to the outdoor one-seater, he used a bedroom fixture — the slop jar. And when older, a chore of his was to empty the contents of the slop jar into the cavity of the privy. But that's not the worst of it.

Making a new cavity a little distance from the old and placing the outhouse on top of it, a necessity once every two or three years, released the vilest, most disagreeable odors that Mickey has ever experienced. He had to live through that more than once, and the thought of it still makes him cringe. The thought returned often when he helped with changing his children's diapers. Privy-moving day made the whole neighborhood reek. But

empathy abounded. All the neighbors had privies that required the same care and concern as the one in the Blackwell backyard.

Conditions slowly improved. Clitus was proud that he could afford to install an inside toilet, serviced

Neighborhood kids and cousins are a part of Mickey's fifth birthday party in Gastonia.

Champion Little League team sponsored by Flint No. 2 Mill with right fielder Mickey (second from left, first row).

by a septic tank, in 1953.

By age two, Mickey had taken up talking — and there are friends who say that he has never stopped. His mother noted on the "Second Birthday" page in his Baby Book, "Mickey has learned to talk very good by now. Can say five nursery rhymes and says anything else he wants to." He is remembered as a pretty child with long "precious" curls. At age six, he became a student at Flint-Groves school, within walking distance from the house. He would go all the way at Flint-Groves, through grade nine, but would ride a bike, not walk, those last few grades. The school, built in the early 1920s, stood at the corner of Ozark Avenue and Lower Dallas Road, now known as North New Hope. But the school, later known as R.K. Hancock School, has been torn down.

Another Baby Book entry reports that Mrs. Blackwell was tipped off by his first-grade teacher, Mrs. Mary Ruth Davis, that her son "answered questions before she could ask them, and [she] told me he was a very smart and bright little boy." Signs that he had been born with the gift of gab were multiplying. He suffered through the diseases and ailments that beset most children. His most painful time was in the fifth grade, when he came down with a case of yellow jaundice.

He liked school and was a good student. His report cards showed it, nearly all A's. Reading he especially liked. He responded well to his mother's constant push to excel, to stand out. She enjoyed feeling as though she had accomplished something herself anytime her son's achievements were recognized.

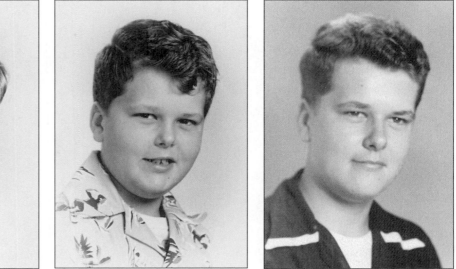

(Left to right) Mickey's school pictures: first grade, third grade and eighth grade

Mickey's piano: here one day, gone the next

Making money soon caught his attention. He became gainfully employed in 1953 as a paperboy, when he was a fifth-grader. (He can boast today that since 1953 not a week has passed when he was not working at one paying job or another.) As a carrier for the twice-weekly ***Gaston Citizen***, he earned around $3 a week. Two years later, he moved up to the ***Gastonia Gazette***, an afternoon daily. For the next three years, he nursed a route of 120 customers and made close to $15 a week.

He played right field for a mill-spon-sored Little League baseball team, and it was a rare time in his life when he was not the fellow knocking in the runs. As a member of Boy Scout Troop No. 1, he advanced rapidly, almost earning the rank of Eagle.

It was a mistake, he has said, not earning the additional two required merit badges (Personal Fitness and Lifesaving) and gaining the top rung before being drawn into other after-school activities. He also wishes that he had stuck with piano study longer. His teacher was Mrs. J. Robert Wright, under whom he took lessons at Flint-Groves School from 1952-1957. By the fourth year, he had gained lead student status. Therefore, at the May 1957 recital, after being the last student to play a solo, "Spanish Gypsy Dance," he helped ring down the curtain by engaging in a duet with Mrs. Wright. Their selection was the sprightly "Doll Dance." Mickey's mother said that he needed to practice more. If he didn't, she was going to sell the piano. He didn't. When he went home one afternoon and stepped into his room, he found that the piano was missing. His mother's only comment was, "I told you

13

Just Call Me Mickey

I was going to sell it."

His picture appeared in a local newspaper for the first of many times when he was a sixth-grader. He had been adjudged winner in an annual essay contest sponsored by the local Daughters of the American Revolution chapter. What made him even prouder was being chosen "the picture machine man" at school. He had learned to handle responsibility so well that he could be trusted to have ready and to operate the motion picture projector that was used to show movies for the students every Friday. He did that three straight years, through the ninth grade.

Of all the honors, none quite equaled the one he received in 1956. He was singled out by his eighth-grade teacher, Louise McKittrick, to present a gift during a school assembly to the Flint-Groves principal, Robert K. Hancock. Years later, Michael would write, "Ramrod-straight Mr. Hancock . . . was my first real hero. He inspired [loyalty and] the confidence of students and teachers, and I shall be forever grateful for his influence in my life." Mickey can recite half a dozen incidents that led up to his turning into a hero-worshiper. "He was a historian, motivator, mathematician . . . an artist of the mind who challenged the limits of learning. He believed in the necessity

PRESENTED GIFT—Robert K. Hancock, principal of Flint-Groves School, is shown receiving a gift from Mickey Blackwell, representing the student body, in chapel exercises Monday morning. Mr. Hancock is retiring after 33 years as principal. He will be succeeded by John H. McClure who served this past year as assistant principal. Teachers of the school presented a gift earlier to Mr. Hancock. (Photo by Ennis Atkins Photography.)

of the intellect, and was determined that [his students] would receive the finest education possible." Hancock had, in turn, taken a personal interest in Mickey, admiring his ambition and industry by assigning him important duties to perform such as running the movie projector.

At the assembly, Hancock was being honored upon his retirement after serving 33 years as principal at the school later renamed for him. Near the assembly's conclusion, Mickey emerged from backstage, to Hancock's surprise, and presented him with a typewriter, a going-away gift from the student body. Without warning, the moment filled Mickey with emotion. He quickly turned away before the principal could respond, disappeared backstage, and burst into tears.

Whenever asked today to name his heroes, he will say, "Well, there's Mr. Hancock, of course."

The year that fol-

R.K. Hancock – childhood hero

lowed was when he "was bitten by the radio bug." His ninth-grade report card showed it. B's had crept in where there had been only A's. His homeroom teacher, Ruth Fulkerson, wrote across the card, "Get hold of yourself and start making the grades you're capable of." But it was too late, Ms. Fulkerson. Mickey, now nearing his full height of 6 foot 1 inch — taller than his father, and a nice-looking young man with a head of wavy brown hair that attracted admiring glances — couldn't hear what any teacher might be advising. The rock and roll music was turned up too loud. His hormones were acting up. His mind was on **Billboard** magazine and girls, not history and math books.

He permitted not only radio work but an assortment of other extracurricular activities, especially his involvement at church, to keep him from scoring as high scholastically at Frank L. Ashley High School as he had the ability to do. (It had been Gastonia High School until May 1955, when Frank L. Ashley retired as its principal, after 26 years in education, at which time the school was renamed in his honor.)

His first year, as a sophomore, he was homeroom secretary-treasurer, was made a member of the Key Club, and, because of a growing

he was holding or standing in front of a microphone. He wrote scripts for high school band performances at sporting events and served as show announcer while also handling the band's publicity. He was the voice on the public address system when school pep rallies were held. His connection with radio led to his providing the play-by-play at broadcasts of some American Legion and a few semi-pro baseball games. After becoming a member of the local DeMolay chapter (his father was a Mason), he was named dance

Frank L. Ashley High

chairman and set up the "record hops" at the Masonic Temple.

Soon after he turned 16, in 1958, his father, pleased with how his son was turning out, bought him his first car, a 1954 Chevrolet purchased from used-car dealer Melvin Cloninger for $100. The color was a shameless orange. It had two names. In public it was called "The Butterscotch Beauty" and in private "The Butterscotch Bomb." Mickey and his close friends piled into it and chased after the girls with new vigor.

(Left to right) High school pictures: tenth grade, eleventh grade and senior Who's Who in American High Schools

reputation as someone who could stand up and speak before an audience without his knees knocking, was chosen the sophomore talent show emcee. Soon it seemed that anytime Mickey appeared in public,

His senior year was a whirlwind: member of the astronomy club, business manager of the yearbook, member of the cast of "Mountain Gal," the senior play (he was also in the cast of a play staged by

Mickey, front center, with high school senior class. (The white shoes were a gift from his parents.)

Gastonia's Little Theater), homeroom president, Class Day lawyer and Junior Rotarian. The senior talent show was "Calendar Capers," with Mickey in the cast as "Father Time." He also wrote the script and was emcee.

Classmates acknowledged anew his facility with the pen as well as at the microphone by choosing him to write their last will and testament. (To the entire junior class, he, on behalf of the seniors, willed all the chewing gum stuck under the desks in the senior homerooms.)

Recognition was hardly stinting. He didn't win either of the major awards for which he was nominated by Ashley High. The first was a Jefferson Foundation Scholarship that paid all the expenses of studies in radio, television, and motion pictures at the University of North Carolina at Chapel Hill. He thought that he'd be a shoo-in because of his radio employment experience, and he was heartbroken when he wasn't chosen. The second was a Morehead Scholarship which translated to $1,250 a year for four years at the university, he moved

up to county level but not beyond.

Still, he was one of the winners of the highest school honor that an Ashley student could reap, being chosen a member of Who's Who. The faculty picked 12 seniors for that distinction every year. Only those outstanding in the areas of leadership, scholarship, character, and service to school were considered. Mickey was one of six boys tapped for membership in 1960. Longer than that of any of the other selectees was his list of involvements and accomplishments.

From dating first one senior girl and then another, he went to going steady with a classmate from childhood, someone he had "liked" since the fifth grade. They remained close from May until the end of summer, or until it was time for Mickey to leave for college. She had failed to interest Mickey in matrimony. She moved to Virginia, married, and still resides there.

Frank L. Ashley High School

This Certifies That

Michael Clitus Blackwell

has completed a Course of Study in the Frank L. Ashley High School and in testimony thereof is entitled to receive this

Diploma

Given in Gastonia, North Carolina, this sixth day of June, nineteen hundred and sixty.

Broadus McSwain
CHAIRMAN BOARD OF SCHOOL COMMISSIONERS

Clyde R. Wright
TREASURER BOARD OF SCHOOL COMMISSIONERS

Woodrow B. Sugg
SUPERINTENDENT OF SCHOOLS

R. E. Carothers
HIGH SCHOOL PRINCIPAL

17

Just Call Me Mickey

As graduation approached, Mickey and his senior classmates encountered a disappointment. More precisely, a weather phenomenon. It snowed each of the four Wednesdays in the month of March. The final exercises, scheduled for late May, were postponed a couple of weeks. It was not until June 8, 1960, that Mickey marched across a stage at Ashley with 350 other seniors — all of whom he knew by their first names — and walked away with his high school sheepskin.

Then two things happened that put him on course to attend the University of North Carolina at Chapel Hill.

His application for admission to UNC-CH was promptly approved, along with an application for financial assistance. The student-aid office would provide a $250-a-year scholarship.

Also, he had won yet another essay contest, one in which many brainy youngsters had competed. The contest topic was "Why I am interested in a broadcasting career." A Charlotte, N.C., television station, WSOC, was contest sponsor and solicited entries through Jimmy Kilgo's show pitched toward the youth, "Kilgo's Kanteen." The prize coveted by so many was an all-expenses-paid participation in the 10th annual North Carolina High School Radio-TV Institute at Chapel Hill from June 12 to 26, 1960.

Mickey enjoyed every minute of it. The curriculum included an introductory course to radio and television and courses in writing, announcing, acting, and production, with opportunities for practical experience in broadcasting. He had a barrel of fun. The taste of college campus life was tantalizing. He came away more determined than ever to make his way in the field of broadcasting. And what could be more thrilling for a teenager than the prospect of leaving home for the first time and spending the next four years on the campus of one of the nation's finest universities.

Also that summer, having turned 18 in May, he boarded a bus for a round trip to Charlotte where he easily passed a physical and returned home a bona fide registrant with the Selective Service System. He was one of thousands who hoped there never would be cause to be drafted into the military.

The years at Ashley High School were three of Mickey's happiest.

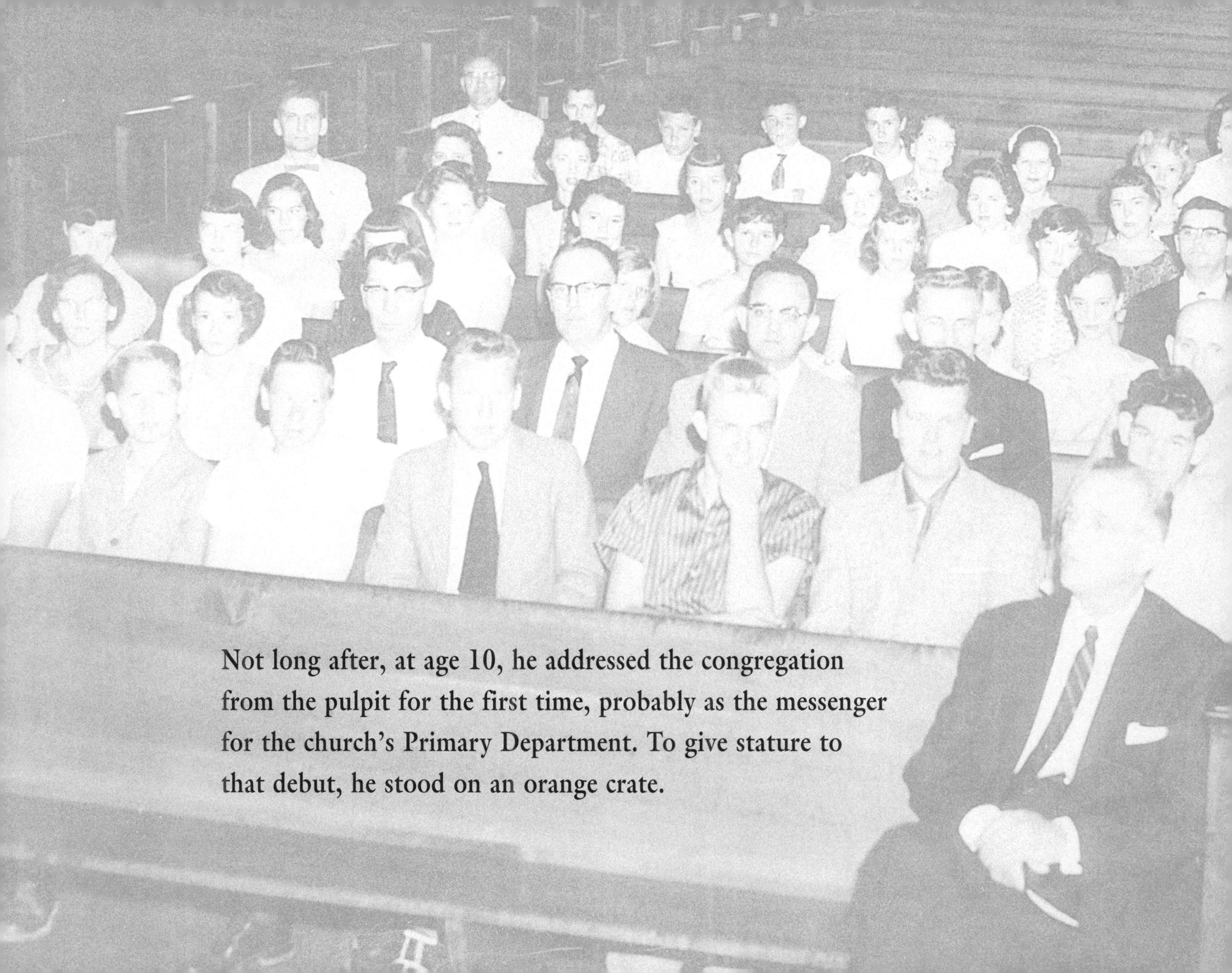

Not long after, at age 10, he addressed the congregation from the pulpit for the first time, probably as the messenger for the church's Primary Department. To give stature to that debut, he stood on an orange crate.

Chapter Three – *Inspiring Connections*

Sunday mornings in the 1950s were routine for the Blackwell family — rise early and dress in their church clothes, and it was a fast trip in Clitus's gray 1947 Ford to Flint-Groves Baptist Church.

"Tuck the corner of the sheet tightly," Clitus urged his son. Early every Sunday, while Viola cleared the breakfast dishes, the Blackwell men made the family's beds.

"Is that right, Daddy?" Young Mickey gazed toward his father for approval. With a nod, the duo pulled the handmade quilt over the pillows.

Beds made, breakfast eaten, the family headed out the door. "Hurry up, Viola," Clitus called. "Mickey, wait in the car."

"I'm ready, Daddy. Tell Mother I've got her Bible." Mickey hurried out, the screen door slamming behind him.

Many Sunday afternoons were spent at his grandmother's home in Gaffney, S.C.

The Blackwell family had chosen Flint-Groves to attend within a month of alighting on Lander Avenue. It was one of about 40 Baptist churches in Gaston County. The number of county residents calling themselves Baptists was far greater than those belonging to any other denomination, and the churches they attended were, for the most part, affiliated with the nation's largest Protestant church body, the Southern Baptist Convention. Moreover, the percentage of Gaston Baptists who offered up their tithes or other monetary gifts was higher than all but the Wesleyan Methodists.

Flint-Groves' address was 2017 East Ozark Avenue in East Gastonia, in 1946 an unincorporated area dotted with spinning mills. It was a mile and a half from Lander Avenue and fairly typical of the Gastonia area's mill village churches. For many years the church had opened its doors to those living in both villages surrounding it, Flint and Groves. Flint was on one side of Ozark Avenue and Groves on

the other (Ozark was the name of a local textile mill that burned down in the 1930s).

Then, as now, in one of these neighborhoods were two Flint textile mills, both with a connection to a textile operation that disappeared long ago — Flint Manufacturing Co. The decision of the Blackwells to settle down on Lander Avenue caused Mickey to grow up in the shadow of one of these. Their street was named for Lander Gray, a member of a family outstanding in the history of Gastonia's textile industry.

Flint Manufacturing reputedly had been named for the stone, with the hope that the company also would be strong and durable.

In Groves Mill Village were three textile buildings that had been erected under the guidance of members of the Groves family, whose patriarch was Gaston County textiles pioneer Laban F. Groves. He helped organize Flint Manufacturing, then left it to build the first of the Groves mills. Upon arrival of the Blackwells, the Groves textile organization was thriving with its two spinning mills and a finishing plant.

Mickey waves to no one in particular and everyone in general.

Gastonia's resounding boast was, "Combed Yarn Center of the World." In 1946, when its population was 22,000, the manufacture of cotton yarns and cotton products to the exclusion of almost any other manufacturing activity dominated nearly everything and touched nearly everybody. The high school newspaper

Groves Thread Company, 1940, was a major economic, religious, and political influence in the community of East Gastonia. (Note the "mill houses" in the background.)

was named "Fine Yarns" and the yearbook, "The Spinner." Under its front-page nameplate, the *Gastonia Gazette* proclaimed

The typical "mill village"

"Gaston County, The Fine Combed Cotton Yarn Center of America." The county fair went by "Spindle Center." A radio station was WLTC ("World's Largest Textiles Center"). A school with grades 1-9 was named Flint-Groves. Mill whistles attempted to keep workers on their toes. They piped up when it was time for the eight-hour shifts to change, at 6 a.m., 2 p.m., and 10 p.m. In the late 1940s, there were between 130 and 140 textile mills in Gaston, more than in any other county in the United States.

With the end of World War II came a wave of changes within the industry. Consolidations, refittings, and unprecedented economic gains occurred even as Gastonia witnessed the first signs of diversification and urbanization.

Flint-Groves Church was founded in 1923, not long before, as matter of fact, the infamous Loray strike that tore Gastonia asunder and made bold headlines the world

Aderholdt

over. In the violence that bloodied the failed attempt to unionize more than a thousand Loray mill hands in the Spring of 1929, two persons were killed, Gastonia Police Chief O.F. Aderholdt and mill worker Mrs. Ella Mae Wiggins. Churches, which with the mills were Gastonia's foremost institutions, were caught in the crossfire of mill owners on the one hand, and on the other, mill workers and union organizers. It was a time when village churches were still mill-subsidized, and in some cases their buildings were owned by the mills. They were rewarded in various ways so long as their pastors assisted mill managers in screening and giving direction to workers. The dilemma for church leadership arising from the fury at Loray — to try to comfort and counsel those in their flocks caught up in union activities and still remain the recipient of mill ownership benevolence — has attracted the scrutiny of sociologists and religion scholars ever since, the most notable examples being *Millhands and Preachers* by Liston Pope in 1940 and its sequel, *Spindles and Spires*, by John R. Earle, Dean D. Knudsen, and Donald W. Shriver Jr. in 1976.

The Flint-Groves Church that the Blackwells became part of in 1946 was little different from the Flint-Groves Church

This Report Card Cover Furnished Through Courtesy of

FIRST FEDERAL
SAVINGS AND LOAN ASSOCIATION
251 West Main Avenue · Telephone UNiversity 7-7248

GASTONIA, NORTH CAROLINA

WHERE THOUSANDS ARE SAVING MILLIONS

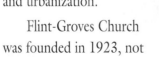
Mickey Blackwell Pupil

IT PAYS TO SAVE
WHERE SAVING PAYS

YOUR COLLEGE EDUCATION

of the 1920s, and it was therefore still a member in good standing within the family of mill village churches. It was no less conservative, no less faithful to Southern Baptist tenets and customs, still a refuge from life's stresses, democratic, and a source of moral guidance that most of its members found to have more appeal than the growing number of other

Flint-Groves Baptist Church in 1952 – The women wore hats, the men wore suits, and Clitus Blackwell led the choir.

places and activities bidding for their attention and participation. By this time, mill management had begun to mollify somewhat its anti-labor stance. The unions were yet to win an election at any of the mills — and would not for years to come — but their spread appeared to be inevitable, and mill proprietors generally did not conceal that they were resigned to that. Most village churches had grown less dependent on mill paternalism

Clitus, second from left, with his barbershop quartet

but remained supportive of management, and it is well-documented that as a rule they remained veiled inhibitors of the labor movement.

Clitus and Viola Blackwell, who had been Baptists growing up, quickly grew comfortable at Flint-Groves. They quickly made the life of the church a significant part of theirs. The two of them, with Mickey in tow, attend services several times a week. Moreover, before the end of their first year, Clitus, a gifted singer (he had been performing with various quartets since the age of 14), was named choir director. Later on, he became an ordained deacon. He wore the title of "Friendliest Man in Church," one of those who had never met a stranger.

Clitus Blackwell

The adult choir could be heard at services on Wednesday night and twice on Sunday. It became known across Gastonia as one of the city's best trained.

As long as they lived, Clitus and Viola were Flint-Groves regulars, and proud of it. When Clitus chose to resign in 1968, he had directed the choir for almost two decades. A church bulletin on that occasion was filled with testimonials, typical of which was this one by assistant organist Patsy Sanford: "It has been a pleasure to work with Clitus in the music program of our church. He always encourages one to do his best, not through flattery but by practice and hard work. My prayer is that he will continue to inspire others to worship God in music." At a party at the church in honor of his retirement, he was given a "This Is Your Life" scrapbook bulging with snapshots of him, his family, church members, and friends. A final entry read: "Thank you for the total per-

2106 Lander Avenue, Gastonia, N.C.

revival time, in which case he was paid $50 because of the many hours of extra work.

Two weeks shy of his eighth birthday, on a Sunday night, April 16, 1950, Mickey was baptized at Flint-Groves by its pastor, the Rev. Love Dixon. Not long after, at age 10, he addressed the congregation from the pulpit for the first time, probably as the messenger for the church's Primary Department. To give stature to that debut, he stood on an orange crate.

(In looking back, he sees that it was when he was about eight that he truly discovered the importance of Christ in his life: "I was led to the Lord by my pastor, Love Dixon. Christ had become very real to me, and all I had to offer him at that early age was what I gave him. Since then, I have sought to give God all that I am and ever hope to be.")

By the time he was 13, Clitus's boy had become one of his choir members. Some might say Mickey fit the image of a choirboy as well: pleasing of visage, well-behaved (except when, on the back of a wooden church pew, he carved his initials and those of a girl he was sweet on), energetic, and neat. He was also inquisitive, plenty bright, as well as a mite large for his age. Other choir members would say, "Well, you can see he's got his daddy's voice." The consensus was, "He looks like his mother and acts like his father."

He sang in the choir and became involved in other aspects of

Mickey, second from right in second row, was Youth Pastor for Youth Sunday at Flint-Groves in 1957.

son you are. First and foremost as a Christian, and then as you have led us through 'fun times' and 'serious times' as we have sought to sing to God's glory."

It had been a labor of love; he received not a penny for it, except at

church life until his high school graduation. He once said, "If the church was open, I was there." It is another of the places he emerged as a leader. Each time he moved up to a higher Sunday school class, he

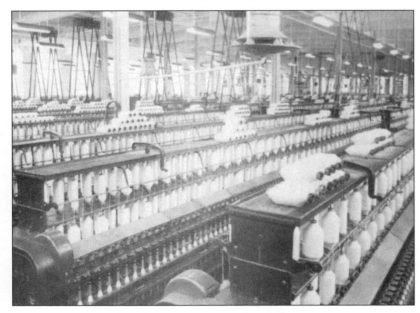

The textile industry dominated the Gastonia landscape for decades.

was elected class president. It's not too much to say he made a difference at Flint-Groves. And the church, in turn, stamped him for life. He never grew too big for it. They have never been apart for any great length of time. And it is most probable that they'll be found arm-in-arm as long as both exist.

Many lasting friendships grew out of his Flint-Groves church connections, one of which put him in close association time and again with a third generation Gastonian textile mogul. This was, or is, Earl T. Groves, now a retiree but still an esteemed Gastonian citizen. His grandfather was the Laban F. Groves already mentioned. Laban, or Labe, got into the yarn-spinning business just after this activity began supplanting the liquor-making business, or when Gaston County went

from "stills to mills."

Historians say that between 1860 and the 1880s in Gaston there were 48 licensed stills and about as many unlicensed. The red clay there produced bumper crops of corn, and the growers reaped a tidy profit by making certain that the corn needs of the still operators never went unmet. Then in 1881, a bill passed by the North Carolina General Assembly, one prohibiting the sale of "spirituous liquors in Gaston County" (well ahead of statewide prohibition, imposed in 1908) sent both the corn growers and the whiskey makers searching for other sources of income. A number of them invested their savings in an emerging enterprise, the manufacture of cotton products. Some of the Southern states were finding a way to imitate what had made New England the nation's textile capital. Southern speculators had begun to capitalize on such advantages as an abundance of cheap labor, accessible waterpower, a mild climate, and proximity to cotton growers.

Starting in 1890, literally dozens of cotton mills were built in Gaston. It was in 1906 that Labe Groves and associates, or Flint Manufacturing, put up one on the south side of Ozark Avenue. It still exists, the well-known Flint Mill No. 1. The new owner of Flint Manufacturing built yet another in 1922, just south of the first, which, too, still is standing: Flint Mill No. 2.

Flint Manufacturing, in 1931, had been acquired by Textiles, Inc., a locally-owned chain, which in 1946 became part of Greensboro, N.C.-based Burlington

The Gastonia mills were known simply as "cotton mills."

Mills. The latter remodeled and enlarged Flint No. 1 and renamed it its R.C.G. Love Plant. Later on, it was sold to Parkdale, and it does business today as one of the cotton yarn mills in the Parkdale system.

Parkdale, based in Gastonia, is presently rated the company that produces more cotton yarn than any other mill. Flint No. 2 also remains an active textile operation as well and is owned by Galey and Lord.

In 1900, Gastonia's population was only about 18,000. Labe Groves and other pioneers solved a textiles boom labor shortage

built. He purchased it from Charlie and Sarah Parker, who bought it from a mill.

Labe's descendants, as he had, belonged to Gastonia's First Baptist Church, but they made themselves familiar with the affairs of Mickey's church and stood by the ministry there. Mickey remembers Earl T. as a dynamic participant in the civic and religious affairs of Gastonia. He led an expansion at Groves Mills in 1954 that produced a spinning plant known as Groves Mill No. 3, a big step forward that Mickey happens to remember for a curious reason — one to do with annexation.

Three generations of the Groves family were powerful forces in East Gastonia – from left to right, Laban, Earl E. and Earl T. Groves.

by luring struggling North Carolina mountain families and others to Gaston County with the offer of steady work and a decent place to live. Manufacturers built houses that they rented to the workers they hired. Transportation to work was not readily available, so the houses were erected close to and around the mills, which is how mill villages came about.

One of the consequences of new directions in management strategies that were adopted soon after the end of World War II was for mill owners to initiate the process of divesting themselves of ownership of the dwellings they had built, many of which were purchased by mill employees. The house that Clitus Blackwell acquired in 1946 was mill-

Prior to undertaking the expansion, Earl T. had assurance from Gastonia's City Hall that there existed no plans to annex East Gastonia and, therefore, no burdensome city taxation. So he moved ahead confidently with the construction of another mill. He most generously made arrangements in the process to have residences in Groves Mill Village furnished with electricity and water and sewer service. Only a year or two later, to his shock and dismay, the city government announced a sweeping annexation program. Part of it called for taking into Gastonia city limits the Flint-Groves and Pecan Grove neighborhoods, or East Gastonia. Earl T. dropped everything in order to organize and direct a campaign to prevent city government from doing what it had said it wouldn't. The ensuing battle created noisy, emotional clashes. The owner of the two Flint plants, Burlington Mills, also was opposed to paying city taxes and quickly lined up with Groves.

Groves Mill No. 1 and No. 2 in 1923

Mickey's seventh-grade teacher at Flint-Groves school, Leary Jenkins Spence, joined the fray by setting up a debate in her homeroom. To be argued was, "Is annexation right for East Gastonia?" Mickey was pleased to be chosen one of the debaters but displeased by his assignment — to defend annexation. When the arguing had ceased, his teacher declared him the superior debater; however, the outcome faithfully reflected the sentiment prevalent in the Flint-Groves community. According to how class members voted, Mickey had been clobbered.

And so, it turned out, was city government. City Fathers had sorely misjudged the effect of their offer to supply city water at inside-the-city rates. They appeared to have lost track of the fact that a goodly number of Flint-Groves families already had

Seventh Grader Mickey

water service and it didn't cost them anything.

On December 7, 1954, Flint-Groves voters had ridden to the polls in cars that were flying banners that warned, "Don't Sell Your Birthright For A Drink of Water."

City Hall's defeat was as humiliating as Earl T.'s victory was scintillating. East Gastonia cast only 69 votes "for" compared to 924 "against." Although there were no fireworks, Mickey has a vivid recollection of how the whistles at the Groves plants, which normally sounded off only to signal the start of eight-hour shifts, spewed jubilation for a full five minutes early in the afternoon following the announcement of the vote. He and the other Flint-Groves students were required to sit quietly so everybody could get an earful of the noise the mills were making.

Mickey's esteem for Earl T. took another leap because of the annexation matter. "Here was a man of integrity who believed so strongly in

29

something that he used all his resources to defeat a measure which he thought was unfair for his people," he would recall later. What's more, the licking that went into the record books as the most lopsided

Downtown Gastonia was a bustling center of activity when the Blackwell family moved there in 1946.

in the history of Gastonia municipal referendums taught Mickey a lesson or two about leadership: "Never try to force your will upon someone else . . . do your homework . . . build personal relationships."

But East Gastonia was not going to remain unannexed forever. In 1963, city government renewed an interest in claiming that territory. Its representatives cautiously and respectfully approached mill owners with a plan. A meeting of minds occurred, and a short time later, without additional sound and fury, the corporate limits lines were extended to make East Gastonia, the Blackwell house included, of course, a part of the city.

Prior to that time, there arose additional cause for Mickey's regard for Earl T. to increase. This was in 1956. Flint-Groves Church had

decided to add an education building, and a drive for the funds necessary had been mapped out. Solicitation assignments were made. It fell to the pastor, the Rev. Wilburn Hendrix, to call on Earl T., for a contribution or pledge. He postponed revealing the response he received until one Sunday morning at the church: "Please wait a minute after the service is over. I have an announcement." Then it was learned that Groves Mill had made a commitment of $50,000 and that the addition would be named in honor of Earl T.'s father. Mickey was there. He remembers, "There was an audible gasp from the congregation. That was more money than any of us could conceive of at the time. Our pastor was quite emotional but was so happy I thought he was going to shout. It was a memorable moment, one that Pastor Hendrix talked about the rest of his life."

Mickey was

to become even better acquainted with Earl T. He had returned to Gastonia after getting his college diploma and functioned as campaign manager for Earl T. when the latter set out to be elected Gastonia's mayor. (The annexation fight may have caused Earl T. to take a more active part in city government.)

ry Hunters
For Area

tential location, they always want to know if there is enough land available.

Robert Stine, chairman of the GIDC, said there still were several buildings available for ... the industry ... new

astonia Lands New
tile Printing Firm

Gastonia Bureau

A large build- ... Pyramid Elec- ... South Caro- ... ago is getting ...

Universal Screen Printing, which has been in business more than 39 years, specializes in screen printing of cotton, linen and rayons by the highly skilled hand-screen-printing method. Universal also will expand into certain lines of machine-printed fabrics.

The company headquarters are in Paterson, N. J., and this is the first time that a branch office has been established.

Gaeto said Gastonia was chosen because "it is in the near geographic center of the tremendous textile industry in the two Carolinas."

Availability of an existing building and the excellent transportation facilities were among reasons for choosing ..., Gaeto said.

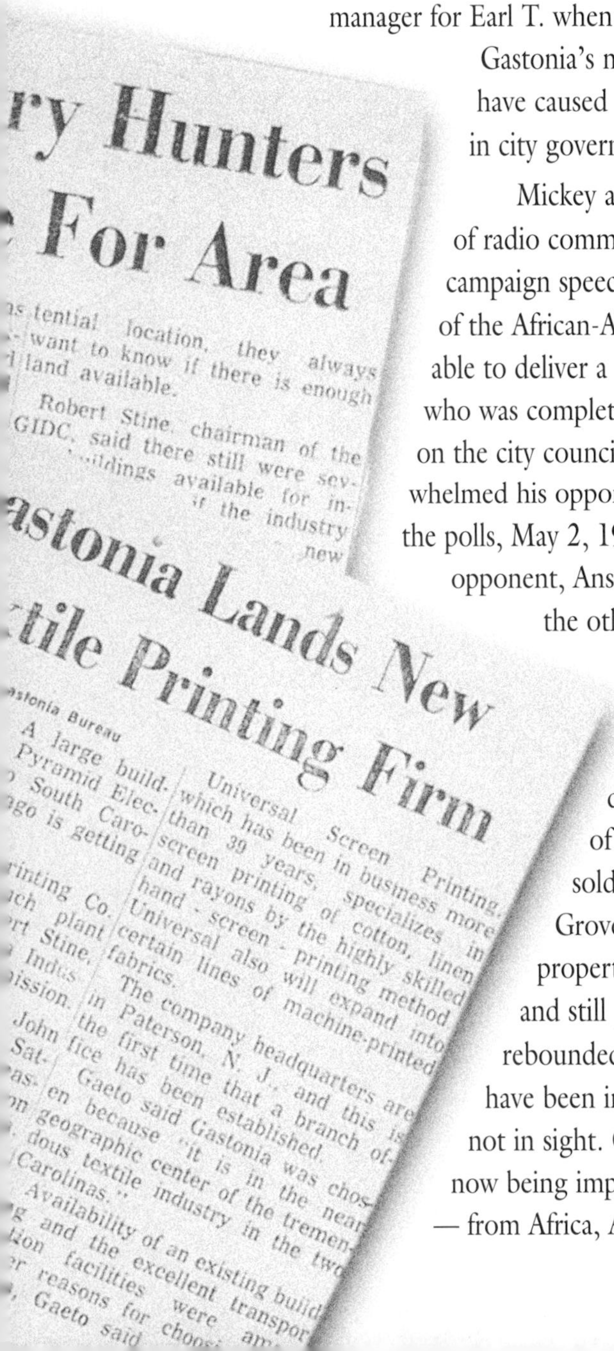

Mickey assisted Earl T. in the production of radio commercials, drove him to the sites of his campaign speeches, and introduced him to members of the African-American community known to be able to deliver a bloc of votes on election day. Earl T., who was completing a term as Ward 5 representative on the city council, as well as mayor pro-tem, overwhelmed his opponent on the day the voters went to the polls, May 2, 1967. He received 2,674 votes. One opponent, Ansel Cavney, picked up only 1,038, and the other, Hero Harrell, a mere 78. Earl T. served as mayor with distinction from 1967 to 1969.

The textile industry became less dominant in 1970s. Earl T., members of his family, and other shareholders sold their interest in Groves Mills, or Groves Thread, in 1978. At present, these properties are owned by American & Efird and still produce textile products. Textiles rebounded a bit in the 1980s but since then have been in a depression, the end of which is not in sight. Great numbers of textile goods are now being imported from many parts of the world — from Africa, Asia, Latin America, and Mexico.

Mills that are still profitable can be found here and there in a city that currently, early in the 21st century, is a vibrant center of diversified manufacturing with a population of 60,000. It is a chamber of commerce claim that more manufacturing concerns exist in Gaston than in any other county in the state. However, the probability that any time soon the spindles in Gastonia will spin out good times — as they did in the period from 1940 to 1960 — no longer exists.

During the second semester as a junior, when his name was posted in the DTH masthead as "contributing editor," DTH used Mickey's stories on ticket-scalping, dorm room rent increases, a Playboy Bunny visit, the season's first panty raid, and complaints about segregated bedding facilities at Memorial Hospital.

Chapter Four – *"Carolina Kid"*

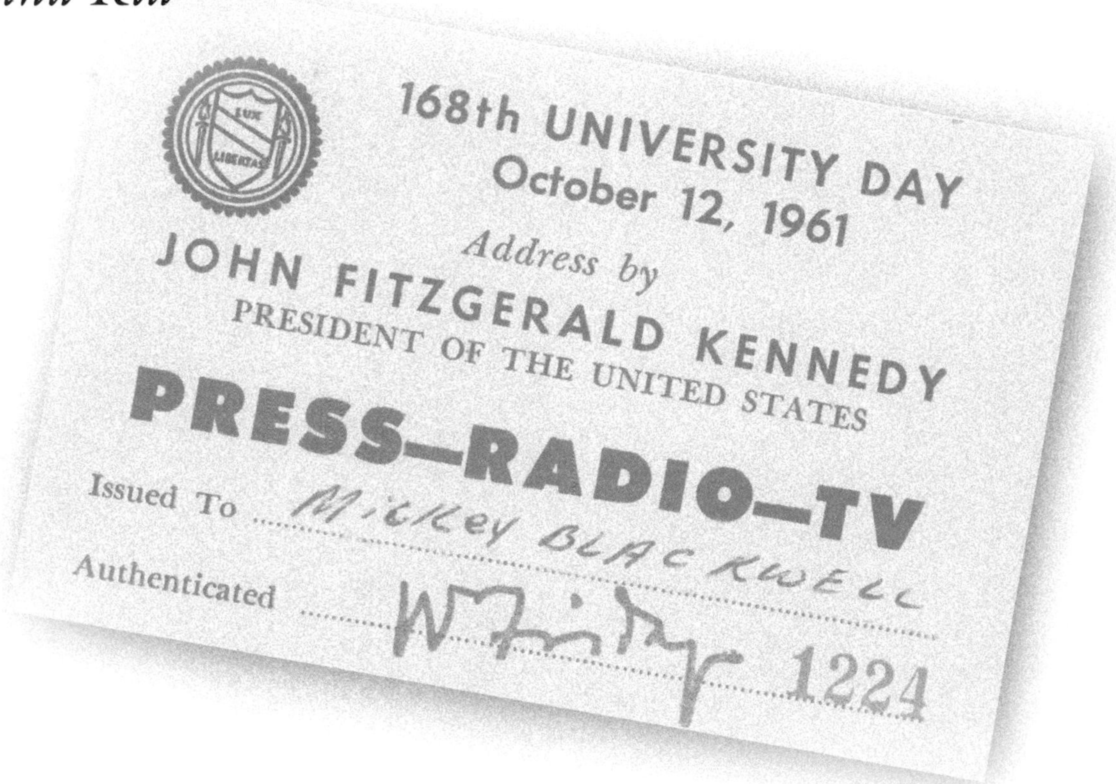

168th UNIVERSITY DAY
October 12, 1961
Address by
JOHN FITZGERALD KENNEDY
PRESIDENT OF THE UNITED STATES
PRESS—RADIO—TV
Issued To *Mickey Blackwell*
Authenticated *W Friday* 1224

Mickey hurried home to see if the letter had arrived. It would be with the other mail Viola placed on the kitchen table each day.

"Did it come yet, Mother?" Mickey called as he walked in from school.

"You know what they say about a watched pot never boiling," Viola replied in a motherly tone.

"Yes, ma'am," Mickey responded. Then, "Well, did it come?"

Viola, with a slow, pained grin, held the letter behind her back. "It came," she said as tears began to form in the corners of her eyes.

The University of North Carolina at Chapel Hill, where Mickey had wished mightily he would become a full-time undergraduate, notified him in a letter dated February 8, 1960, that he had been approved to enter this, the oldest state university in the country, effective the fall semester, which was to begin September 8, 1960. Mickey never considered applying to any other college.

He did a lot of hip-hip-hooraying.

So now he had to buckle down and determine how to get the money he would need.

He wrote the office of student aid at UNC in quest of assistance. By his estimate, he explained in his letter, he'd have to come up with $1,160.50 for the 1960-61 school year. He thought he could produce maybe $450. He hoped, because of his knowledge of radio, to find work at the university radio station, WUNC. Student aid wrote back that the best it could do was a $250 student aid scholarship. He replied that he was eager to accept even that. It was renewable for a total of four years, provided that he maintained a grade average of no less than "C" and would forgo ownership of an auto.

A buyer for "Butterscotch Beauty" was found. He then packed his bags and stowed them in the family car for the trip to Chapel Hill.

In a time-honored ritual new to the Blackwells, his parents deposited him and his belongings lovingly at the front door of Mangum Hall. The comparatively long separation looming was also something totally

UNC – the oldest state university in America

new. Mother was dabbing at tears as she hugged and kissed him goodbye and prayed he would be a good boy. From his dad, a strong, manly handshake. An awkward moment had arisen. There was no college experience in Clitus's background on which to base parting dos and don'ts. But there was no attempt to hide how proud he was that a kid of his would be getting a college education.

And this kid of his was rarin' to go after it.

Also not unusual was the student housing situation. Mickey not only was assigned to a room in which there were two others; he also discovered that not one of the students from Gastonia he knew would be sharing a Mangum address. His two roommates were upperclassmen who could have comforted a somewhat lonesome freshman occasionally bewildered by the new world he had entered. Instead, "They made life miserable for me," he would say later. His treatment at their hands would have qualified as hazing if he had been a fraternity pledge and the roommates had been fraternity brothers. They deeply resented having to share their space. The abuse was designed to drive him away. They opened his mail and scattered it about, and fouled his bed clothing with bits of cigarette tobacco. Replacement of the lock on the door came as one of many infuriating surprises.

Mickey suffered in silence. He kept the vow he had made to himself not to give in and move out. At the end of the first semester, the roommates did the moving — into an off-campus apartment. They were replaced by a freshman Mickey knew, Steve Norris of Spindale, N.C.. These two got along just fine. Mickey knew Norris from when, the summer just past, they attended UNC's high school radio-television institute.

The work Mickey found in radio was not at WUNC but as part-time announcer at the commercial station in Chapel Hill, WCHL, owned by Village Broadcasting Co. Commercial radio work was, in fact, his preference. Since he had no car (freshmen at UNC weren't allowed to have one, anyway), WCHL arranged for a taxi to pick him up at 5:30 a.m. so he could put the station on the air at 6 each weekday morning. The cabbie reappeared at 7 a.m. and returned him to campus in plenty of time for classes. He also held down the WCHL morning shift on Sundays.

Mickey was hired there by Ty Boyd, with whom he formed a lasting friendship. Soon after, Boyd went to work for WBT in Charlotte and

"Where Chapel Hill Listens," WCHL, with Mickey at the controls.

became a radio and television celebrity with a huge following.

Mickey's pay at WCHL was $2 a day, and a dollar an hour for Sunday duty.

His freshman year, he also worked at the University's Lenoir Hall, where most students took their meals. At first he was the dining hall's employee around whom the crowds formed, the dipper of the ice cream. A heaping scoop commanded only five cents. Seldom were there fewer than 20 to 25

Mickey with friend Eddie Weiss, right, who later becomes NC radio legend "Charlie Brown."

waiting in line to be served. In this case, he was paid in script, redeemable only at Lenoir Hall. When dangerously low on personal funds, Mickey might sell $10 worth of script to someone he knew, say a student from Gastonia, for eight bucks.

The student blue plate special at Lenoir — a meat, two vegetables, bread, and a drink — costs 40 cents.

When promoted to manning the Lenoir Hall cash register, to his relief, his remuneration was in the form of cash — plus an evening meal of no more than 90 cents on the days he worked.

His parents paid his first-semester tuition, but most of the funds he needed came from what he had saved while working in high school and what he was picking up as a self-help student. Once he completed the first half of his freshman year, he made it through without financial aid of any kind from Clitus and Viola.

Working at WCHL made him eligible to cast a ballot when the Associated Press set about selecting its All-American collegiate basketball team for 1961-62. The five players for whom he voted became the AP's all-American first team. It was a feat duplicated by only seven of the 322 sports writers and radio and television broadcasters across the country who participated in the balloting. Mickey insisted that he was knowledgeable, not simply lucky.

—Mick Picked 'Em Down The Line

WANT TO KNOW who'll be crowned the 1962 champion of of NCAA basketball?

Chances are Mickey Blackwell, a University of North Carolina student from Gastonia, can.

Out of 322 sports writers and radio-TV broadcasters across the nation voting for the Associated Press All-America basketball team, only seven hit the first team on the head.

And Mick, a part-time announcer at WCHL in Chapel Hill, was one of the seven.

Young Blackwell, a WGNC staffer while a student here at Ashley High, is the son of Mr. and Mrs. Clitus Blackwell, this city.

greater than what he needed to spend on himself, so for a while he sent his parents $20 a week, or more than enough to reimburse them for that one semester of tuition. His summer residence was Joyner dorm, and he attended summer school. He would say years later, "Work in radio was an important part of my life. I learned the real art of communication while I worked in that medium."

His sophomore year was barely underway when WCHL turned to him as someone to represent the station when state government undertook to dock a discarded World War II battlewagon, the U.S.S. North Carolina, at Wilmington as a war memorial. This was in September 1961. To be where he could see and describe the act of docking for WCHL listeners, he set out for the coast in a Piper Cub piloted

His Chapel Hill radio days provided the 18-year-old Mickey with many memorable experiences.

USS North Carolina being berthed in Wilmington, N.C..
(Photo: Hugh Morton)

The summer of 1961, he remained in Chapel Hill, a full-time employee at WCHL, 2 p.m. until sunset, $48 a week. The pay was

John F. Kennedy during UNC's 168th University Day
(Photo copyright by Jim Wallace)

by Pebley Barrow, the UNC fencing instructor. Unfortunately, heavy weather moved in. High winds pitched the small plane this way and that. Mickey and the plane did not cease to shake — this was his first time to fly — until Barrow managed the approximation of a crash-landing at Elizabethtown, 50 miles west of Wilmington. There the two narrow-escapees hopped a bus and returned to Chapel Hill. Instead of September, the berthing of the big ship took place in October — without Mickey's supervision.

He continued at WCHL full time, same schedule, same pay.

John Fitzgerald Kennedy, elected president in 1960, had won the heart of Mickey, as he had hordes of other young people. Therefore, Mickey was extremely happy to learn JFK was to be the headliner at the 168th University Day celebration on October 12, 1961. He did more than attend this event; he described it "live" for WCHL listeners. That put him in the thick of things, so close to the president that he got to shake his hand and later declare it "a great day!"

WCHL now knew for certain that he could handle a microphone expertly, outdoors as well as indoors.

Some 32,000 persons jammed into UNC's Kenan Stadium to see JFK receive a UNC Honorary Doctor of Laws degree, presented by Consolidated UNC President William C. Friday, and to hear him make a speech. He pledged every effort "to prevent the world from being blown up." Still, he warned, pointing to the prevailing crises stretching from Berlin to Vietnam, "We are destined — all of us here today — to live out most, if not all, of our lives in uncertainty and challenge and peril."

The rip-roaring politics of 1960 that produced figures that still stand tall in the histories of the state and nation helped convince Mickey that he wanted to be a member of the Democratic party and work for its causes. He celebrated not only the election of Democrat JFK, but

37

also that of Democrat Terry Sanford, graduate of the UNC law school, who had won the governorship of North Carolina — and consequently the chairmanship of the Greater UNC board of trustees. He lost no time registering as a Democrat once he turned 21, in 1963 (this was before 18-year-olds had been enfranchised), and has been faithful to the Democratic party ever since. The commitment he made pleased his parents, both longtime registered Democrats, especially his father, who did not deny he was, indeed, a "yellow-dog Democrat."

His summer of 1962 was spent in Gastonia. Most of the time he was employed at WGNC, where he had been a sensation as a high school disc jockey and where his new rate of pay was $1.25 an hour. Luckily for him, an announcer's job had opened up just as he began job-hunting. WGNC's owner, Pat McSwain, having learned Mickey was available, hired him over the phone. He would work from 6 a.m. to 2 p.m., and what he was told to do was very much to his liking.

With his junior year at UNC under way, in the fall of 1962, he could be found reporting in a limited fashion for the

student newspaper, *The Daily Tar Heel*. He was somewhat ambivalent. Maybe his future lay in print journalism, not radio, although he was still

*Mickey, center, got "ink in his blood" while working for **The Daily Tar Heel.***

an employee of WCHL, working Sunday mornings and available for part-time work other days. He continued to spin records, this time as the "Tar Heel Dance Party." His sponsor was not anything to write home about — Schlitz Beer. But, after all, from time to time UNC-Chapel Hill was ranked "the beer-drinking capital of the country."

There appeared in the *DTH*, under his byline, an article about an appearance by Hal Holbrook as Mark Twain. His hometown paper, the *Gastonia Gazette*, purchased and used news clips of Chapel Hill that he sent in. While in New York City during the Christmas break — with other students on a UNC YMCA-sponsored visit to the Big Apple — Mickey, thirsting for action of some kind, flashed a *Gastonia Gazette* press card and otherwise finagled admittance backstage at a theater

The Daily Tar Heel
University of North Carolina at Chapel Hill

PRESS 19 · 19

MICKEY BLACKWELL is accredited to the staff of *The Daily Tar Heel* and is commissioned to procure news and photographs for this publication. Please extend all privileges and courtesies that the duties require.

Hugh Stevens Editor-in-Chief

It is a night out for Mickey at Ram's Head Rathskeller in Chapel Hill (1961). These shoes and white socks soon gave way to Bass Weejuns and Gold Cups.

and an interview with veteran entertainer Rudy Vallee, appearing in the sold-out "How to Succeed In Business Without Really Trying." The performer proved to be less than generous. Rather than give Mickey

On December 2, 1961, in UNC's Woollen Gym, new basketball coach Dean Smith led the Tar Hills to a 80-46 victory over Virginia. The game was the first of Smith's record setting 879 wins. Mickey is with high school and college buddy Larry Ledford.

a ticket to the play, he sold him one, good for "standing room only." Outside the theater after the show, he had a pleasant 20-minute conversation with future movie and television star Eddie Albert, who was waiting for a ride. Mickey then went back to his hotel and quickly assembled a story about Vallee. Off it went to NC's Raleigh *News & Observer*, which published it. Vallee had uttered profanities a number of times. Mickey faithfully included almost all of them in his story, and to the surprise and chagrin of a multitude of readers, the *N&O* printed everything Mickey sent in.

During the second semester as a junior, when his name was posted in the *DTH* masthead as "contributing editor," *DTH* used Mickey's stories on ticket-scalping, dorm room rent increases, a Playboy Bunny visit, the season's first panty raid, and complaints about segregated bedding facilities at Memorial Hospital. By early spring, he had become the UNC correspondent for the *Raleigh Times*, to which he also fed stories throughout his senior year.

Much later on, William Friday would look back on the time he was UNC president and Mickey was with the *DTH*: "The student paper was full of opinion and spirited comment by the staff. It was the duty of the university president to read it each morning and get his instructions for the day." He paused. Then, "Mickey never let me down."

Mickey tested other waters, of course. He emceed "The Junior Class-Faculty Variety Show," a parody of popular television variety productions. The cast did not lack for celebrities. They included President Friday, UNC varsity football coach Jim Hickey, and Chapel Hilllian Norman Cordon, a former Metropolitan Opera star. He made his plunge into campus politics his first and last. He also lost by a margin of less than one percent when he ran for treasurer of the senior class on the University party ticket. The reason being he neglected to campaign in Cobb dorm, a female domicile, most of whom were juniors and there-

fore eligible to vote. His opponent, Mal Lesavoy, capitalized on this oversight. The opponent's fraternity brothers enlisted the support of girls they knew at Cobb, and these in turn campaigned for Lesavoy votes among their dorm mates. It was a lesson in the power of the female vote that Mickey would never forget.

He had decided that fraternity life was not his cup of tea. Early in his sophomore year, he pledged Sigma Phi Epsilon, but after getting a good whiff of what becoming a Greek might be like, he, as he put it, "depledged." Not all fraternities had been ruled out, of course. He was eager to join, and later on proud to be accepted as a member, of Sigma Delta Chi, professional journalistic society.

This Gastonia mill village product looked, acted, and partied conservatively. All around him were students with flattops, but his hairstyle remained the same as it had been in high school. Finding a date among the comparatively few

Yum-Yum near UNC-Greensboro campus

females on campus was not for the faint of heart. For female companionship, he and a buddy from Gastonia, Johnny Parker, would hitchhike to Woman's College, an institution now known as the University of North Carolina at Greensboro. Hooking up with a girl for the evening usually necessitated only a phone call or two. He and Parker liked to walk their dates around the campus and then down Spring Garden Street to Yum-Yum, a celebrated, historic source of king-size servings of ice cream. Yum-Yum was virtually a clone of Tony's Ice Cream and Sandwiches on Franklin Avenue in Gastonia, where while growing up Michael regularly partook of large servings of ice cream and delicious hot dogs. (Tony's is still going strong 50 years later.)

Chances of catching a "Carolina Coed" improved when he was an upper classman, but he never went steady, and spent many Saturday nights as a stag, attending a free movie at Carroll Hall, congregating with other fellow students at someone's residence, or hanging out at Graham Memorial, the student union, where he seldom lost a ping-pong match.

He skirted a popular student pastime, which was drinking, and never came close to taking up smoking. And he later needed no greater discouragement than that his father had been a chain-smoker and died of emphysema. If sufficiently provoked, he could swear with some vigor. For him it was somewhat like Mark Twain said: swearing

41

could provide relief not available through prayer. He was not a regular churchgoer after reaching Chapel Hill, but he always attended services at Flint-Groves Baptist whenever in Gastonia. His first week at college, he attended the worship service of a church still in its early stages of formation. This was Binkley Memorial Baptist, whose members were meeting in UNC's Gerrard Hall. He went only that once. (Years later, Dr. Olin T. Binkley, for whom the church was named, would help plot one of the major twists and turns in Mickey's professional career.)

His second Sunday at UNC, he was present for worship services at University Baptist, after which he abandoned regular attendance at any Chapel Hill church.

Settling on a journalism major did not come until late in his junior year and only after he had been introduced to the UNC Journalism School's Walter Spearman. The next fall, Spearman would be teaching

"Introduction to News Writing" (Jour. 53). He said enrollment would be open to Mickey, who did take that course and eventually every other course Spearman taught, including "Editorial Writing," "Reviewing," and "Advanced Reporting." "He became my mentor — and strongest critic . . . . The way I felt, you couldn't get a higher compliment than one from him. . . . More than anybody else he pushed me to excel."

Mickey's major could have been quite different. If he had won the scholarship for which he yearned and thought he would surely receive because of his radio experience, the $1,000-a-year Jefferson Foundation award, he probably would have been on his merry way to a UNC degree in radio, television, and motion pictures.

"But things have a way of turning out for the best for me," he said. He would have missed the experience of working his way through college, and, far more importantly, missed taking journalism and learning the proper

6-A THE CHARLOTTE OBSERVER Wednesday, Feb. 19, 1964

MICKEY BLACKWELL, an Observer correspondent based in Chapel Hill, sits forlornly on the back bumper of his stricken automobile as John Montague walks off in search of gasoline. The picture was staged, but the situation was from real life. (Photo by Jim Wallace)

The Country's Nice—But Not When You're Out Of Gas

By MICKEY BLACKWELL and JOHN MONTAGUE
Observer Carolina News Service

"Mornin'," says an overall-ed native of those parts as your 1953 Plymouth rolls silently into

what time this station opens?" you holler at two kids wheeling their bikes around the sta-

way to write news stories and features.

At the end of May of 1963, he made a beeline for home and found summer work, this time with the vaunted **Charlotte Observer**. At first, he commuted from the home of his parents and worked in the newsroom there. "**Observer** Staff Writer" was part of the bylines on his stories the paper published. Then, during the months of July and August, he was one of the news reporters in the **Observer**'s Gaston County bureau in Gastonia, an exciting learning experience.

He was owner of an auto again, a 1953 Plymouth his father had found for him to buy.

Summer sped by. Before striking out for Chapel Hill to start his senior year, both he and the **Observer** seemed pleased that it had been arranged for him to be the paper's new UNC "stringer." He had saved enough to see him safely through the few remaining months of school.

After having resided three years at Mangum, room 205 — and being elected Mangum dorm president — he would move across the upper quadrangle to Ruffin, room 210, where he'd have a place to himself for the first time, and where he'd serve as resident advisor (who was, if not the problem-solver for the second floor, the one who imparted counsel and advice freely — and who got his room rent-free).

As a senior (1963-64), Mickey allowed newswriting to eat up great chunks of his time. By now, he liked transferring excitement onto newsprint with a typewriter, maybe better than, putting it on the radio with a microphone. His old Underwood was one of the busiest at the **Daily Tar Heel**, but also, as their campus news representative, he was now dispatching story after story to two of North Carolina's most influential publications: the **Observer** and the **Raleigh Times**.

At the start of the year, his title was reporter, assigned to covering university administration. By the end, he was in a leadership role — executive editor, in close association with the paper's co-editors-in-chief.

CHAPTER FIVE – *"Carolina Gentleman"*

The interview with Dean of Student Affairs C. O. Cathey was going well. Mickey had scheduled the appointment more than a week ago. He had prewritten all his questions. He even had anticipated the dean's answers. Suddenly in mid-question, the door opened and Dean of Men William Long interrupted, "President Kennedy has been shot."

Mickey was stunned, but it was only a second before he closed his notebook, gathered his things, excused himself, and left. His thoughts were only, "Get to the newsroom!"

Running across campus to the **Daily Tar Heel** newsroom in Graham Memorial Hall, his thoughts spanned all the questions: "Was the President alive? Who could have shot him? How will the country react?"

President Kennedy was elected in Mickey's freshman year. He had visited the UNC campus his sophomore year and was now shot, possibly murdered, his senior year.

Mickey was not alone in the newsroom when the teletype machine's bells began to ring. Click! Click! Click! Standing at the wire machine, he read the words, "FLASH . . . The President is dead."

The murder of President Kennedy in Dallas, Texas, on November 22, 1963, provided a stern test of a collegiate journalist and news publication's ability to get the big story in print quickly, accurately, and completely. *DTH* appeared to earn high marks. Its four-page issue the next morning was devoted almost exclusively to the shooting, what went on just before and just after, and to reaction the world over. The front page consisted of a big portrait of Kennedy and the dates 1917-1963, all in a heavy black border, and nothing else. Mickey teamed with staff writer Peter Harkness to produce a long article recapping the life of the President. Most of the *DTH* staffers, Mickey included, were among the great number whose affection for Kennedy had never wavered. For them, rushing about to fill column after column with information pertaining to his sudden, stunning death was a tearful, emotion-packed, unforgettable experience.

Three days later, Mickey was in the nation's capital. He was the pick of *DTH* to behold the majesty of the

John Fitzgerald Kennedy funeral on November 26, the interment of the President at Arlington Cemetery. His eyewitness account appeared in the *DTH* the morning after.

(A *DTH* presence at such history-making times was not unprecedented. *DTH* Editor Sylvan Meyer sped from Chapel Hill to Washington after the bombing of Pearl Harbor in December 1941, and while standing on the Capitol steps, heard President Franklin D. Roosevelt's declaration of war.)

Every way he turned, there was a momentous event to report on, it seemed. If he had been able to pick a year to be a student newspaperman, could he have done any better? The beatniks and peaceniks were in full swing. The President of the United States was assassinated. The sit-ins of the civil rights movement

46

proliferated. Freedom of speech underwent a severe test.

The Ku Klux Klan was on the loose again. Demonstrations were a dime a dozen. In sports, Cassius Clay burst on the scene, and on the campus hardwood, future basketball hall-of-famer Billy Cunningham was collecting sports page superlatives. The Psychedelic '60s were aborning — the years, as *Time* magazine noted, "when everything changed." More social cataclysms loomed.

It is also during this time that Mickey formed acquaintanceships with the governor, the university president, and a federal judge that grew into warm, long-lasting friendships.

As he was wont to do, he moved ahead rapidly at the *DTH*. At the start of the year, his title was reporter, assigned to covering university administration. By the end, he was in a leadership role — executive editor, in close association with the paper's co-editors-in-chief. (While an editor-in-chief could

name an executive editor, only the vote of the student body could name an editor-in-chief.)

But being a reporter was the most fun.

Stunned Chapel Hill residents gather on Franklin Street to listen to radio broadcast news of Kennedy's assassination.

In the fall, the papers he represented published his exclusive interview with Floyd McKissick of Durham, N.C., national chairman of CORE (Congress of Racial Equality). McKissick was the first black to be enrolled in an all-white public school in North Carolina. He, as a student in the law school at North Carolina College at Durham (now North Carolina Central University), had joined other blacks in a lawsuit contending that the NCC school was not equal to the one at UNC in Chapel Hill. A U.S. Court of Appeals agreed in March 1951 and ordered the admission of the plaintiffs to UNC. By then, McKissick had earned a law degree at NCC. He took one summer course at UNC, then joined the national civil rights movement, and eventually became a well-known constitutional lawyer. (He died in 1991.)

The first integration at UNC had taken place at its law school in June 1951. A black student was enrolled in the medical school in the fall of that year, and three blacks enrolled as freshmen in the fall of 1955. Today, around 25 percent of the undergraduates at UNC are black.

In 1963, McKissick organized first one anti-segregation demonstration, then another. Mickey earned his trust and was allowed to witness how the firebrand in lawyer's garb trained demonstrators, after which Mickey would tag along so he could watch the trainees, the young blacks and a few whites, descend on some public place and take a noisy stand against separation of the races. (CORE preached nonviolence.)

Once having covered some event or finished an interview, Mickey would dispatch himself back to the *DTH* office to write and turn in his story. Then, if the subject merited it, he would furnish the state dailies

6-A THE CHARLOTTE OBSERVER Thursday, October 3, 1963

CORE Chief Is Fighting Back

By MICKEY BLACKWELL
Observer Carolina News Service

DURHAM — The law office of McKissick and Berry is tucked away over a jewelry store at 113½ Main St. in the Durham business district.

You go up one flight of creaking wooden stairs to a busy office that is one of the key civil rights planning centers in the country.

The man seated behind the cluttered desk is Floyd McKissick, who became the first Negro to break the color barrier at a state-supported school in North Carolina when he was admitted to the UNC Law School in 1951 under a federal court order.

Today McKissick, 41, is national chairman of the Congress of Racial Equality (CORE), and in his small office with its constantly ringing phones and steady parade of visitors he plans his antidiscrimination campaigns for the nation.

McKissick is a quiet, mild-mannered person, who decided when he was 14 years old that he would spend his life fighting for racial equality.

"I was a Boy Scout at the

FLOYD McKISSICK

time," McKissick said. "I was helping to direct traffic in Asheville. We all had on skates so we could get around to the various intersections.

". . . Suddenly this white policeman comes up to me and asks me what I am doing there.

"I told him I was doing what I was told to do. He told me I didn't have any business being there, and then without any reason at all he hit me across the face with a glove which had three large reflectors on it.

"There was another policeman with him. He asked the first man to quit hitting me, but he didn't stop.

"Then he really started beating me and whipping me for no reason at all. I kept telling him that I thought I was doing what was right, and he kept saying, 'We don't want any niggers around here.'

"All I could taste was blood and asphalt. "Up until that time I was trying to decide whether to be a preacher or lawyer. I knew from then on that I couldn't be a preacher, so I decided to be a lawyer.

"I vowed to do what I could so that no other member of my race would ever have to go through what I did on that day."

McKissick is tall and lean and speaks in a straight-forward way. He is not a shouter but when he speaks, crowds listen.

"North Carolina has made progress in the civil rights movement," McKissick said. "But I will not be pleased until every bit of segregation is abolished and until we can live as citizens and people without regard to race."

Asked about Gov. Terry Sanford's remark that a march on Raleigh would not be a good thing, McKissick said:

"Let's face it, there has never been a demonstration held at the right time or the right place in the eyes of the people we are demonstrating against.

"When they admit that there is a right time to demonstrate, there will be no need to demonstrate."

McKissick, whose four children are attending desegregated schools in Durham, does not put the blame for inequality entirely on the white man.

"Many Negroes have given up the fight . . . they are defeatists," he said.

"Some Negroes who work for segregationists won't express their true feelings because they are afraid they will lose their jobs. He sells part of himself for a small bit of security." In other words, McKissick said "he sells his self-respect."

with a copy of what he had written for the *DTH*. It was not uncommon for a byline story of his to appear the same morning on the front pages of the student paper and the Charlotte paper and the same afternoon in the Raleigh paper.

All of this reporting could have been called "still working my way through college." The state papers paid him "by the column inch." That is, if a story of his filled 10 inches of a column in one of the papers, Mickey was paid one dollar, or 10 cents an inch. The *DTH* only recently had begun paying its reporters. He and the others were then receiving $25 a week.

There were two ways to transmit a story to Charlotte or Raleigh: dictate it over the phone or send it by Western Union "night press rate collect." Also, he used the mails to transmit features. Mickey was fortunate in being able to finish a story quickly, partly because he had taken typing in high school and had mastered "the touch system." He would later say that typing had been of more benefit to him than any other single course he had ever taken.

Jesse Jackson leads a civil rights march in Greensboro, NC, covered by Mickey and Jim Wallace, who took the photo.
(Photo copyright by Jim Wallace)

Also, in the fall, he wrote his first of several reports on the opposition abroad on the UNC-CH campus to the Speaker Ban that Rep. Phillip P. Godwin Sr. and other conservative Democrats sneaked through the General Assembly as it was closing down in June of 1963. Often referred to as the gag law, it required trustees of all state-supported colleges and universities to prohibit any known Communist from speaking on campus. Mickey's first report, one he's not likely to forget, conveyed the strong distaste of Chapel Hill's Pulitzer Prize-winning playwright Paul Green for the gag and his complaints about the reticence of UNC-CH professors to condemn it. Mickey could only exclaim after meeting Green, "What a gentleman!"

Some of the people upholding the law, noting the argument that it stifled free speech, asserted that it is not the duty of the state to provide a forum for those who would destroy that state. But many endorsed the position that academic freedom was threatened and that politicians were tampering with the educational process. They passionately insisted upon recognition of the unbounded right to consider diverse views.

A broadside was fired off in November 1963 by the chancellor at UNC in Chapel Hill, William B. Aycock. According to articles under bold headlines and Mickey's byline in the **DTH**, *Charlotte Observer*, and other papers, Aycock called the gag law "a stigma, an insult and a limitation upon higher education." In a speech before the annual meeting of the UNC alumni board of directors in Chapel Hill, he also panned it as "the poorest drafted legislation that I have seen, and is the

Chancellor William B. Aycock

most serious challenge to the university since the monkey bill of the '20s" (which prohibited teaching Darwin's theory of evolution but never was enacted). Aycock wanted alumni to join with the university in fighting for repeal.

It was not until November 1965 that the law was amended to provide for the governing body of each affected institution to draw up its own regulations concerning the use of campus facilities by speakers said to be subversive. If nothing had been done, the Southern Association of Colleges and Schools might have made good on a threat to strip UNC of SACS accreditation. Then in a court challenge, the law was declared unconstitutional, after which the Speaker

Ban devolved into a non-issue.

On the eve of final exams in 1964, Mickey and *DTH* photographer Jim Wallace should have been poring over class lecture notes. They opted instead to go to Greensboro to report on history being made. For the *DTH*, they covered a crucial civil rights march from the campus of a black university (then A & T College) into and through the downtown area that was led by a passionate young civil-rights activist who would become internationally known: Jesse Jackson. Police were braced for incidents of violence, but the only casualties to come out of that event were the grades that Mickey and Jim made on their exams. (Jim would later become director of printing and photographic services at the Smithsonian Institution and a member of the Board of Visitors of UNC's School of Journalism and Mass Communications.)

Some assignments, of course, were far removed from grave matters of state. Mickey interviewed sultry songstress Julie London after her campus concert while she relaxed with a menthol cigarette. "Miss Barefoot of 1964" (Sandra Morgan of Sanford, N.C.), far prettier than Miss London, cast a spell that had him gawking when he should have been jotting down the answers she gave to questions he asked. An interview with Chapel Hill's "Queen of Manners," Otelia Connor, who persistently scolded UNC students for their defiance of social behavior standards, got off to a bad start. Miss Otelia put her foot down: "I am not going to talk to you, Mr. Blackwell, as long as you are chewing gum." She was unmindful that ashes were falling upon an expensive-looking rug from the lighted coffin nail she was holding. He liked Benjamin Swalin, 62, conductor of the North Carolina Symphony for 25 years, but he didn't like what he had to say. "Rock and roll," Swalin said with a grimace, "is nothing but a chaotic sound

6-A THE CHARLOTTE OBSERVER Monday, Sept. 14, 1964

Bill Frida

Baseb

By MICKEY BLACKWELL
Observer Carolina News Service

CHAPEL HILL — William C. Friday never played center field for the New York Yankees, but then Mickey Mantle never became president of the Consolidated University of North Carolina.

Today, at 44 years of age, bespectacled Bill Friday, the state's top educator, still remembers his ambitions on the ball diamond.

WILLIAM C. FRIDAY, president of the Consolidated University of North Carolina, has another title. To daughter Betsy, he's daddy. (Observer Photo by David Nance)

Mickey stands beside the white pole under the "B" of Brady's Restaurant sign. He was covering this civil rights demonstration in Chapel Hill for the **Charlotte Observer** *and* **Raleigh Times***. (Photo courtesy NC Department of Archives)*

combined with great shouting. It's just beyond the definition of what you call music." It so happened that he was being interviewed by an inveterate rock fan who had become captivated long before he met the famous baton wielder, and never expected to be — or wanted to be — freed.

Through other interviews, he became friendly with Terry Sanford during the time he occupied the governor's mansion and L. Richardson Preyer of Greensboro, a Democrat and one-time federal judge who campaigned for votes in Chapel Hill while trying to be elected governor. A close association with President Friday dates from the time Mickey became administration reporter for *DTH*, when Friday was the youngster in the driver's seat at the "Greater University" of North Carolina. Mickey's three-part profile of Friday, also a Gaston County product, then 43 and in his eighth year as UNC president, appeared in *DTH* issues in April 1964.

Historic Woolworth's in Greensboro – future site of the International Civil Rights Museum

Thirty-five years later, Friday would provide the foreword for a book Mickey had written.

Before that, Mickey the reporter had covered more of the disruptions staged by CORE foot soldiers, including sit-ins at popular Chapel Hill dining establishments and at campus sporting events. Thirty-six arrests were made during four days of protesting at the restaurants. Police dragged the demonstrators to one side when they blocked the exit to a UNC gym parking lot.

Some of the arrests took place at Leo's Restaurant on Chapel Hill's West Franklin Street. Mickey was an observer, in the role of reporter. Leo mistook him for a demonstration leader and called for his arrest. A trip to jail was averted only because detective Howard Pendergraft of the city police department happened to recognize him as a member of the *DTH* staff. For a tense moment, Mickey could commiserate as never before with those being pushed and packed into waiting patrol cars.

There appeared in *DTH* in February a full-page ad with the headline "Proclamation to the Editors of *DTH*" and a preamble that read, "We the undersigned would like to have it known that, even though we may or may not approve of the tactics of the Chapel Hill Freedom Committee, we agree with its basic ideals, those of racial equality. Although some of us have no desire to become involved in the Civil Rights demonstrations and have never so much as carried a picket's sign, we intend to at least do our own small part by boycotting those businesses which refuse to admit that all men are created equal, regardless of race, creed, or national origin." Below this were about a thousand names, the last of which was — Michael C. Blackwell.

(The first sit-ins took place in Greensboro in February 1960. Four black students at North Carolina A&T College occupied stools

UNC Journalists Win State And National Merit Awards

Kirkpatrick And Blackwell Win 1st

Six Others Win Observer Awards

J-School 1st — 3 Are In Top 10

Clotfelter Win Clinches Top Spot

By DENNIS SANDERS

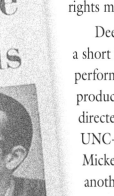

JIM CLOTFELTER
Another Win

MICKEY BLACKWELL SEATED AND CURRY KIRKPATRICK
Journalism Win Kids
—Photo by Jim Wallace

"Carolina Gentleman"

Greensboro is slated to become a national civil rights museum.)

Deep inside one issue of *DTH* was a short item announcing the opening performance of the Carolina Playmakers production of Archibald MacLeish's *JB,* directed by Harry E. Davis. A listing of UNC-CH students in the cast included Mickey Blackwell. So here was Mickey in another brush with acting and a new temptation to get serious about the stage. Davis also in this period was directing episodes of the long-running outdoor drama *Unto These Hills* in Boone, N.C.. He issued an invitation to join the cast of "Hills" that Mickey declined. Mickey explained that he was simply too occupied with completing requirements for a B.A. (If he succeeded, he would be the first in either branch of his family to earn a higher education degree.)

Courses at the journalism school provided experiences both memorable and of infinite value. He was assigned to do writing chores at the UNC news bureau under supervision of its famous director, Pete Ivey, and to do much the same at the *Chapel Hill Weekly* with its legendary editor looking over his shoulder, one of North Carolina's finest writers, Jim Shumaker, later a journalism school professor.

With May 1964 came Judgment Days. Some 17 college and university newspapers in North and South Carolina learned how they fared in the contest sponsored annually and jointly by the *Charlotte Observer* and the *Charlotte News.* Judges looked at 257 entries and

---

at the all-white lunch counter in Woolworth's on Elm Street and refused to leave. This sparked a national movement to end segregated public accommodations. Today, an eight-foot section of the lunch counter and four of its stools are a display at the Smithsonian Institution in Washington, D.C., in an exhibit entitled "Sitting For Justice: The Greensboro Sit-in of 1960." The old Woolworth location in

NORTH CAROLINA'S

Tribute

TO JOHN F. KENNEDY

For the benefit of the John Fitzgerald Kennedy Library
Featuring Addresses by Dr. Billy Graham and Others.

North Carolina's Tribute to
President JOHN F. KENNEDY

Featuring
An Address
by
DR.
BILLY
GRAHAM

4 B 00913

FIELD SEATS

Kenan Stadium
Chapel Hill
3 P. M.
MAY 17
1964

Kenan Stadium, Chapel Hi.

OBTAIN YOUR TICKETS FO... HIS HISTORIC
EVENT FROM YOUR COUNTY CHAIRMAN OR
...THE GOVERNOR'S OFFICE.
KENNEDY LIBRARY FUND.

gave 13 of the 23 press awards to *DTH*. Mickey won a first in news writing, $25 for one of his Speaker Ban stories, "Aycock Looses Blast at Speaker Gag," and an honorable mention for his interview with Julie London. Curry Kirkpatrick of Niagara Falls, New York, *DTH* sports editor, won a first in sports writing for a column on the retirement of baseball star Stan Musial.

DTH received honorable mention in the "best college newspaper" competition.

When they appeared together in a photo in the *DTH* as prizewinners, Mickey and Kirkpatrick rated identification as *DTH's* "Whiz Kids."

Also, the William Randolph Hearst Foundation, which rewarded outstanding work of college and university journalists and their institutions with cash prizes, announced three *DTH* staffers as winners. As a result, the UNC-CH School of Journalism was declared No. 1 among similar organizations across the country vying for foundation honors. The staffers picked up $1,950, and the school received the same amount. Mickey, Curry, and Jim Clodfelter of Atlanta, Georgia, a *DTH* co-editor prior to joining the ***Durham Morning Herald***, finished among the top 10 collegiate journalists nationally for the year 1963-64. Mickey wound up in eighth place in investigative/interpretive-writing and spot news writing for a series entitled "Rebels – do they have a cause?" (the story he was researching when he heard of JFK's assassination), which earned him $100, and his reports on local sit-ins, worth another $100. With these wins he accumulated enough points to put him in ninth place among all students competing in the Journalism Awards Program and made him the recipient of a foundation bronze medallion and scroll. Kirkpatrick was first in news writing with his account of how President Kennedy's death impacted Chapel Hill, which paid $750. Clodfelter's story in the news-writing category about the Ku Klux Klan won him $500.

Curry Kirkpatrick, undoubtedly one of the *DTH's* best writers, was summarily dismissed by Co-editor David Ethridge after he took the

Billy Graham

blame for the "Ad Staff Takes It In The Ear" article that appeared within one of the small boxes at the top of the sports page (known as "the ear") of a February 1964 issue of the *DTH*. The editor would not abide Kirkpatrick's disgust that big ads had eaten up space in the *DTH* that should have been filled with hot sports news. On the other hand, the sports department won only applause for this banner headline after the Tar Heel football team walloped the State Wolfpack and its noted school of agriculture: "Moo U goes down to udder defeat 31-10" (October 1963). Kirkpatrick found his way to **Sports Illustrated** and was one of its top sports writers for many years. His work there earned him recognition by the National Basketball Hall of Fame. When it came to getting married, Kirkpatrick arranged for his old friend Mickey Blackwell to officiate at the knot tying, a ceremony held on the beach at Hilton Head, S.C.

Mickey participated in, as a reporter for the *Observer*, North Carolina's last goodbye, one last salute, to JFK. The milieu once again was Kenan Stadium. Proceeds from gate receipts went toward strengthening the John Fitzgerald Kennedy Library.

Mickey officiated close friend Curry Kirkpatrick's wedding at Hilton Head.

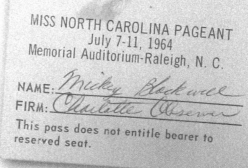

MISS NORTH CAROLINA PAGEANT
July 7-11, 1964
Memorial Auditorium-Raleigh, N. C.

NAME: *Micky Blackwell*
FIRM: *Charlotte Observer*

This pass does not entitle bearer to reserved seat.

Edward, and mother, Rose, both attended the event.

By waiting until a late hour to decide on journalism as a major, Mickey had to stay in school longer than four years. He was in classes through the summer and fall terms in 1964 in order to meet all journalism degree requirements. He continued to "string" for the **Raleigh Times** and also handle assignments from the *Observer*, one of which was the "Miss North Carolina Pageant" at Memorial Auditorium in Raleigh July 7-11.

The title was won by Sharon Finch of Thomasville. (In joining the Thomasville Rotary Club years later, he would make friends with Sharon's father, Rotarian and wealthy properties owner Harry B. Finch.)

His Bachelor of Arts in Journalism was awarded in January 1965. With that in his clutches, he was ready to choose from among the five news organizations that had offered him a job. Not included, he deeply regretted, was the **Charlotte Observer**. He had performed satisfactorily

Gov. Sanford was honorary chairman of the committee that arranged the tribute. Hugh Morton, UNC Class of 1943 and state tourism leader, was state chairman. Delivering the principal address was North Carolina's world-renowned preacher, Billy Graham. Kennedy's brother,

The Bell Tower is one of the enduring symbols of the University of North Carolina at Chapel Hill.

for that publication while in its Gastonia bureau and then as its campus representative, and he fully expected an overture after he interviewed at UNC with the paper's managing editor, Tom Fesperman. Yet, he was looking at offers from the **Richmond News-Leader** and the **Kansas City Star**, which knew of the awards he had won, as well as Jim Shumaker at the **Chapel Hill Weekly** and Pete Ivey at the UNC news bureau. But somehow he felt he would profit the most — well, he just knew intuitively, he has said, that it would be his best career move if he responded to the Durham (N.C.) **Morning Herald**. So early in February, he became the Herald's county government reporter and feature writer, Monday through Friday, at $90 a week. He also disc-jockeyed Saturdays and Sundays 7 p.m. to 1 a.m. at WKIX, an 850-AM radio station in Raleigh. Therefore, he was working seven nights a week. "But I loved both jobs," he said. The personal attention he received from each one produced instant gratification.

He could look back on his stay at UNC with pardonable pride. Though he never made the Dean's List, his grades were at least average or better. He studied only enough to get by. But the kid from Gaston County had toughed it out and had gone all the way — without much help. He received $250 each of three years by way of the student-aid scholarship, but what else was needed to cover costs, he earned with his own sweat.

Mickey was one of the fortunate for whom college turned out to be everything for which he hoped. A growing-up process, an awakening, a seasoning that he would always cherish. "I loved that school from the first day I walked on the campus until the day I took the last exam," he said. And among his pleasures late in life would be to tread the campus from time to time, rekindle his reverence for Old East, the Old Well, and the Davie Poplar, and feel blessed once more for the privilege of having sat at the knee of the likes of William Aycock and William Friday.

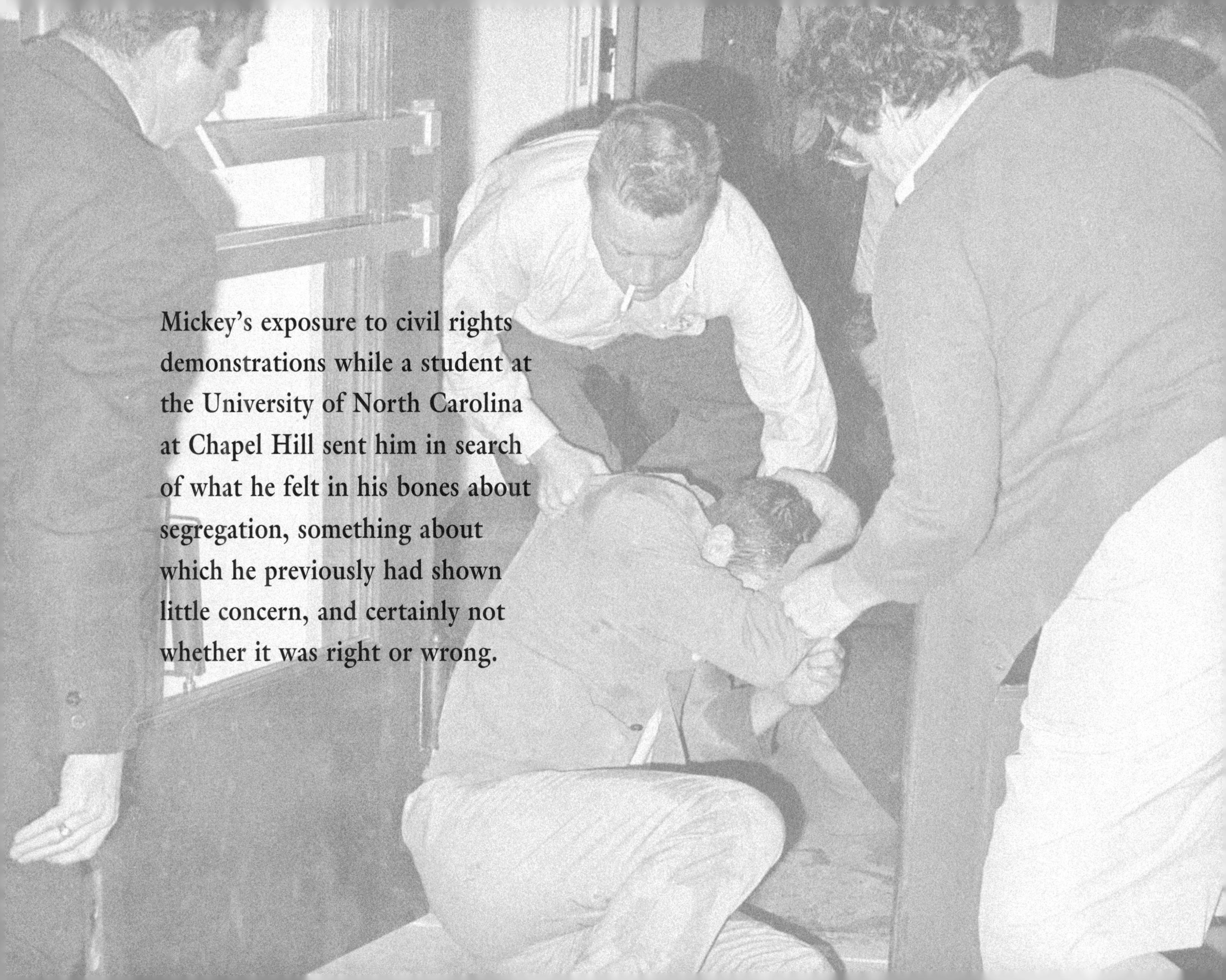

Mickey's exposure to civil rights demonstrations while a student at the University of North Carolina at Chapel Hill sent him in search of what he felt in his bones about segregation, something about which he previously had shown little concern, and certainly not whether it was right or wrong.

CHAPTER SIX – *Standing for Equality*

By the age of 12 or 13, Mickey was finding it puzzling that blacks and whites were being kept apart. Traveling with his father working his insurance debit in Gastonia's black community, Mickey never detected any cause or necessity for separating the races. The custom made him curious more than anything.

"Come on, Mickey, I dare you," coaxed Eddie. "You ain't scared, are you?"

Mickey and Eddie Taylor, with whom he had a "blood brothers" bond, looked for ways to defy entrenched southern behavior.

"I ain't scared. I'll show you."

Mickey took Eddie's dare. He drank deeply from the "Colored Only" water fountain in a downtown Gastonia store, Eagle 5 & 10. Somewhat to his surprise, the water tasted pretty much like any other coming from a fountain, except that maybe it was kind of warm instead of cool.

Civil rights marches and demonstrations were a regular part of the Chapel Hill landscape in 1963-64. (Photo copyright by Jim Wallace)

Mickey was an inquisitive child and curious about everything. Another time, he and Eddie went to the Gastonia railroad station and seated themselves in the "Colored Only" section, but they soon left when it became apparent this daring feat would produce no repercussions. After that, they went to the Lyric Theater, a cinema, where blacks were allowed to purchase a ticket, enter the theater through a "Colored Only" doorway, and climb stairs to a balcony for their exclusive use. One person occupied the ticket booth. She would swing on her stool to a window on her right to sell tickets to whites and swivel to the opposite window to serve blacks. Mickey said to her that he and Eddie would be able to see the screen better from the "colored" balcony, and therefore he wanted two tickets for this black section. Without an argument, she sold them two, for the regular price, 10 cents each, but could have been fired for selling a ticket to a black that allowed him or her to sit among the whites. Once in the balcony, the lads saw two black

Demonstrators vowed to remain non violent.
(Photo copyright by Jim Wallace)

persons mesmerized by the movie, but nothing held the attention of the white trespassers, the movie included. So they left.

In this period, Gastonia had three other movie houses. The others were totally segregated. Anti-segregation demonstrations were held in front of two of them, the Center and the Webb, during the 1960s.

Mickey's exposure to civil rights demonstrations while a student at the University of North Carolina at Chapel Hill sent him in search of what he felt in his bones, something about which he previously had

In his copyrighted photo, Jim Wallace captures the spirit of the "standing for equality" movement.

61

shown little concern, and certainly not whether it was right or wrong.

Mickey was a senior at UNC before he got to know a black person. Early in the 1963-64 year, he attempted polite conversation with Karen L. Parker, a junior journalism major from Winston-Salem. She responded in a friendly manner. Here was a remarkable, courageous young woman. Mickey thought she was loaded with personality — and an excellent writer. She is remembered as the first black female undergraduate at UNC, became the first black female to serve as editor of the School of Journalism's UNC *Journalist*, and was the first black female to graduate from UNC. But nothing shows that Mickey saw her as

Karen Parker

black and himself as white. He soon learned of her loneliness and isolation, how shut out she was. They worked side by side for a time at the *Journalist*, where he was an assistant editor. As they became better acquainted, at her request, he led her out of some of her problems and did it compassionately.

She would say long afterward that Mickey became her confidante. She disclosed her fears, her despair. "He was just an unusual guy — and a good journalist." She thought there were other students who wanted to socialize but were kept at a distance by the fear of being ostracized by their peers. "He stuck his neck out, helped me keep my

sanity." When Mickey graduated and left, "There was a big void . . . It was like one of my limbs had been cut off."

On one occasion, the big brother/little sister thing they had going raised suspicions at the administrative level. They were seen walking together through Polk Place, which was within sight of the office of the dean of men in South Building, while on their way to a story assignment on behalf of the *Journalist*. The next day, the dean, William Long, with whom Mickey was acquainted, called him aside to try to learn whether he and Karen were dating, as it appeared they might be. That, if true, harbored the potential to cause yet another ugly incident on a campus that at the time was on the lookout for any sign that segregation customs were being flaunted. The dean seemed relieved when Mickey assured him that his relationship with Karen was strictly that of good friends. Mickey doesn't remember that he was offended by the suspicions. Maybe

George Miller: At 18,

By MICKEY BLACKWELL

George Mason Miller is a prodigy with a capital P. He:

—appeared on a nation-wide quiz show when he was 11;
—lectured in Africa when he was 12;
—finished high school at 14;
—spent the following summer at Columbia University;
—graduated cum laude in History from Livingstone College when he was 17.

And now — at the ripe old age of 18 — he's beginning his second year as a graduate student in Political Science here. While others his age are taking Carolina's library orientation tour as entering freshmen, Miller is preparing to

George skip the f
His progress wa
enal that he also w
skip the fourth grad
of the seventh and ei
Now he is attendi
with graduate students
from five to 25 years o
he is.

And, there are drawba
attending classes with thos
are much older than hi
George quickly admits.
"I'm not as stable as mo
the other graduate
are," he says. "I don't
things through to the
most of the older stude
I have to let the cro
over a

the dean was just doing his job, just trying to keep the lid on a seething caldron of racial prejudices ready to spill out even from the slightest encouragement. Or maybe he intended to warn Mickey that a male student thought to be courting a black risked physical harm from the campus' most rabid segregationists. It was not until years later that he related this incident to Karen.

Before graduating in 1965 and as the campus civil rights movement picked up speed, Karen became an activist and discovered that she liked to "speak out." She considered herself "one of the beatniks, hippies," and ended up taking two trips to the jailhouse.

Slowly, Mickey arrived at the conviction that segregation was morally wrong and totally unacceptable. He was pushed along by vicious acts he witnessed, one of which occurred in 1963 in front of Watts Grill on Highway 15-501 a little south of Chapel Hill, where a sit-in demonstration was in progress. While one of the male demonstrators was sitting on the ground, a white waitress popped out of the restaurant, straddled him, and urinated. **Daily Tar Heel** carried a bare mention of it, but

Mickey recalled that the big dailies "wouldn't touch it."

Mickey didn't march against segregation, but he was, nevertheless, a demonstrator on behalf of civil rights for all and equal opportunities

Waitress at Watts Grill in Chapel Hill assists in removing a demonstrator.
(Photo copyright by Jim Wallace)

for everyone through how he acted and by the decisions he made — sometimes against the tide of public opinion — once he was in a leadership position, once he was at the forefront of institutions of one kind or another.

Many years later, Mickey could look back at his record in race relations and be confident that he chose to stand for equality and against discrimination.

Karen Parker went on to have a long career as a newspaper copy editor, including 14 years at the *Los Angeles Times*. She gave Mickey and his wife Kathy a tour of the paper when they were in town for a meeting of what was then called the National Association of Homes for Children.

Years later, John Railey of the *Winston-Salem Journal* was surprised to discover that Michael and Karen — now back home and a co-worker of Railey's at the *Journal* — were friends in college days.

"I get the feeling that Michael has

The purpose of the civil rights movement is summed up in this copyrighted photo by Jim Wallace.

a whole other side that people don't always see," said Railey, an editorial writer who got to know Mickey when Railey was the *Journal's* religion reporter. "We get a lot of press releases about all the good works he and Baptist Children's Homes do, but I never got the sense until recently that he's someone who has really pushed the status quo. He was one of the first and few whites to befriend Karen when she entered Carolina, and they remain friends to this day.

"A lot of Southerners," Railey continued, "would probably love to flaunt such a story, especially in these days when segregation is all but forgotten, but Blackwell doesn't. Maybe he felt he was just doing what was right, and there was no need to boast. Whatever his reasons, this very public guy's silence on that story tells me there's something very good at his core."

The Michael-Kathy romance and marriage had its beginning where the days were filled with excitement and surprises, at Big WAYS in the summer of 1965. Kathy was there for the summer months only, as a secretary. "Michael and I met over the Xerox machine," she said.

CHAPTER SEVEN – *"Here's C. Michael"*

"You've got to go for the interview," urged Mickey's roommate, Eddie Weiss.

"I'm a newspaperman now," insisted the young journalist.

"Well, it's a chance to be a part of something from the ground floor," his friend said, unrelenting.

Eddie had heard his radio friends talk of a Charlotte investor with grandiose ideas. Stan Kaplan and his wife, "Sis," had purchased New WAYS, a 5,000-watt radio station at 610 on the dial that was barely breathing. On charts that rated the popularity of Charlotte's eight or nine stations (all of them AM), 50,000-watt WBT was the favorite. New WAYS was in last place.

The enterprising Mr. Kaplan had in mind a number of things to do. One was a name change. His station became Big WAYS. For another, after an interview, Kaplan acquired the services of Mickey. He was an arm-twister who usually got his way. Mickey agreed to report for work June 1, 1965, although still without a convincing argument that he would be better off forsaking newspaper work in Durham and returning to radio in Charlotte. "I just trusted my gut," said Mickey.

Mickey's first broadcast, from a slightly makeshift control room, was proceeding without a hitch. "And in the local news," he said, stopping in mid-sentence. Looking up, there was a horse standing, looking back at him. Beside the horse, "Sis" Kaplan was standing, laughing uncontrollably.

"Well folks, it seems I have a special guest," he said, working the practical joke to his advantage. "I have a horse in our newsroom — yes, a horse."

C. Michael Blackwell works in the WAYS newsroom. "Big WAYS news...at your service."

Mickey was pleased, almost from the start, with the decision he had made. The time he spent helping to rescue a loser and putting it on top would prove to be as much fun, as exhilarating and as stimulating as anything he had ever done, or, for that matter, would ever do at a newspaper.

Kaplan gave Mickey the title of news/public affairs director and harnessed him with the veteran radio man he had hired to be program director, Jack Gale, a lively individual bursting with tricks and ruses to catch listeners.

Mickey took a liking to Gale, and Gale to Mickey, but the idea-man quickly set about making Mickey somebody else, or inventing a persona

Blackwell standing beside the WAYS "news wagon."

designed to gain him the attention of, and maybe popularity with, the owners of radios all across Charlotte and beyond. First, he tinkered with the name. Mickey became C. Michael Blackwell. Gale said it had a nice sound, or sounded better. Mickey approved — and found he could, as well, abide the other moniker Gale devised and to which he switched on occasions, "Sweet C."

It was at this point the determination arose to ditch the name he grew up with, and in its place use, and ask others to use, nope, not "Mike," but something he thought came across as less adolescent — maybe, well, more

dressy — possibly more suited to the professional life he had begun to live. It was the beginning of the struggle that has never ended to be addressed simply as Michael, or when in the guise of a radio newsman, as C. Michael.

Jingles had become commonplace in radio. Announcers had their

C. Michael, left, with WAYS crew in a Christmas parade in Waxhaw, N.C.

own to establish identity readily with an audience. Gale, a skillful jingle writer, created one for C. Michael. Gale said that during his 46 years in radio, he never knew another newsman to have one of his own. It went like this: "C. Michael Blackwell . . . Big WAYS . . . Number One." Another jingle ended . . . "Here's C. Michael." He usually played it or sang it as a cue for C. Michael to begin his first newscast of the day at 6:55 a.m.

They were on duty each weekday from 5:30 a.m. to 2:30 p.m. (and on the air together from 6 to 9). Michael had moved back in with his parents in Gastonia. He had to be an early riser in order to have break-

69

Just Call Me Mickey

fast, drive the 27 miles to Charlotte, and be at work on time. Gale made "Sweet C" his straight man in the banter they generated when not spinning records, reporting the news and weather, and airing commercials. He gave free rein to "Sweet C's big, booming voice . . . . I found him to be a great, quick-thinking ad-libber . . . . It was terrific having him on the news, and he was a wonderful fun guy, one you couldn't have replaced . . . . If he'd stayed with radio, he would have become a network star."

Kaplan spent great sums of money on promotions, thinking he would get it all back, and then some. And he was right. Big WAYS billboards appeared all over Charlotte. The Big WAYS message on one that businessmen could read as they left the airport and headed home read, "While you were away, we entertained your wife." A treasure hunt was staged every week for 10 weeks. The station would hide or bury a $1,000 certificate someplace, then broadcast clues to its location until somebody found it. Hundreds and hundreds of listeners went treasure hunting — and sometimes caused traffic jams. Ten thousand dollars was given away. Annual Big WAYS birthday balls were inaugurated at the Charlotte Coliseum. They were open to the public for an admission charge of 99 cents. The coliseum filled up. Entertainment was provided by some of the biggest names in show business: The Four Seasons, Stevie Wonder, and the Monkees.

The WAYS staff appeared weekly at area charitable benefits. Here, C. Michael rouses the crowd.

"We turned Charlotte upside down," C. Michael said. The number of listeners grew steadily and the volume of advertising shot up. A Big WAYS national sales office was opened in New York City. In charge was Jim Beaty, a former University of North Carolina track star who was the first to run a sub four-minute mile indoors. Soon, C. Michael was heading a staff of five in the news department. He was given a station wagon to use (he said "goodbye" to his 1953 Plymouth), on the sides of which was emblazoned "Big WAYS."

Recruited from among station employees were the "Big WAYS Good Guys," a team that made appearances all over Charlotte and several counties. They might pour out of their "Fun Wagon" van at an local high school sporting event and engage the school's cheerleaders in a game of powder-puff football. Such shenanigans usually were a fund-raiser for some local cause. C. Michael was a "Good Guy." He oftentimes spent half the day in the studio and most of the night helping with some "Good Guys" stunt. They went up against the Harlem Globetrotters at the coliseum, an encounter that made C. Michael's head swim. He had to play the legendary Meadowlark Lemon man-to-man. The spectators cheered wildly when Michael, with the ball and unable to escape Meadowlark's defensive maneuvering, simply surrendered it to his tormentor, who dashed away and executed a two-point goal with

The courageous Big WAYS good guys played friendly games of football against local girls teams.

as much grace and skill as any basketeer who had ever lived.

"It was hard work, long hours, but exciting good times," according to C. Michael. "I thrived on it. Jack Gale made a celebrity out of me. I became as well-known as any of our more popular disc jockeys."

Gale, who went on to win national disc jockey and program director awards, has credited much of station's success to programming that appealed to bubblegum-chewing 13-year-olds. Within a year, Big WAYS had moved ahead of big-time WBT. A new ratings report placed it first, not just in Charlotte, but in 36 counties in the central and western part of North Carolina. Kaplan turned down $4 million for his $500,000 investment with, "You ain't seen nothing yet."

When C. Michael had time for himself, WAYS remained in his

At the Ridgecrest Baptist Conference Center in 1967, Blackwell, left, is named a national speaker of distinction.

thoughts. He went to New York City for a radio news directors conference. During a recess, he took a walk on Third Avenue. A motorcade with police sirens stopped near him. A man stepped out of a limousine that Michael recognized immediately as Russian Premier Kosygin. He wanted to stroll the remaining five or six blocks to the Russian Embassy. Michael watched as he did, then later called in a report of what he had seen to Big WAYS.

C. Michael Blackwell

The North Carolina Associated Press Broadcasters Association named him one of its directors.

To be a celebrity was to receive invitations to give speeches. He developed a knack for being able to pon-

BLACKWELL NAMED
C. Michael Blackwell of Gastonia was elected as one of directors of the North Carolina Associated Press Broadcasters Association.
Blackwell is affiliated with Station WAYS in Charlotte.

tificate on a wide range of subjects. "Speaking and emceeing turned out to be really harder to do than I expected, but if a person goes into something with the attitude of enjoying it, he usually winds up doing so." He spoke before a Baptist Brotherhood and at various civic club meetings. In his only speech about radio, he let an Optimist club in Gastonia know the industry was not all he wished it to be. "Radio just ain't what it used to be," he lamented while contrasting the old-time shows, such as "The Shadow" and "The Fred Allen Show," with modern-day programs featuring little more than disc jockeys spinning records. Still, "Radio remains a potent force in America. As a matter of fact, the transistor radio is the single most valuable piece of equipment a family can own in time of crisis.

Radio can probably lay claim to being the greatest discovery of science. No other science has so dramatically changed the path of man."

Another Optimist Club heard him express regret that "Failure of the parents and the church to give sufficient direction to youth has resulted in their drifting into demonstrations of protest, into illicit drugs and other forms of immorality."

C. Michael emceed the Lake Norman Beauty Contest, and "the familiar voice you hear each morning on Big WAYS as news and public affairs director" was also master of ceremonies at the Miss Stanley Pageant. He kept the Jaycees' "Battle of Bands" at Hunter Huss High School moving smartly along as the man in charge of the microphone. These experiences boosted his ego, and his billfold, to the tune of $50 to $75 a pop.

He worked long and hard at Big WAYS from mid-1965 to mid-1967, during which short span of time he also, believe it or not, was an active leader in his home church, tried to derail a liquor vote in his hometown, met Kathy Kanipe and married her, won an important declamation contest, helped a friend win the office of mayor of Gastonia, finished making up his mind to leave radio and study to become a Baptist minister, and received

a license to preach.

No doubt about it anymore, Michael had really learned how to hustle. He was certain by then, "I'm hard-wired for work."

He wrote and memorized a speech titled "What Is Success." Then he used it to win a speaking contest at his home church. He also won in a competition at the association level and at the regionals, to advance to the state finals. Competing in Boone, N.C., in April 1967, he, having been declared winner of the State Speakers Tournament, received a Certificate of Merit from the Training Union Department of the

First In Better Speakers Contest
Voice Key To Blackwell Success

By ALICE ANGIER
Gazette Staff Reporter

When C. Michael Blackwell was born in Gaffney, S. C., the first cries heard by his parents, Mr. and Mrs. Clitus Blackwell, were of course, special.

But they could not forecast that, in later years to come, the sound of his voice would have a special meaning to thousands of other people as well.

This deep, clear voice which resounds over the pulpit of Flint-Groves Baptist Church on occasion, recently helped Mickey Blackwell place first in a local "Better Speakers" contest, sponsored by the Baptist Training Union.

From here, he went to the Gaston County contest in Cherryville, where he also placed first. At the regional contest in Hickory, he walked away with top honors again, and remarked, "I was lucky."

At the state contest, held in Boone, he expounded once more on his topic, "What Is Success?", and was selected all-state winner. He will represent North Carolina in the south - wide "Better Speakers" contest, in July in which seven states will partici-

pate.

★ ★ ★

Blackwell has also spoken at various churches in this area, where he grew up, as well as to youth groups, clubs and organizations, such as the Red Cross.

"If you feel you have something worthwhile to say, and the opportunity to say it arises," he said, "then I feel it is your duty to say it.'

On several occasions, he has emceed beauty pageants and band contests throughout the state. "It's really harder to do than I thought it would be," he admitted, "but if a person goes into something with the attitude of enjoying it, he usually winds up doing so."

Blackwell applies this particular philosophical phrase when he works with young people, and he especially enjoys working with them in the church.

He is president of the Baptist Young Men at Flint-Groves Church, where he is a member, and is also superintendant of the intermediate department, which is designed for 13 and 14 year olds.

C. MICHAEL BLACKWELL

"Besides talking about our lessons which are provided each week for the intermediate group," he said, "we discuss everything that concerns the teen-ager today, such as drinking and smoking, as well as current events. I feel that the church

can play an important role in helping a teen-ager to cope with these things."

Another area where Blackwell enjoys applying his time is at his job as news director at WAYS radio station in Charlotte.

"I feel that my getting this job was fate, as I believe fate plays a great role in all things."

"When I was offered the job, something inside me said, 'take it', so I did.

"Somehow I knew that I would be a happier person for having done so, and that's exactly how things have worked out. Besides enjoying writing editorials and covering elections, I met Kathy Kanipe, a girl who has reshaped my future plans and will become my wife on Aug 12."

As a result of being news director at WAYS, Blackwell was recently elected to the board of directors of the Associated Press Broadcasters Association, whose job is to find better ways of covering the news of the Carolinas. Only two members were elected from North and South Carolina.

★ ★ ★

Also in line with his job at the radio station, he was recently in New York for the Eastern Regional News Directors

Baptist State Convention of North Carolina and the right to compete in a national tournament at Ridgecrest Assembly near Asheville, N.C., on July 8. There, he came out on top once again, during the annual Baptist Training Union leadership and youth conference. He was one of 17 state winners who spoke before an audience of 1,000. Six of these, including Michael, were adjudged worthy of the premier award, the designation of "Speaker of Distinction," conferred by the Sunday School Board of the Southern Baptist Convention. For yet another time, Michael's rich baritone had served him extremely well.

It was his home church pastor, the Rev. Hoyle Allred, who drew him into the liquor controversy. Allred had called together a number of scorners of John Barleycorn, and an organization they called ALERT was created. Its major concern was the movement underway to lower Gastonia's bar to Alcoholic Beverage Control stores. But they made their mission also to stamp out prostitution, end the traffic in narcotics, and deter other civic evils. An executive committee was named. At Allred's request, Michael agreed to serve as youth advisor. Plans were laid for an ALERT

THERE IS STILL TIME
TO OPPOSE LIQUOR FOR GASTONIA

I want to personally thank the hundreds of people who showed up at City Hall Tuesday in opposition to liquor, beer and wine in Gastonia. Believe me, your presence was not in vain, even though the council members in favor of a vote on liquor refused to be swayed.

Your support and prayers are needed now more than ever. Even if we lost the battle Tuesday, we shall win this war, and final victory WILL be ours.

You can begin now by joining with other Christian friends in organizing opposition to the upcoming liquor election. In two years, don't forget those Councilmen who Tuesday disagreed on the issue at a time when city unity was desperately needed.

There IS still time . . .

MICKEY BLACKWELL

CHRISTIAN YOUTH AGAINST LIQUOR

membership drive. A goal of 10,000 memberships was set. ALERT was to be a permanent organization. Allred explained, "We hope to be influential far beyond Gastonia city limits, into the county, state, and nation."

Michael made several speeches to promote the ALERT agenda. And he was one of its spokesmen when ALERT standard-bearers descended upon a Gastonia City Council meeting May 16, 1967, at which was scheduled a vote for or against calling on the North Carolina General Assembly to authorize a referendum in which Gastonia citizens could agree to or oppose ABC stores. Councilmen heard Michael express regret that liquor was a growing problem but pointed out that Gastonian youth had not yet been exposed to dangers inherent in legalized liquor sales, and he hoped they would not be in the future. For council members to help make possible a referendum would be a mistake, he argued. For one thing, it would precipitate a citizens' fight. The council would be labeled pro-liquor. Anyway, a majority of citizens didn't want a vote. The justification for one did not exist. "Just because a vocal minority wants to withdraw from Vietnam, we don't put it up for a vote," Michael said.

Before adjourning, the council gave Michael and the others an answer: a vote of 4-3 to seek a referendum. Michael answered that with an ad he placed in the Gastonian paper a few days later: "Don't forget in two years those councilmen who Tuesday disagreed on the issue at a time when city unity was desperately needed." Which could be translated as, in the next municipal election, please vote out of office those who showed favor for a liquor vote. Michael signed the ad on behalf of "Christian Youth Against Liquor." It called on other Christians to join the youth in organizing opposition to any attempt to establish a store at which liquor could be purchased.

But the old college try was not enough. The influence of the church people and the "dry" forces did not reach quite far enough this time. An act to permit a referendum breezed through the General Assembly. On September 19, 1967, voters favored ABC stores by a 28-vote margin, or 5,409 to 5,381. The first legal sale of liquor in Gastonia, in modern times, occurred December 1, 1967, the day on which the first ABC store opened.

Michael was then found to be flirting with local politics again, yet, although now a loyal Democrat, he had limited himself to taking an interest in nonpartisan issues — the liquor store controversy and the Gastonia munici-

ALERT Organized
Dry Forces Seek 10,000 Members

By ALICE THOMPSON
Gazette Staff Reporter

An organization known as ALERT has been created to fight liquor legislation, and to stamp out illegal liquor, prostitution, and narcotics, its leaders announced Saturday.

In order to halt "civic evils," the Rev. Hoyle Allred, pastor of Flint-Groves Baptist Church, a leader in ALERT, announced the organization had selected an executive committee.

A goal of 10,000 members has been set with a membership drive underway.

"Our organization will be a permanent one and we hope to influence far beyond the Gastonia city limits into the county, state and nation," Allred said.

ALERT has been designed, the minister noted, to help schools strengthen students morally and, in addition, to boost the morale of city policemen in trying to halt what has appeared to be a growing disrespect for the law.

The ALERT executive committee members are: Ward 1, Mrs. W. C. Rucker and Ray Kayler; Ward 2, Mrs. Clyde Wright and Bill Powers; Ward 3, R. L. Schooler and Ray England; Ward 4, Mrs. John Wright and J. S. Mitchell; Ward 5, Jewel Lynn; Ward 6, Douglas Childress and Forest Roberts Jr.

The Rev. M. O. Owens Jr. is pastor advisor and youth advisor is Mickey Blackwell.

pal elections.

(The friend he helped win the office of mayor was Earl T. Groves, who took office in May 1967. Therefore, his friend was presiding at the council meeting at which a vote in favor of an ABC store referendum took place. It was not the mayor's place to vote that morning — there were no ties to break — yet Groves asked that the record show he was personally opposed to the holding of a referendum.)

At Flint-Groves Church, Michael served as president of Baptist Young Men and superintendent of the Intermediate Department, for 13- and 14-year-olds. His specialty was to engage the young people in discussions of current events and show them how answers to current problems, those related to drinking and smoking and such, could be found in the Christian faith.

While in New York City to attend the conference for news directors — the time he encountered the

First date: June 19, 1965, at Charlotte's La Roma Restaurant. Kathy's dog, Patsy, was very protective.

Premier Kosygin motorcade — Michael talked with a CBS producer, Joseph Dembo, about working for his network. The job interview had been set up by Charles Kuralt, a one-

With her brother in front, her sister to her left, and her father by her side,
Kathy prepares for the walk down the aisle.

time WAYS announcer who had been at CBS several years but was yet
to become famous and beloved for his "Sunday Morning" and "On The
Road" shows. Kuralt, from Charlotte, had offered to open a door or
two for Michael at the time that Michael had called to say he would be
visiting New York City and would also like to visit with him. There had
been no meeting face-to-face up until then, but in the course of collecting news for Big WAYS, Michael had become acquainted with his father,
Wallace Kuralt, director of the Welfare Department in Mecklenburg,
Charlotte's county.

The professional compliments received over the years that Michael
prizes as highly as any are those rating his voice and delivery on a par
with the speaking style that helped make Charles a television star.

The producer offered Michael a position on a news rewrite desk.
It was a place from which one could break into the big time. The inter-

viewee bowed and promised to respond without delay. But he never
seriously considered accepting. He kept wondering whether his future
might be behind a pulpit. And his head had become filled with thoughts
of getting married.

The Michael-Kathy romance and marriage had its beginning
where the days were filled with excitement and surprises, at Big WAYS
in the summer of 1965. Kathy was there for the summer months only,
as a secretary. "Michael and I met over the Xerox machine," she said.
She had completed one year at a two-year institution, Brevard College

August 12, 1967, at Charlotte's First ARP Church

at Brevard, N.C., where she was studying secretarial science and had
been elected to serve as president of the Westminster Fellowship.

She was born Mary Catherine Kanipe on November 5, 1945, in
Winston-Salem, N.C., daughter of Jack Edgar Kanipe and Mildred Deal
Kanipe. Not long afterward, the family left the Twin City and settled

in Charlotte, at 4941 Tewkesbury Road. Kathy received a high school diploma at North Mecklenburg High, graduated at Brevard in the spring of 1966, and went to work as a secretary at Charlotte offices of Piedmont Natural Gas Co.

The newlyweds

She and Michael began dating soon after she went to work for Piedmont. At one point he disclosed to her that she was keeping company with someone who might become a preacher. That failed to discourage her, and the courtship continued.

To his pastor, the Rev. Mr. Allred — but not to others, not even his parents — Michael also explained how he felt drawn toward devoting his time to expounding the gospel and that he was thinking about going back to school, to enroll at a seminary. The response he got was: Godspeed.

He received clearance from the pastor to appear before the congregation at Flint-Groves Church on a Sunday in December 1966. It was Christmas Day. In the large attendance were Clitus and Viola, of course. Michael made two major announcements: he had become engaged to marry Kathy Kanipe and he had decided to dedicate his life to the ministry. As he would explain regarding his calling, he had kept resisting, but the ministry had just kept beckoning. "If I was to have any peace, to get any sleep, I had to do what God wanted me to do."

On that most special day, he could hear the pews murmur an approval and see his parents quietly rejoice that what they thought

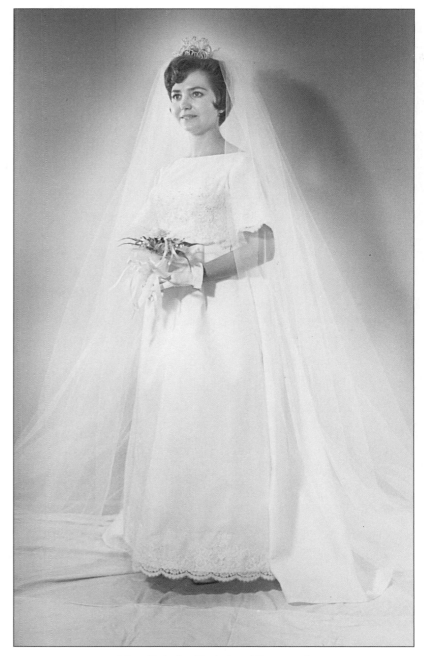

Mary Catherine Kanipe's wedding portrait

might happen would happen. For the only time ever, Michael witnessed his father weeping openly.

The Blackwell-Kanipe marriage bonds were formed in a ceremony  on Saturday, August 12, 1967, at 7 p.m. in surroundings selected by Kathy — First Associate Reformed Presbyterian on Tryon Street in Charlotte. Officiating was her pastor, the Rev. W. Nale Falls, who was assisted by Michael's, the Rev. Mr. Allred. The church in which they were married later suffered heavy

The newlyweds honeymooning on the Outer Banks in Nags Head, N.C..

interior fire damage, but in time was fixed up, and today is the Hugh McColl Arts Center.

The bride's attendants were sister Rachel Kanipe Denham as matron-of-honor and Brevard College classmates as honorary bridesmaids. The groom's best man was his father, and ushers were brothers-in-law Bob Denham and Stephen Kanipe, Big WAYS announcer Mike Greene, and Gastonia schoolmate Bob Culp.

A canceled check shows the newlyweds spent their wedding night in the honeymoon suite at the Voyager Inn in Durham. Charge for the suite was $14.42. The next day, they headed for Nags Head, registered at the Sea Foam Motel, and began partaking of the many pleas-

ures the vacationer can find along North Carolina's Outer Banks. For Michael, it would have been far more fun had he not allowed himself to acquire a most painful sunburn his first day on the beach.

Managing Editor Tom Fesperman phoned him with a chance to do something Michael once itched to do, work full time for the ***Charlotte Observer***. Fesperman would have put him on track to be in charge of the paper's Gastonia bureau. But the call came much too late. Michael responded politely with a "Thanks very much, but I've got these other plans," and hung up.

His experiences in journalism, radio, and speaking to church groups and youth organizations had awakened in him "an interest in the human condition." He began to feel that his place in life should be somewhere he could help make this condition a little better. "But I was always rationalizing. I thought I could do just as well by being a good Christian witness in my chosen career." When he couldn't hold out any longer, he reasoned, "Well, the ministry is communicating, too."

MICHAEL C. BLACKWELL
2106 LANDER AVE.
GASTONIA, N. C.

66-127
531

Day to the order of VOYAGER INN, DURHAM   August 13 19 67   No. 147

Fourteen Dollars & Forty Two Cents $14.42   DOLLARS

For Honeymoon Suite

FIRST UNION NATIONAL BANK
OF NORTH CAROLINA
GASTONIA, NORTH CAROLINA   Michael C. Blackwell

⑈0531⑈0127⑈   12 02 381⑈   ⑈000000 1442⑈

He would add later, in 1967, "My career to date, and any fame or fortune I may have achieved, is all part of God's master plan. I'm going from one extreme to another, from a lot of money to no money, but that's not everything. Most people can't understand it. But I know it's the Lord's will and that he will take care of us . . . . This has been on my mind a long time. If it were up to me, I probably would have stayed in the radio business. But it's up to God."

At Flint-Groves church Sunday night, August 27, 1967, he was licensed to preach in a dedication service. His first official act minutes later was most unusual. He baptized his wife, the Southern Baptist way — total immersion. She had put aside her Presbyterian affiliation and embraced her new husband's denomination. Michael said that baptizing her was "a wonderful experience for both of us, one we will never forget."

Two days later, a headline in the *Charlotte Observer* read: "Blackwell Leaves WAYS For Pulpit." The story below reported that he would be enrolling at the Southeastern Baptist Seminary at Wake Forest, N.C., two

Blackwell Leaves WAYS For Pulpit

By SUSAN JETTON
Observer Staff Writer

A local radio newsman has quit show business to enter a seminary in preparation for full-time Christian ministry.

Radio WAYS news director C. Michael Blackwell said Monday that he had submitted his resignation to the radio station and would enter Southeastern Theological Seminary at Wake Forest next week.

Blackwell, a native of Gastonia, said, "This has been on my mind for a long time. If it were up to me, I probably would have stayed in the radio business. But it's up to God."

C. M. Blackwell
. . . 'All God's Plan'

Sunday morning, dedication services for Blackwell were held at his home church, Flint-Groves Baptist Church of Gastonia, and he was licensed to preach.

His first official act as a Baptist preacher was to baptize his bride of two weeks, the former Kathy Kanipe, daughter of Mr. and Mrs. Jack Kanipe of 4941 Tewkesbury Road in Charlotte, on Sunday night. She has been a Presbyterian.

It's a rather unusual situation when a preacher baptizes his own wife, and Blackwell said that it was "a wonderful experience for us both, one we will never forget."

For several years, Blackwell, 25, had considered entering some form of Christian service.

"But I always rationalized, I thought I could do just as well by being a good Christian witness in my chosen career."

On Christmas morning last year, he told the congregation at Flint-Groves, where he fre-

quently has preached, that he had made up my mind.

"If I want to have any peace, to get any sleep, I have to do as God wants me to do."

Blackwell, who joined the radio station a little over two years ago, formerly had been a reporter in The Observer's Gaston bureau and a correspondent for The Observer in Chapel Hill where he majored in journalism at the University of North Carolina.

"My career to date and any fame or fortune I may have achieved is all just a part of God's master plan," he said.

"I'm going from one extreme to another," he said. "From a lot of money to no money, but that's not everything. Most people can't understand it. But I know it's the Lord's will and he will take care of us."

weeks later. The all-business owner of Big WAYS was astonishingly charitable. Usually when an employee of his spoke of leaving, Stan Kaplan sent him packing that very day. He permitted Michael to work a two-weeks notice, which was fortunate for the future preacher's pocketbook. Kaplan gave him a pat on the back, and he remarked as he turned to staff members standing close by, "You can't go any higher than where C. Michael's going." It was his way of saying, "The only way a person can do better than work for Stan Kaplan is to go to a seminary and work for the Lord."

Michael purchased a used car, a 1963 Plymouth Valiant, and he and Kathy made ready to move to Wake Forest. And so it was that he traded delivering bad news to preaching *Good News*.

He and other seminarians attended classes on a Tuesday-Friday schedule. On the weekends, he worked, which included supply (fill-in) preaching. Most other students did the same.

CHAPTER EIGHT – *On Higher Ground*

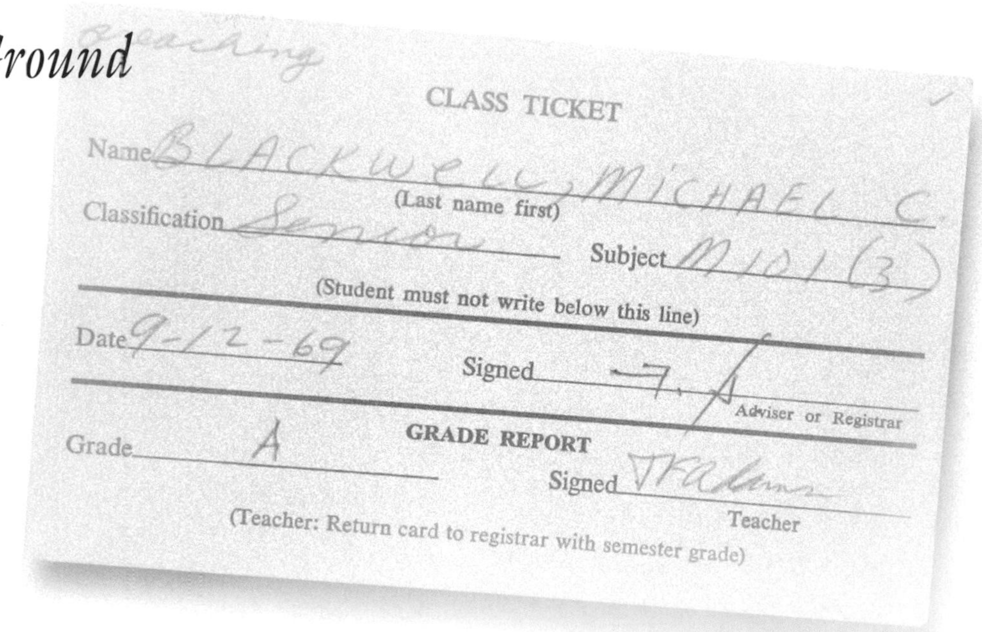

CLASS TICKET

Name BLACKWELL, MICHAEL C.
(Last name first)

Classification Senior   Subject M 101 (3)

(Student must not write below this line)

Date 9-12-69   Signed 7. A.
    Adviser or Registrar

Grade   A   GRADE REPORT
    Signed JR Adams
    Teacher

(Teacher: Return card to registrar with semester grade)

This first day of classes at Southeastern Baptist Theological Seminary in Wake Forest is not much different from the first day of classes any other semester at any other school. Students hurry to class. The rooms fill up, books are opened, and students look to the front of the class. The professor proceeds with his roll call.

"Here," answers one student.

Two desks away another sounds off, "Here."

The professor had taken roll call for years, class after class. It was a standard, almost hypnotic exercise — a necessity nevertheless. "Michael C. Blackwell?" he droned.

"Present," Michael says.

Slowly looking up, the seasoned theologian notes his new student.

The Olin T. Binkley Chapel is the focal point on the campus of Southeastern Baptist Theological Seminary in Wake Forest, N.C..

In contrast to when he entered UNC, Michael, now 25 years old, answered his first roll call at the seminary in September 1967 having resolved to post a record in scholarship commensurate with his abilities to speak, write, and think better than average. He was one of about 600 students, and there were close to 30 faculty members. Dr. Olin T. Binkley was president. In the back of Michael's mind was earning all three of the degrees then being offered. As he said, he was a married student who had settled down, was more mature by a mile, and knew a thing or two about what he wanted to do, where to go, and how to get there.

Whereas UNC-Chapel Hill, where Michael enrolled to earn an undergraduate degree, was a venerable institution, the one at which he enrolled for postgraduate study was younger than Michael himself.

The date on which Southeastern Baptist Theological Seminary had its beginning was May 19, 1950, when the Southern Baptist Convention voted to create it among the shade trees in the North Carolina town of Wake Forest.

For a long time, Wake Forest had been best known as the home of Wake Forest College. Then, once the decision was made to relocate the college, also a Baptist institution, those dedicated to fulfilling The Great Commission set about replacing the college with yet another Baptist seminary, on behalf of the SBC, by appropriating the beautiful campus the college was vacating.

Removal of the college to Winston-Salem, N.C., where it rapidly gained stature and became Wake Forest University, was not completed until 1958. Meanwhile, seminary classes were inaugurated in the departing college's Appleby Hall in September 1951. Three faculty members were available to steer 85 students toward a Bachelor of Divinity degree. By 1958, the seminary had achieved recognition from the American Association of Theological Schools and was well on the way to becoming one of the nation's most respected seminaries.

The Wake Forest community gradually shed most of its small-town trappings. It grew in population as Raleigh, the state capital, only 20 miles to the southwest, rapidly expanded. The town morphed into a bedroom community. Raleigh, Wake Forest, and other close neighbors now make up a region often ranked as one of the most desirable places in the country to live and make a living.

Capitol Broadcasting shown here in 1967, has become one of the nation's most progressive media outlets.

He and other seminarians attended classes on a Tuesday-Friday schedule. On the weekends, he worked, which included supply (fill-in) preaching. Most other students did the same. What most others did not do, but he did, was earn mostly A's, a few B's, and never a C in the 36 courses he took during the three years from 1967-70.

To benefit his checkbook balance, he put his news-writing skills to work in Southeastern's public relations department. But for more

money and more excitement, he quit after four months and accepted a job with one of the leading television stations in the state, A.J. Fletcher's WRAL (Channel 5) in Raleigh. His hiring followed an interview with Fletcher's right-hand man, Jesse Helms, WRAL's general manager and editorialist. This is the same Jesse who in 1972, after having switched his registration from Democrat to Republican, was elected U.S. senator from North Carolina on the Republican ticket (he and Jim Holshouser, named governor, were the first GOPers to be elected in statewide balloting in the 20th century) and by the end of year 2002,

A.J. Fletcher

when he retired, had distinguished himself in the Senate for 30 years as an archconservative, a bane of the Democratic party. (In a year-end interview in 1972, Helms credited his election primarily to his having become well-known and popular with the political right wing while doing WRAL broadcasts, voicing his scathing criticism over the course of seven years, "every night preaching the sound gospel.")

Michael, the staunch Democrat, was mainly part-time to start with — a reporter and 11 p.m. news show co-anchor. In the summer, he worked full-time. He was an employee when WRAL aired its

EMPLOYEE IDENTIFICATION

Michael Blackwell

IS AN EMPLOYEE OF
CAPITOL BROADCASTING COMPANY, INC.

Station WRAL-TV ☒
Station WRAL-FM ☐
Woody Hayes Music ☐

SIGNATURE OF EMPLOYEE

Louise Stephenson
AUTHORIZED SIGNATURE

153

first programs in color.

While at the station on a night in April 1968, he did something many newsmen dream of doing but seldom have reason or an excuse to. It was two hours or more before the 11 p.m. newscast. What had fallen into his lap simply couldn't wait. He, acting alone, dared to interrupt the station's regular programming in order to air a dynamite news bulletin: Dr. Martin Luther King Jr. had been shot — as it would turn out, fatally wounded by an assassin. He and WRAL most likely were the second announcer/station in the country to disclose via a public broadcast this sensational turn of events.

Such a brash act on his part was followed almost immediately by a jolt of self-doubt. What if, after all, King was alive and well, that the source of the bulletin was in error? But anxiety was fleeting. Within minutes, the American Broadcasting Co. (ABC), with which WRAL was affiliated, broke in with an announcement that, yes indeed, the life of the famous civil rights leader was over.

The scoop was made possible only because Michael was in cahoots with Jim Goodmon. Goodmon was A.J. Fletcher's grandson and now president of WRAL's parent, Capitol Broadcasting Co. of Raleigh. In April 1968, he was in the U.S. Navy, stationed at a naval base in the city in which King was slain, Memphis, Tennessee. Goodmon worked part time at a Memphis television station.

Michael C. Blackwell Licensed to Ministry

Michael C. (Mickey) Blackwell has been licensed to the ministry by the Flint Groves Church in Gastonia. Earlier this year, Blackwell, 25, was awarded first place in the N. C. Training Union Better Speakers Contest. He was later awarded a Speaker of Distinction award at Ridgecrest.

For the last 2½ years, the graduate of the University of North Carolina School of Journalism served as news director at Radio Station WAYS in Charlotte. Prior to that, he was reporter for the *Durham Morning Herald*. He has entered Southeastern Seminary and while there will be working in the Seminary's Public Relations Department.

Blackwell

While in the newsroom there (it being supper time, he was alone), he heard a highway patrol radio issue the bulletin that King had been shot. Goodmon, about Michael's age of 26, listened while that shocker was almost immediately confirmed, and then quickly called his TV station to break the news in Memphis, after which he quickly telephoned Michael.

Jim Goodmon, right, is the grandson of A.J. Fletcher, and is President/CEO of Capitol Broadcasting.

It seems a safe claim that the shocking news reached the public, first, from Goodmon and his station in Memphis, and second, from Michael and his station in Raleigh.

In other ways, Michael was once again enjoying the excitement peculiar to newsgathering. He covered phases of the 1968 elections in North Carolina, for example, and, where more than words were being fired off, the riot at Raleigh's Central Prison, on April 17, 1968, in which six inmates were killed and 77 injured. The riot was an outgrowth of prisoners complaints. They didn't like the food or the incentive pay they were receiving.

In 1969, he left the station when two jobs became too much. The other was of far greater importance to achieving his goals, serving as interim pastor at a beautiful town on the North Carolina coast at the First Baptist Church of Beaufort.

He made a round trip to Beaufort, about 300 miles, practically every weekend in his aging Valiant for almost all of 1969. First Baptist there served as the church to request his ordination, which took place in March 1969 in the same place he had been licensed to preach, at the place he dearly loved, Flint-Groves Baptist in Gastonia. The ordination rites were led by three men whom Michael has declared more than once had as much influence on the kind of life he chose to lead as any others — three former pastors at Flint-Groves: Love Dixon,Wilburn Hendrix, and Hoyle Allred. (Michael once wrote that Love Dixon "taught me the most about being a pastor . . . . He led me to the Lord when I was 8 years old . . . . I copied Hendrix's evangelistic fervor . . . . From Allred I learned about administration. Allred's wife says she can see much of his leadership style in me, and I am proud of that.")

Music at the ordination service was under direction of Clitus Blackwell, Michael's father.

Southeastern maintained a service it called the field education office. Here one could find a list of places and organizations looking for assistance that students at Southeastern might provide. Students kept an eye on the list if they were in need of money or practical experience or both. It enabled Michael to make his Beaufort connection.

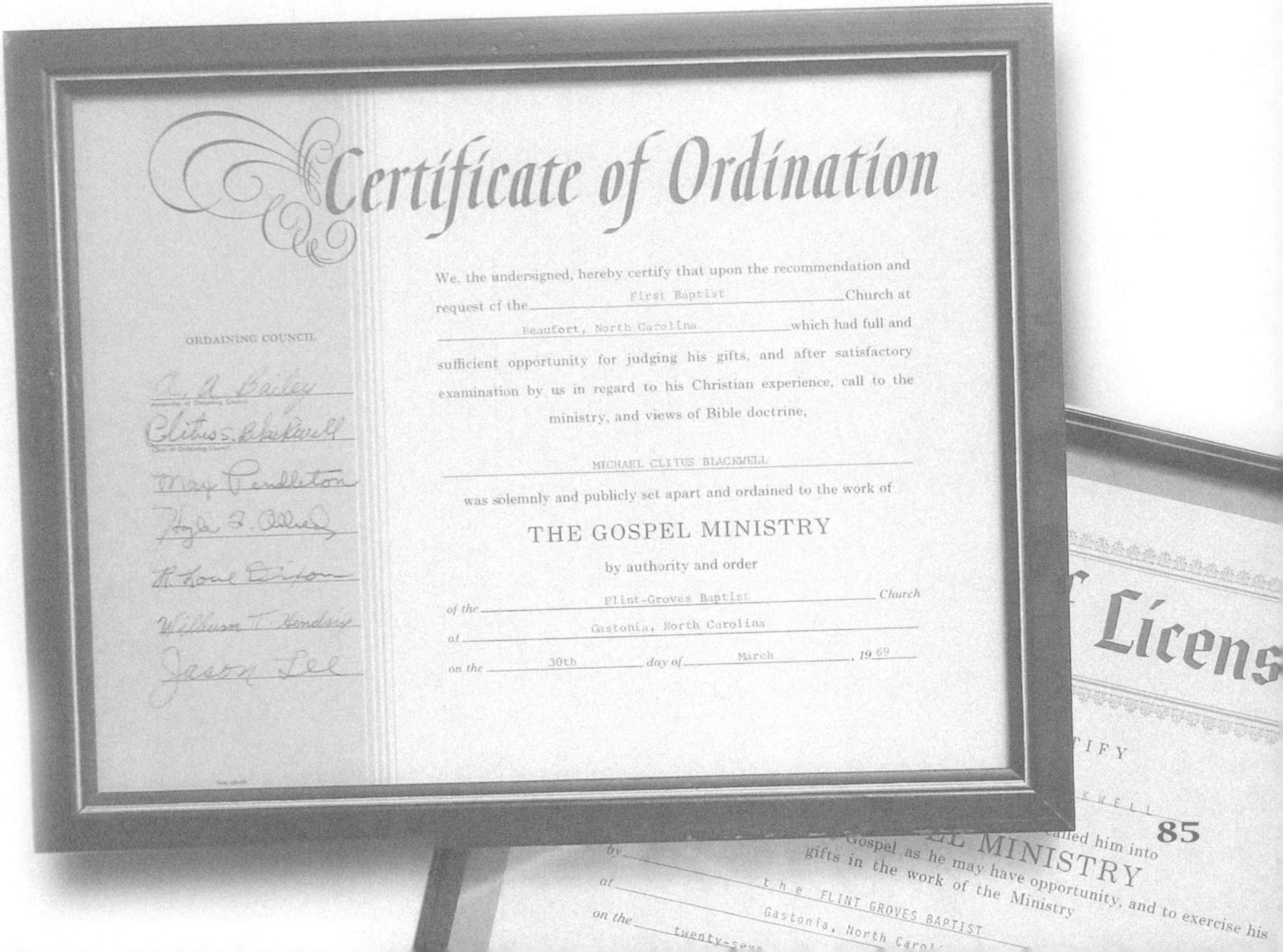
Certificate of Ordination
ORDAINING COUNCIL
We, the undersigned, hereby certify that upon the recommendation and request of the First Baptist Church at Beaufort, North Carolina which had full and sufficient opportunity for judging his gifts, and after satisfactory examination by us in regard to his Christian experience, call to the ministry, and views of Bible doctrine,
MICHAEL CLITUS BLACKWELL
was solemnly and publicly set apart and ordained to the work of
THE GOSPEL MINISTRY
by authority and order
of the Flint-Groves Baptist Church
at Gastonia, North Carolina
on the 30th day of March, 1969
License
MINISTRY
Gospel as he may have opportunity, and to exercise his gifts in the work of the Ministry
the FLINT GROVES BAPTIST
Gastonia, North Carol

With its help he also, as a student, lined up youth rallies to lead and revivals to conduct. He preached several times at Flint-Groves, appearing once as revival speaker. After the stint at Beaufort, he was interim pastor for a while at New Bethel Baptist Church in Garner, near Raleigh.

At his ordination, Michael is flanked by two of his childhood pastors, Wilburn Hendrix and Love Dixon. Another former pastor, Hoyle Allred, took the picture.

One of the faculty members at the seminary, who got to know Michael as well as anybody else on the teaching staff, has not forgotten that he was a standout student. Long afterward, Dr. Thomas A. Bland of Wake Forest, professor of ethics at Southeastern for 37 years remembered "what an energetic person he was." He still did quite well in the classroom, although he was involved in a range of outside activities. Student and professor were drawn to one another in part because they were UNC alumni. Bland was one of Michael's instructors throughout

his time at Southeastern, and during one period, Michael served as Bland's fellow, therefore helping with grading papers and with other chores. Bland was confident Michael would make an outstanding preacher, hoped he would pursue the preaching ministry, and admitted to being a bit disappointed when he gave up the pulpit for a much different kind of service to humanity.

The Blackwell residence during the Southeastern experience was at 103 Rankin Court, a seminary-owned duplex apartment. Michael and Kathy were meeting the cost of living and cost of education by combining Kathy's salary as secretary for Fred Sandusky, registrar at Southeastern, with what Michael could pick up working as a part-time TV man and part-time beginner-preacher. Kathy worked for Sandusky all the time that Michael was a seminary student.

One thing Kathy and Mickey cherished was the chapel service, held on campus in the mornings, Tuesday through Friday. Michael would call for Kathy at her office, and the two of them would stroll to the seminary chapel for worship that began at 10 o'clock and lasted about 30 minutes. They always looked forward to that time together, to becoming a bit refreshed, to being spiritually uplifted. Classes and other activities were suspended for an hour in deference to this worship period. "Going to chapel"

Kathy, seven months pregnant, stands with her in-laws at her and Mickey's seminary apartment.

was optional, but many attended, including most faculty members, which inspired Michael. Sometimes the speaker was a faculty member; sometimes it was a student. Michael spoke twice as a student and has

Southeastern's Class of 1970 – mostly men – has served Christ throughout the world.

been back to speak three times since graduating.

The building would become known as the Olin T. Binkley Chapel, in memory of the seminary's second president.

Near the end of his third, or senior, year at Southeastern — dozens of term papers later — Michael and other seniors eager to put their education to work full time assembled at the school to be available for interviews with representatives of churches in need of pastors or staff members – for, in student lingo, a "cattle call." By then, all hope he would land a job with the Radio and Television Commission of the Southern Baptist Convention had vanished. He had been pretty sure he preferred that over taking a pastorate and had kept such an option in reserve by declining seminary financial help for those willing to obligate themselves to serving in a local church for two years after graduation.

Blackwell, right, wins the American Bible Society Award for excellence in Public Reading of Scripture.

Seminary President Olin Binkley, right, leads the graduation procession.

A committee from Raleigh's Ridge Road Baptist was at the "cattle call" in search of a dynamic person with the potential to start and inject plenty of life into a Ridge Road program for young people. The committee stopped looking after interviewing Michael, and in a letter to him, dated May 28, 1970, from committee chairman David W. Gaylor, a call was officially extended "to serve as Associate Minister of Youth and Education, a joint effort of you and Ridge Road pastor William B. Rogers, to develop and coordinate youth programs." Salary would be $6,000 annually. He also would receive a housing allowance of $1,800, hospital and retirement benefits amounting to $600, and an auto allowance of $600. Michael quickly accepted. It would be a match made in heaven.

Shortly thereafter, he graduated from Southeastern with the degree of Master of Divinity. His hope to excel scholastically had been realized: he was second in the Class of 1970 with a 2.72 grade average out of a possible 3.0. Along with his diploma, he was awarded one of the prizes available to those graduating — the American Bible Society Award, which was for the public reading of the Holy Scriptures.

As a graduation reward he provided for himself, he bade farewell to his trusty 1963 Valiant and purchased a 1970 Ford LTD — brand-new.

On August 1, 1970, Michael Clitus Blackwell, newly ordained Baptist minister sporting a postgraduate degree — his first — appeared at Ridge Road to begin his first full-time assignment as a minister of the Gospel.

But his work at Southeastern was not so much as half done.

Father and mother rejoiced that they had been blessed with both a girl and a boy child. The family had moved by now, to a more comfortable, more expensive apartment on Charles Drive, in the Crabtree Valley Mall neighborhood.

CHAPTER NINE – *The Fountain of Youth*

I In the fall of 1970, while Michael had started working on his doctoral degree, Kathy was about down to her last nerve with a baby daughter in diapers, a drafty apartment with the leaky plumbing, and an old vacuum cleaner that kept breaking down. Sometimes she saw very little of the very busy Mickey, who had just started work at Raleigh's Ridge Road Baptist Church. She had met few people in the community, and she dearly missed her family and friends back in Charlotte, but the young Blackwells didn't have much money to spare for long-distance calls.

"Sometimes I got pretty frustrated trying to juggle so many things alone. I wanted to scream or just take Julie and go back home," Kathy said. "But I kept in mind how devoted Mickey was to what he was trying to accomplish and figured it wouldn't be that way forever. And I kind of loved the guy."

Kathy with Julie Renée Blackwell, born August 14, 1970.

For his part, Michael admits that he had his head so far in his books while working 60-hour weeks at the church that he didn't fully appreciate how she was struggling. "I could have been more helpful and paid more attention had I recognized her struggles. I was only 28 and determined, and sometimes it was like I was wearing blinders," he said. "But I have to give her and the Lord credit for keeping the home front going at that time. And when I look back on it, I am ever so grateful for her patience."

Kathy would have even more patience over the years, and early on, Mickey sometimes got a figurative nudge in the ribs so he would appreciate the fact. As time went on, he needed no reminders.

The first two weeks at Ridge Road were a whirlwind. Michael was trying to settle in while also preparing to preach in the absence of the church's minister — not to mention preparing, or bracing himself,

for the arrival of his and Kathy's first child. Pastor Rogers was not to be found. The sign on his office door: "On Vacation." Michael pulled out his only two sermons. They were barely enough. After a bit of rewriting, he would give one on his first Sunday at Ridge Road and the other on his second Sunday. Both had been used often when busy as a supply or interim pastor.

The first time out, he expounded for 20 minutes on "The Eternal Commitment." All went fairly well, he felt, a feeling confirmed at the door as he shook hands with departing worshippers. Most offered warm congratulations and encouragement.

Bringing him back to Earth momentarily was a young son of Ridge Road with whom he had made friends while temporarily in youth work at the church a few months before. This was Mark Warren. His solemn, terse comment when his time came to face Michael: "Nice try." Then he grinned broadly. Only someone who thought well of the sermon and the one giving it would have chosen to cloak his congratulations

The proud poppa with Julie

accordingly. The two have remained friends for many years. Warren is now a medical doctor in Greenville, N.C..

Much later, Michael would recall something he wrote: "My first day [at Ridge Road], I was poised to thrill the world with the wisdom of Solomon, the courage of Paul, and the insight of Jesus. By the end of the first week, I was still thrilling people — with the bumbling of Peter, the excuses of Moses, and the timidity of Jeremiah." Then he mentioned having only two well-worn homilies at his disposal when

The young Blackwell family in front of their Farrior Road apartment, Raleigh, N.C.

having to sub for the minister, as well as the excitement and anxiety of becoming a father for the first time. "In the midst of those chaotic 14 days, however, I was sure of two things: I knew what the church expected of me and I knew what I had the ability to do."

The first child of Michael and Kathy's was a healthy girl. They named her Julie Renée. She was born at Rex Hospital in Raleigh on August 14, 1970.

Their home now was on Farrior Road in Raleigh, a down-at-the heels duplex apartment that rented for $90 a month.

Ridge Road could be classified as an up-and-coming suburban church. It was founded in 1954 and had about 500 members.

Before the end of his first month, Michael had made big strides in what he had been mainly engaged to do, to minister to youth, to afford direction in righteous living. He conceived an outreach plan and took it to Pastor Rogers. The church had never attempted anything like it before, but the pastor thought it ought to and that perhaps the time to do it had come. So on August 30, Ridge Road launched its college ministry.

The church sat only about a mile and a half from Meredith College, a Baptist-affiliated school for girls, and about two miles from NC State University (the name since 1965), a key member of the University of North Carolina system. Michael arranged for incoming freshmen of all faiths at both institutions to receive invitations to attend Sunday services, morning and evening, at Ridge Road. Transportation from the two campuses to the church was furnished, along with snacks at the church. Only a few students responded in the beginning; however, the response kept growing, and in time as many as 200 collegians were enrolled in Ridge Road Sunday school classes and other programs.

Michael, of course, gave it heart and soul. On a typical Sunday morning, he would take his car into downtown Raleigh, purchase 10 dozen doughnuts at the Krispy Kreme outlet, pick up students at Meredith and State, and return to Ridge Road to assist with the opening of Sunday school. At the outlet, he shelled out $4.80. If as many as 10 dozen doughnuts were purchased, the charge for a dozen came

Julie Renée Blackwell

to no more than 48 cents. What a bargain. A snack of doughnuts and a soft drink or coffee was a potent, palatable ingredient in the attraction the church had for students. Michael remembered, "The girls came for the doughnuts, and the boys came for the girls."

He served four years at Ridge Road. Working with young people of all ages, preaching in the pastor's absence, and coordinating all evening activities, including Sunday night worship – well he has said, "it was a beautiful experience."

And there exists plenty of evidence the youth ministry there amounted to a life-changing encounter for some of the participants. Michael counseled more than he preached, but when he preached, he reminded his congregation that "in a world so unsure of tomorrow,

Come . . . Be Yourself

Youth and College Ministry

Ridge Road Baptist Church

2011 Ridge Road

787-4423

Raleigh, N. C.

William B. Rogers
Pastor

Michael C. Blackwell
Associate Pastor
Youth and College Minister

94

with its numerous philosophies, shifting moral standards, and questionable goals, there is no doubt of the urgency of giving Christ a pre-eminence in our lives. Our time on this earth is far too short to 'enjoy the pleasures of sin for a season.' Only what is done for Christ will count in eternity."

From out of the college ministry came much:

– Two morning worship services to accommodate a large turnout of teenagers and students.

– A large number of students joining the

church in full membership. Some were elected to church leadership positions. Ten among them indicated a desire to enter full-time Christian service, and four of these became licensed to preach.

– Students forming a drama group, The King's Players, which toured in North Carolina dramatizing the message of Christ.

– Meredith students forming a singing group, The New Wind.

– Two or three Sunday school classes "sponsoring" students, or helping them financially. Four scholarships for college students were created.

– A Watchcare arrangement, by which a church-member couple would "adopt" two college students, making available worship, fun, and fellowship.

– College students being enlisted as Big Brother or Big Sister to a high school junior or senior.

Michael also produced something called the weekly college supper forum at Ridge Road. At 5:30 p.m., Meredith and NC State students who had been provided transportation to the church were served a free snack

Michael's Ridge Road years were a great ride!

Lively discussions and group support were hallmarks of the Ridge Road youth ministry.

supper, after which they heard a talk by someone well-known in the Raleigh area or the state. For example, Charles Dunn, director of the State Bureau of Investigation, spoke on "Youth and the Drug Culture." Other speakers included Dr. John T. Caldwell, chancellor of NC State; Dr. King Cheek, president of Shaw University; and E. Bruce Heilman, president of Meredith College.

Then there was the coffeehouse, which overshadowed all other youth programs and activities. This time, the initiative came from a contingent of college students who in the second year of the Ridge Road college ministry, in 1971, decided to test and share their faith in the marketplace. They felt they wanted to do more than just talk about being a Christian.

So they went to the most popular teenage hangout in Raleigh, North Hills Mall, and made a stab at low-key evangelizing among some of the youthful loafers there, most of whom were clearly the non-church type and a few who were clearly into the use of drugs. They went

Blackwell with youth leader Pam Sloan (Annas).

more than once, and after one trip came away with the inspiration to open a coffeehouse as an answer to "we don't have any place to go."

They borrowed the Boy Scout Hut on church property, called it "Tranquillity Base," and decorated the inside to look like a refuge from the bright lights, a place for a little guitar-strumming and heady conversation, and some earnest socializing. A name for what they were doing was chosen: "Operation GYST (Get Your Self Together)." The grand opening on a Friday night in March 1972 drew 300, mostly high school junior and senior boys and girls, alarmed some of the neighbors, and filled a page in the Saturday entertainment supplement of the *Raleigh Times*.

Good purposes were being served,

95

Tranquility Base, Ridge Road's innovative coffeehouse outreach, touched the lives of hundreds of non-churched youth.

Michael assured the *Times* entertainment reporter. "We're all trying to solve the personal identity crises a lot of these young people are trying to solve for themselves . . . . They are facing these crises as they try to find out what they're about, what they should be doing, how they should relate to their parents, to themselves, and to God. It's not a club. It's a unique environment. It's

Church youth and college students blended into a cohesive force.

the kids' place . . . . I think we can do something for them this way, something lasting . . . . With this outreach we show the kids that we love them and care about them . . . . One of the kids knew of another coffeehouse. The will of the young people had little meaning there. It flopped. But here, he said, smiling, 'WE are the coffeehouse.'"

It lasted for about two years, or until perhaps its life cycle had been completed. Most everybody involved agreed at that point the time had come to move on. Their hangout may have passed away, but the memories are still alive.

Other means of drawing the teenagers into the House of the Lord were devised, and programs were concocted to attract those far younger, down to the kindergarten level. There were film festivals, retreats at Kerr Lake, ice-skating parties, Halloween projects, progressive dinners hosted by Ridge Road adults, ping-pong tournaments, cookouts, Bible schools, New Year's Eve parties, assistance to needy families, and trips to Camp Caraway, Camp Kanata, Crescent Beach, S.C., and the Baptists annual State Youth Conventions.

One of the most popular of the Michael innovations was Children's Worship Service for ages 5-8 as part of the Sunday morning service in the sanctuary. The only one causing him to hold his breath was his Interracial Dialogue program. On several occasions, he arranged for both white and black college students, as well as representatives of both races from among Raleigh's Broughton High School seniors, to meet at the church, become introduced one to the other, mingle, and exchange points of view in amicable discussions. In that period, whether any mixing of the races was desirable remained hotly debated. But nobody burned down the church, and Michael saw nothing to regret. Some good had resulted, he concluded. It was clear to all that pathways to understanding one another better were found and were used.

Through it all, the Ridge Road youth ministry remained true to its purpose: not to try make the young people swallow a little religion, nor

On his last day at Ridge Road, January 28, 1974, Mickey is "roasted" and presented a new typewriter by the youth of the church.

97

Mickey is treated to a surprise 30th birthday party at Raleigh's Shakey's pizza parlor.

was character development ever an objective, but, as Michael once noted, "What we've tried to do is to help persons to be aware of God's self-disclosure and seeking love in Jesus Christ and to respond in faith and love — to the end that they may know who they are and what their human situation means, grow as sons and daughters of God rooted in the Christian community, live in the Spirit of God in every relationship, fulfill their common discipleship in the world, and abide in the Christian hope."

He believed they "accomplished a lot," and for one reason more than any other, "because we gained the respect and the trust of those who came and took part. That was the key."

The Sunday evening snack supper for youth and college students was very popular.

An "amen" is sounded from Steve Sumerel, who as a student at NC State helped establish the coffeehouse, and as long as it was viable,

worked hand-in-hand with Michael. He developed a high regard for the leadership Michael provided, called him his mentor, admired how he handled the sensitive political ramifications of the coffeehouse, applauded his sense of humor, and respected him for the partnership he created between himself and those to whom he ministered. As Sumerel saw it, many of the youths were looking for an alternative family, and they found one at Ridge Road. Some grew close enough to their minister to address him only as "Mick."

Sumerel also was a Watchcare participant. The couple to whom he was assigned and who had children of their own treated him — somebody a long way from home — like one of their own.

Michael's command of counseling made a deep impression, in particular how he guided those trapped in the misuse of drugs. Sumerel, a product of Asheville, N.C., gave up studying to become a medical doctor, earned a Master of Divinity at Southeastern, and today is with the Baptist State Convention of North Carolina as director of the Council on Christian Life and Public Affairs. He spends considerable time counseling those with AIDS.

Somehow, Michael found time to continue

College Ministry at Ridge Road Baptist Church

by Mickey Blackwell

August 30, 1970, marked a turning point in the ministry of Ridge Road Baptist Church. The suburban church in Raleigh, North Carolina, is located about a mile and a half from North Carolina State University and Meredith College, a Baptist school for women. On that August Sunday morning the church launched its college ministry, a ministry that is now felt throughout the church.

Now, more than three years later, the college ministry

his seminary studies. In his second year at Ridge Road, he also managed to make way for a workshop/cruise, destination Nassau, sponsored by the Sunday School Board of the Southern Baptist convention, an event billed as a period of self-examination. And he squared himself with local draft board No. 36 back in Gaston County, where he had been a registrant since 1960. (The Vietnam War would not play out until 1975.) As a minister, he applied to be classified as 4-D. The draft board wrote back that this deferment was reserved for those who "as a regular and customary vocation, preach and teach principles of religion and be able to administer the rites and ceremonies of the church." Did he qualify? The draft people agreed he did once they had in hand a letter written November 3, 1971, by Alvin W. Jenkins Jr., chairman of the deacons, stating that, indeed, the Rev. Mr. Blackwell

"Doctor" Michael C. Blackwell

was a full-time minister, at Ridge Road Baptist Church, no less, where he in fact preached and taught and performed rites and ceremonies.

Michael had set a goal of earning a doctorate — Doctor of Ministry — at Southeastern as soon as possible after having received his Master of Divinity. To meet one of the requisites, in the summer of 1972, he had six weeks of Clinical Pastoral Education at North Carolina Memorial Hospital in Chapel Hill. This was, he would insist later, another of the pivotal events in his spiritual growth. The most unforgettable

College class leaders discuss some of the options for the next semester's curriculum. Left to right: Michael C. Blackwell, Dixie (Mrs. Roger) Fisher, Roger Fisher, and Norman Williamson.

aspect of it was the donning of a mask and visiting with patients in the hospital's tuberculosis ward. He did that time after time, talking to the sick — often the hopelessly sick — to whom he had been assigned, attempting to reassure them, to comfort them, to renew their hope. It was a humbling, gut-wrenching experience.

Southeastern Seminary's first Doctor of Ministry class in 1973

He worked diligently from October 1972 until March 1973 to meet all the requirements of yet another degree. His seminary schedule was set up to avoid conflict with his duties and activities at Ridge Road. Title of the doctorate project he adopted was "The Will to Relate: Depth Relationships Through Growth Groups in the Local Church."

Two groups were formed at the Ridge Road church, one being Self-Discovery, made up of six college students, the other, Marriage Enrichment, in which the participants were three couples whose marriages were less than nine years old. With assistance from Dana

Scrivner, chaplain in outpatient counseling at North Carolina Memorial Hospital in Chapel Hill, Michael sought to show, and document, how, within the interaction of these small circles of individuals, previously unrecognized human potential is revealed and the power of healing is released. He reported observing "moments of spontaneous celebration, soul-to-soul sharing, persons becoming aware of their uniqueness under God, the emotional reuniting of a husband and wife, the shedding of masks, the connection with the Source, all of which makes small groups in the local church an effective means of declaring the Gospel of Christ to all people." A person often grows or starts growing again when confronted by fellow strugglers, when accepted and loved by them, when a new lease on life is gained. To Michael, small groups were "growth groups."

A small-group movement had found its way into many segments of society, but the church was yet to open up to it. Michael said, "I believe the key to church renewal is through small groups."

Michael Jr. – a bundle of joy

The second, and last, Blackwell child arrived just as the project was being concluded. The birth of a robust Michael Clitus Blackwell Jr. occurred on March 13, 1973, also at Rex Hospital. Father and mother rejoiced that they now had both a girl and a boy child. The family had moved by now, to a more comfortable, more expensive apartment on Charles Drive, in the Crabtree Valley Mall neighborhood. Kathy had become a full-time mom.

Two months after the boy child's arrival, Ridge Road pastor, Rev. Rogers, in his church bulletin dated May 23, 1973, announced

The young family in Raleigh

that big Michael would "receive the Doctor of Ministry from Southeastern this week. He has made many sacrifices in order to attend school and at the same time carry on his regular duties as Associate Pastor.

We certainly congratulate him on this significant scholastic achievement."

When another six months had passed, Michael stood up during a Ridge Road Sunday morning service and announced that, regretfully, the end to his "beautiful experience" was nigh. This was in November. He, still the associate minister of youth and education, would be leaving effective February 1, 1974, to be the pastor at First Baptist Church in Carthage, a folksy, no-frills community of about 1,000 souls in the North Carolina Sandhills, near the famous resorts of Pinehurst and Southern Pines. Pastor Rogers wrote in the bulletin again, noting, "Michael will leave a void in our hearts that will be difficult to fill . . . . We have grown to love him as a friend and as a fellow minister. Our youth responded to his creative leadership from the beginning, and this area of our ministry was greatly enhanced due to his compassionate

concern for this age group."

Before he left, Ridge Road Baptist discovered Michael was good at something unsuspected — rescue and recover.

Proof showed up one day in the spring of 1973. He had stopped in traffic at a signal on Wade Avenue before turning onto Ridge Road. Right away he could see that

PICKLE PACKERS INTERNATIONAL, INC.
ST. CHARLES, ILLINOIS 60174

"for those who think pickles"

PICKLE PACKERS INTERN

P. O. BOX 31
ST. CHARLES, ILLINOIS 60174

108 E. MAIN
PHONE (3

Reverend Michell Blackwell,
2250 Charles Drive,
Raleigh, N.C. 27607

101

on the lid of a trunk of an auto headed out Wade toward the Raleigh-Durham Airport was a bulging briefcase. Obviously, in packing for a trip of some kind, the driver absent-mindedly had failed to stow the briefcase securely. It tumbled to the pavement and exploded when the traffic signal changed and the driver accelerated. Dozens of folders and sheets of paper soon scattered across the street.

Michael never hesitated. He parked, then, alone, set about retrieving the case and, it turned out, its priceless contents. The need to parry the streams of cars made it a 30-minute rescue-and-recover exercise.

Clearly, the owner was a NC State University professor, Dr. John L. Etchells. Michael was to learn that Etchells was one of the world's foremost authorities on pickles and pickling. By the time Michael could contact Mrs. Etchells, she already had received the cries of anguish of her husband. She was overjoyed to learn she could assure him a disaster

had been averted, and when Michael declined to be personally rewarded, she sent a $25 check to the Ridge Road church.

News of the professor's close call spread far and wide. Soon, Michael received word from the executive vice president of Pickle Packers International Inc. of St. Charles, Illinois, that declared: "Your living example of Love for Fellow Man in the case of the errant briefcase is gratefully acknowledged in behalf of

Grammer and Paw Paw Kanipe with Julie and Michael

our industry which is dependent on the creative scientific knowledge of Dr. J.L. Etchells of Raleigh.

"Under separate cover we are arranging to have a planter sent to you in hopes that it will provide further reminder to you and your friends of the great appreciation we have for someone who would brave traffic, realize a fellow man's momentary forgetfulness with something most of us have done at one time or another, picked up, gathered up loose sheets and returned them to the very, very worried Etchells family.

"We are very proud that the thoughtfulness of the type you have displayed still exists."

Kathy's first day back home with her newborn son

Michael became a familiar figure
all across Carthage — which, by
his account, is where he learned to
be a community person. He served
two one-year terms as president
of the Parent-Teachers Association
at Carthage Elementary, where
daughter Julie was a student.

CHAPTER TEN – *At Home in the Pulpit*

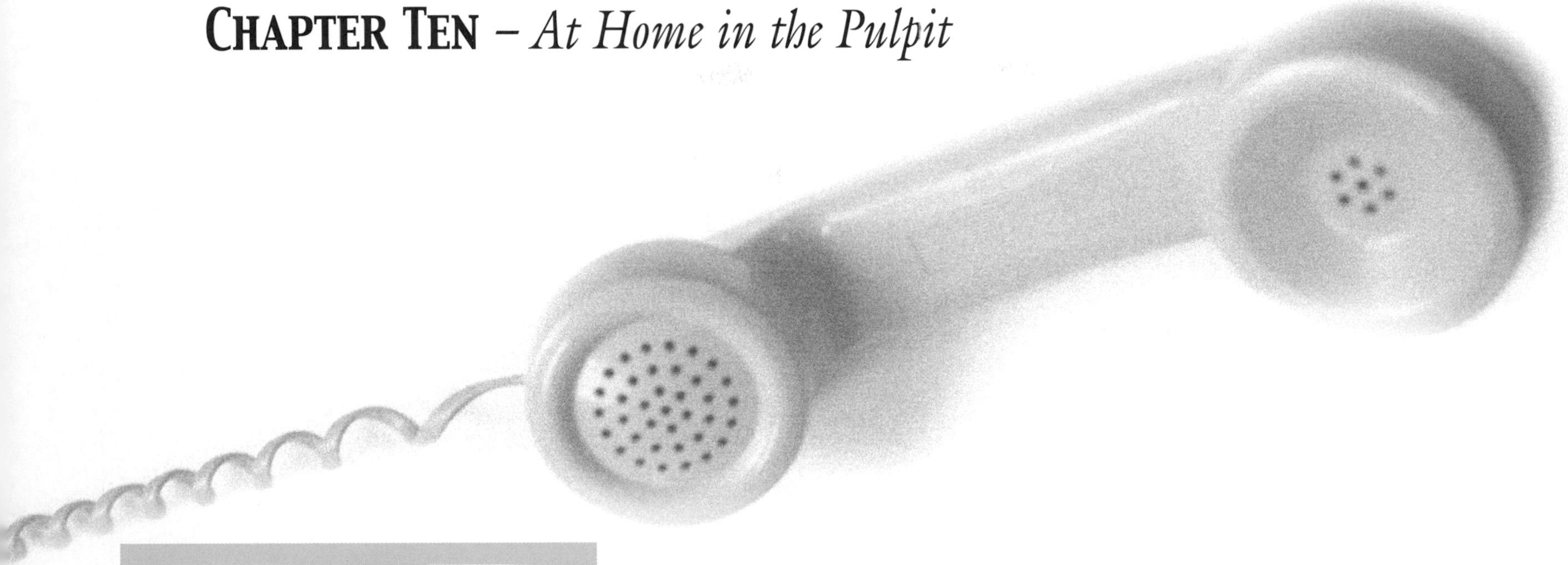

The phone rang. Reverend Gene Booker, pastor of First Baptist Church in Robbins, reached across his desk and picked up the receiver, "Hello?"

"Gene, this is Bill Walton," chairman of the pastor search committee said. "We're looking for a new pastor; I was wondering if you could recommend someone?"

Dr. William Walton was the associate superintendent of Moore County schools and an active member of the First Baptist Church in Carthage.

Booker assured Walton he could get a name and that he would call him back. A quick call to Dr. Thomas A. Bland, Professor of Christian Ethics at Southeastern Seminary, yielded Walton a good lead. Bland suggested Michael, the-up-and-coming-staffer-of-Ridge Road.

Just Call Me Mickey

Michael is remembered as Carthage's first choice and one who was unanimously approved by the members. Recommending someone of Michael's age, only 31, did not raise eyebrows. The congregation was accustomed to youth in its pulpit. The beginning salary was quite small, one that over time has been forgotten. He and the rest of the family moved into the big, aging parsonage standing next to the church.

A new preacher has come to Carthage and the folks at First Baptist Church have rolled out the red carpet for Dr. Michael Blackwell. He's being greeted here by Wayne Adams and Alex Caddell. For a look at a pounding the new members gave the Blackwells, see page 12.

He became pastor at First Baptist on February 1, 1974. His pastorate would span almost seven years, putting him in one place longer than any before – well, since leaving the nest in Gastonia.

And there was hardly a dull moment.

In addition to giving the comparatively small church (founded in 1858 with 22 members) in the somewhat small town an energetic preacher, he also did a great deal of civic work, considerable writing, some teaching, more studying, and a bit of traveling.

Adding members, increasing the budget, and improving physical facilities is a measure of a successful pastor, and Michael earned high marks.

Once having discovered that he possessed a knack for raising money, he made use of the skill in creative ways. The sanctuary incurred heavy water damage when the First Baptist furnace blew up (a steam valve malfunctioned). It was rendered almost unusable. The pastor immediately drew up a fund-raising plan he named "Remember the Church." (What had happened to the Alamo in Texas must have wandered into his thoughts.) A goal of $10,000 was set. With Michael pushing and prodding, members pledged $10,322 — in just two weeks.

Another time, he devised what he described as an exercise in tithing. Members were introduced to "The 10-4 Experiment in Faith." They were exhorted to give 10 percent of their income each of the four weeks in the month just ahead. Collections rose dramatically for a brief time.

Looking ahead, the pastor noticed that in February 1976 there were five Sundays — and that there would not be a repetition until the year 2004 — he dropped everything and mapped out a "Five Fabulous Sundays" campaign, an evangelistic effort of the church Sunday school. It paid off. Sunday school attendance increased each of those five February Sabbaths. Newcomers were entertained by Michael and Kathy at their residence, at what he called a "People Warming."

Pastor and wife gradually adjusted to the loss of the many amenities they enjoyed in Raleigh.

As First Baptist members were added and the budget grew, ways were found to construct a parsonage to replace the one that was 67 years old and to add a fellowship hall. Long before Michael left, the budget had grown by 50 percent. It took a $13,000 leap in one year alone. The church staff expanded from two — Michael and a secretary — to three when a person was hired to serve full time as Minister of Music and Youth. Michael also introduced and sustained Dial-A-Prayer. It became a custom of his, when a member died, for the church to present a book in memory of the deceased to the public library. His weekly church newsletter, which he named "The Front Pew" and was mimeographed in the church office, won a first prize in a design competition sponsored by the Baptist State Convention of North Carolina. He and the membership kept growing closer. In a letter to a friend he noted, "We have a special group of people here, and the relationship between the pastor and the people has developed into an intimacy that few churches have." When he asked for something, more times than not he got it. That included time off to do other things.

Michael and Julie stand in front of the Carthage church sign.

For a while, he attended class one day a week at Southeastern, moving ever closer to meeting all the requirements of a research degree he desired, Master of Theology. Off and on he spent time on his thesis, "The Ethical Thought of Carlyle Marney." Marney was a controversial Baptist minister who referred to his Southern Baptist heritage as "south of God." He was a dynamic preacher, a scholar and a friend of bedraggled ministers who found solace at the Interpreter's House at Lake Junaluska. Marney had fascinated Michael from the time they had met in 1966. At that time, Marney was pastor at Charlotte's Myers Park Baptist Church, and Michael was at Big WAYS.

Michael spent the morning hours in the pastor's study.

Michael became a familiar figure all across Carthage — which, by his account, is where he learned to be a community person. He served two one-year terms as president of the Parent-Teachers Association at Carthage Elementary, where daughter Julie was a student. Here his reputation as a fund-raiser gained stature. Enough was cleared from the raffles and bake sales he promoted to purchase two new, deluxe typewriters. The prize in a series of little contests for teachers he devised was the afternoon off; Michael taught in the winner's absence. For three years, he taught at Union Pines High, two mornings a week, a course in the Bible. A column he wrote, "Coping," appeared regularly in issues of the weekly *Moore County News* over a three-year stretch. He opened his church not only to the annual community Thanksgiving

During the 1970s, the Blackwells enjoyed summer breaks at the Baptist Assembly at Caswell Beach, N.C..

service, but also to various civic groups. Sundays were set aside to pay honor to volunteer firemen, to city policemen, to service organizations. Rotarians would come on Rotary's Sunday and sit as a body, for example. He was secretary of the Moore County Prison Advisory Unit and, as a Democrat, a precinct delegate. It is little wonder the Carthage Jaycees, for his impact on the community, presented him with their annual Distinguished Service Award (or "Young Man of the Year" title).

Winning the award brought to attention that he also was a member of the board of trustees of the N.C. Baptist Homes for the Aging, member of the business management committee of the Baptist State Convention's general board, certified to conduct deacon training in conferences throughout the Southern Baptist Convention, and youth director of the Sandhills Baptist Association.

AWARD WINNERS: The Carthage Jaycees held the annual Distinguished Service Award banquet Monday night and several persons came away with awards for their community service. Seated, l-r, are these winners: John Frye, Young Educator; Judi Kelly, Boss of the Year; Dr. Michael C. Blackwell, DSA recipient; and Wayne Matthews, Young Farmer; standing, l-r, Hurley Thompson, Mr. Spark Plug; Bobby Preddy, Jaycee president who received a new gavel from the Jaycettes; Attorney James Van Camp who was the guest speaker; Trip Johnson, Mr. Jaycee of the Year; and Talmadge Baker who presented the young farmer award.

Julie on the first day of first grade

In response to an invitation from Clyde Aumen, representative of Moore County in the North Carolina House, he delivered the opening prayer at a session of the General Assembly in Raleigh.

Michael emerged as one of its busiest members after joining the Rotary Club. First he was elected president, then Rotarian-of-the-Year.

He made his mark there, too, partly by, while president, hounding members into living by the letter of one of its cardinal rules, which was, come hell or high water, thou shalt not miss a single club meeting. A goal of perfect attendance by all 25 Rotarians at each of the weekly meetings for three consecutive months was set — and met, creating a precedent. This would not have been possible had Michael not, for 13 weeks, picked up delinquent members and driven them to meetings of nearby clubs so they could "make up" for the ones they missed in Carthage. "He was a slave-driver," one Rotarian recalled, "but we were proud of our accomplishments under his leadership."

109

As an adjunctive instructor at Union Pines High School, Blackwell taught "The Bible As Literature."

The attendance record was established in the Carthage club's Rotary District, composed of about half the clubs in the state, and is believed to be still standing.

Also, in a membership push over which Michael presided, Carthage's roster grew by 25 percent.

Members of his church never knew what to expect. One Sunday morning, the guest speaker was a Chinese minister from Taiwan, the Rev. Stephen Liao. Another time, it was no less than Dr. James L. Sullivan, the president of the largest Protestant body in the country, the Southern Baptist Convention. He was elected for a yearlong term in June 1976. Michael gambled, and to his great surprise, Sullivan agreed to arrange a Carthage stopover. Sullivan, retired from 20 years as president of the convention's Sunday School Board, was a giant in Baptist circles. In addition to preaching at a crowded First Baptist in March 1977, Sullivan was guest of honor at a dinner in Southern Pines that Michael arranged and to which local denominational and civic leaders were invited.

Blackwell with Carthage youth during a downtown fund-raiser

For 11 days in May 1977, Michael was in Nashville, Tennessee, for a course in "Personal and Professional Growth" offered by the Sunday School Board of the Southern Baptist Convention. As it turned out, he was one of only two enrollees. The experience there, because it forced intense personal self-examination, is rated by Michael as another turning point in his life. It was while there that he made contacts that led to assignments to produce articles for various Sunday School Board publications. He would write for these for the next 15 years.

The Nashville trip was sponsored by his church, which did not find his laundry list of outside activities to be cause for concern. Dr. Walton, also chairman of the board of deacons during part of Michael's tenure, says Michael never was accused of neglecting his First Baptist responsibilities — blessing the newborns, presiding at weddings, helping to bury the dead (the hatched, matched and dispatched), along with visiting the sick and baptizing those of newfound faith. Walton remembers him as a gifted speaker, good organizer, and a "people person," an effective leader. "We were fortunate to keep him so long . . . . I guess [while with us] he was honing his skills."

Within a couple of years after arriving in Carthage, Michael had caught the eye of other Baptist churches. But he and the Blackwell family had finally found much to like in Carthage, and for quite some time he never seriously considered relocating. To one of his correspondents, he confided, "I've turned down several good churches because I don't see that I'm anywhere near through here. When a church contacts me, I realize that I'm still happy and fulfilled as a pastor in Carthage."

Attention from either of two churches he had grown to admire greatly might have caused him to change his tune. One was First Baptist in Hickory, N.C., the other, First Baptist in Winston-Salem, N.C.. But neither ever undertook to solicit him.

Other opportunities for his self-improvement were seized. "My church didn't object," he has noted. "I would take a course, and then, once back in the Carthage pulpit again, I'd be full

of fire." Twice in two years, he attended intensive biblical study at Union Theological Seminary in New York City, and twice in two years

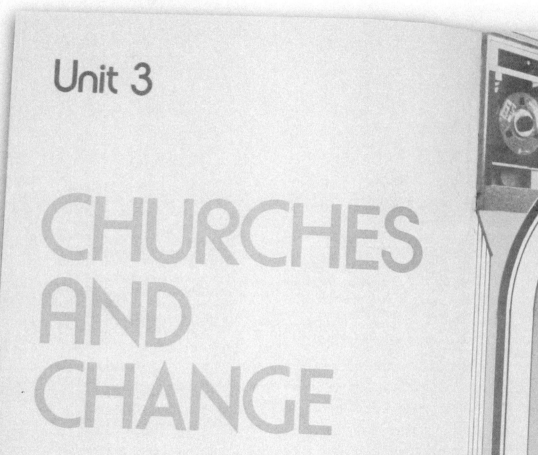

Unit 3

CHURCHES AND CHANGE

Speaking of change, Mickey (Michael C.) Blackwell, writer, has changed jobs since he last wrote for *Come Alive.* He is now pastor of First Baptist Church, Carthage, North Carolina. He has written this unit during his own personal decision making and change of locations. He's an exciting young pastor on the scene today.

On being a change agent

111

OPENS HOUSE SESSION WITH PRAYER — Dr. Michael C. Blackwell, minister of Carthage First Baptist Church, center, opened Thursday's meeting of the N.C. House of Representatives. Majority Leader Horton Roundtree who was standing in for Speaker Carl Stewart, w̶ father died the day before. T̶̶̶

The job offers from Nashville, three of them, were flattering, but he never gave much thought to any of them. All were from the Sunday School Board, two of which were to be a consultant and one to be editor of the board's *Deacon* quarterly.

He was juggling the many demands on his time. The children were ages six and three. Michael always tried to be present at their bedtime. Making up fun characters that the children still remember today is a fond memory from that time.

But Friday nights were inviolate times for Michael and Kathy. It was date night, and nothing interfered with that. A "third grandmother" in the Carthage church, Masal Barbour, showed her love by taking care of Julie and Michael Jr. every Friday night for five years.

as well, he was a student briefly at Southeastern Seminary's Pastors School. At the invitation of the Church Administration Department of the Baptist Sunday School Board, he conducted motivation workshops in such distant places as Detroit, Michigan, and Carbondale, Illinois. From his typewriter in the pastor's study flowed articles that appeared in 17 Sunday School Board periodicals, such as his thoughts on youth and death, musings on citizenship and politics, and a series of sermons based on First John. And he found pleasure in reviewing books for the weekly *Christian Century*.

(One piece he worked hard on but failed to finish in Carthage. This was his Master of Theology thesis. He asked for and received from Southeastern an extension of time but did not complete it until later.)

On the steps of the church parsonage

In one 12-month period, by using some of his personal vacation time and part of the annual two weeks granted by the church for outside preaching, training, and teaching, he led revivals at four other Baptist churches. What finally slowed him down briefly was sickness — something he rarely encountered.

The annual meeting of the Baptist State Convention in Raleigh in November 1978 proved to be, for more than one reason, a particularly stressful time. After an irksome motel reservation problem popped up, he came down with a rapid heartbeat. The sensible and expedient thing to do, it seemed, was to drive himself to a hospital. Which he did, to Rex Hospital. It took a while, but normal heart rhythm returned under a medication regimen provided by the hospital staff. No heart damage resulted. Word raced through Carthage that he had suffered a heart attack. Back home, he mistakenly was thought to be a very ill individual, or was until his reappearance in Carthage the following week, when he was already up to speed again. The palpitations did not recur, and to ward off their reappearance he did some dieting and some exercising — well, at least for a while he did.

He resumed an activity of which he was extremely fond: jogging. In Carthage, he was as well known as a jogger as he was a preacher. A part of Carthage folklore is how he subjected a friend to a punishing afternoon. This was Joe Lynch, one of his deacons and an elementary school teacher in Robbins, a town near Carthage. He had been challenged by Michael to join his preacher in jogging to Cameron, or to try to. They made it, a grueling 10 miles. Then they stumbled into the car of Joe's wife, Ann, and she drove them home. Thereafter, Joe remained wary of other ecclesiastical challenges.

At the close of the Sunday morning worship at First Baptist on August 17, 1980, he disclosed to his congregation that a sizable church in Richmond,

Baby Michael with Mom and Dad on their first day in Carthage

Virginia, wanted him to be its pastor. He had been in Carthage exactly six years and eight months, having hung around much longer than those who knew him best had figured he would. Michael explained

"Books are my best friends," says the new pastor.

to his audience: "Monument Heights in Richmond was both unsought by me and unknown to me. Yet, as matters developed, it became obvious that this was the direction that God was leading my family and me."

Only a week before, on August 10, he had preached there — at the Monument Heights Baptist Church, that is. The sermon he used was "The Time of Your Life," the one he selected for what anybody could see was his "trial" appearance. A few days later, there arrived in his mail a letter from T. E. Coleman, chairman of the Monument Heights' pastor selection committee, and stewardship committee Chairman Rodney Johnson. It read: "Members of Monument Heights in a special meeting voted to call you as our pastor effective September 28, 1980." The salary would be $29,500 annually. Four weeks vacation

113

time would be provided along with two weeks for enrichment activities. In his reply, in which Michael joyfully accepted the call, he said he would participate in the Annual Leadership Retreat for the Monument Heights church staff and church council August 22-23 and preach his first sermon as the new pastor October 5.

By Michael's calculations, Monument Heights had potential with a capital "P."

The Blackwell family would move into the first house they ever owned, at 9202 Minna Drive. The family car would be a Ford LTD, a carryover from life in Carthage, the one purchased to replace their first LTD.

Monument Heights, founded in 1950, was at the corner of Libbie and historic Monument Avenue. It was a full-service, cosmopolitan institution on one of the main roads in Richmond, itself a metropolis, Virginia's pride and joy, the state capital, and one of the Southland's treasures. The church had 1,366 members. Michael would head a staff of five: two additional ministers and three secretaries.

Messages congratulating him on the move he would be making came from all directions. Cornell Goerner wrote, "I have rarely seen a more unanimous and enthusiastic call." He was a Monument Heights member and was associated with the Southern Baptist Convention's Foreign Missions

Blackwell was Santa Claus for the annual Carthage Christmas parade.

Board in Richmond. His grandson is Monument Heights pastor today. From Fred Anderson: "Your new congregation . . . is known across the city as a creative and very friendly people. You will enjoy your days of ministry with them." Anderson was executive director of the Virginia Baptist Historical Society, whose offices were near Monument Heights.

There were prayers as well as congratulations. From a close friend, J. George Reed, director of the department of Christian Citizenship Education of the Baptist State Convention: "I pray for you a decent moving company."

Michael would be succeeding at Monument Heights the Rev. Aubrey J. (Buddy) Rosser, who then served at Richmond's Bainbridge-Southhampton Baptist Church. He and his wife, the Rev. Dr. Anne Rosser, were co-pastors there. Another of Michael's letters was from Monument Heights members Red Eagles and his wife, Nellie, who wrote him a welcome just after his "trial sermon." The Eagleses marveled, "We could not help but notice your warm, friendly personality and apparent wit was so similar to our beloved former pastor, Buddy Rosser."

Michael would return to Carthage to speak at First Baptist several times, so the "goodbyes" exchanged as he and his family prepared to depart were a far piece from forever. Such revisiting would afford him great pleasure — a warm "welcome back" was guaranteed. Still ready with an invitation, more than 20 years later, is the Rev. Thomas V. Herndon, now Carthage First Baptist pastor. He was pastor at Bethlehem Baptist, the mother church of First Baptist, during Michael's pastorate. The two were about the same age, but Michael "was somebody I looked up to." Michael's legacy, according to Herndon, was that of "wonderful preacher, one who was well-loved and well-respected . . . one of the finest ministers ever to preach in Carthage."

There would be repeated invitations to revisit each of the churches he had served. He had made sure of one thing: whenever he moved on, good feelings were left behind. In every case, it was an amicable parting of the ways. Once, in looking back, he said, "I never burned any bridges."

He liked where he was. There was so much he hoped to accomplish. Wouldn't leaving so soon be an affront to his flock? For a long time it had been his conviction that where he would be the happiest in the years ahead and where he could do the most good was in a Baptist pulpit.

CHAPTER ELEVEN – *Monuments to Climb*

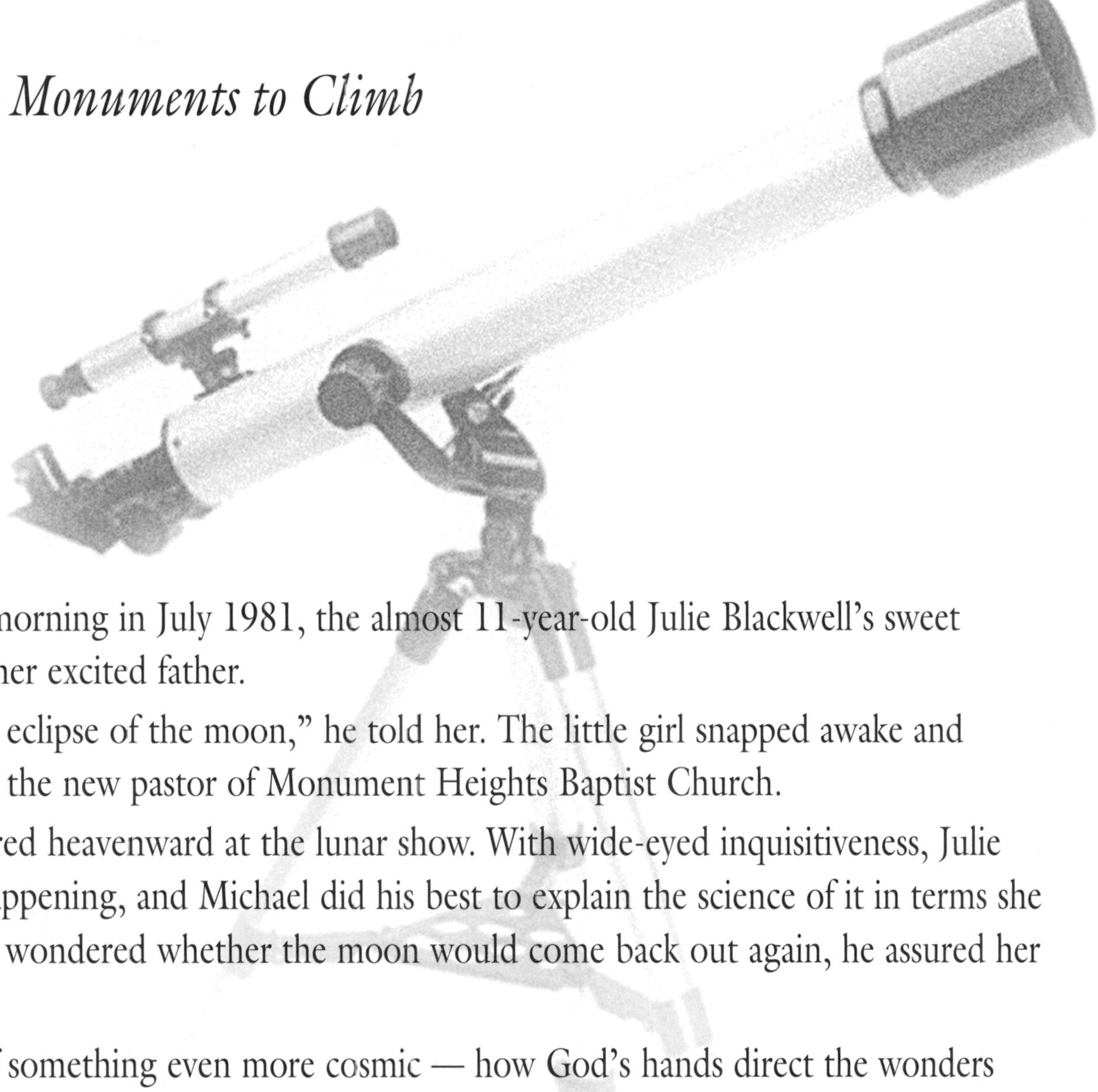

In the wee hours of one morning in July 1981, the almost 11-year-old Julie Blackwell's sweet dreams were interrupted by her excited father.

"I want you to see a total eclipse of the moon," he told her. The little girl snapped awake and trudged out in the yard with the new pastor of Monument Heights Baptist Church.

For 20 minutes, they peered heavenward at the lunar show. With wide-eyed inquisitiveness, Julie wanted to know what was happening, and Michael did his best to explain the science of it in terms she could understand. When she wondered whether the moon would come back out again, he assured her that it would.

But Michael was aware of something even more cosmic — how God's hands direct the wonders of nature, and how sometimes it is necessary to step outside at 2 a.m. to witness His handiwork.

As for Julie, it was a precious moment between father and daughter — one that she would still be talking about nearly 25 years later.

The Monument Heights pastorate offered Michael the opportunity to hone his preaching skills.

October 1980 had rolled around, and the large, urbane congregation at Monument Heights Baptist Church was on the verge of learning whether its new preacher, Michael Clitus Blackwell, the 38-year-old from the hinterlands with only one pastorate under his belt, was really as good as he seemed at his "trial" appearance, and otherwise as good as he was cracked up to be.

As for Michael: nervous but confident. He didn't intend to disappoint anybody, not himself, not his family, especially not those who had recommended him for such a major step up.

The Monument Heights pastor search committee had been told by Theodore F. Adams, for 32 years pastor at Richmond's First Baptist Church and then professor of preaching at Southeastern, that Michael was "one of the finest men I taught at Southeastern." They were

You are cordially invited to
The Service of Installation
of
Dr. Michael C. Blackwell
as pastor of
Monument Heights Baptist Church
Monument Avenue at Libbie

7:30 P.M.
Sunday, November 2, 1980

Dr. W. Randall Lolley to charge the minister
Dr. Charles B. Nunn to charge the congregation

Dr. Michael C. Blackwell

Dr. W. Randall Lolley

told by the Rev. William B. Rogers, pastor of Ridge Road before moving to First Baptist in North Wilkesboro, N.C., that "his ability to communicate and relate to the youth and college students helped ensure a strong ministry, and he proved to be a blessing to the total congregation. He appeared to have a strong sense of call to the Christian ministry. It was a real privilege to work with him and watch him grow spiritually. You will find he is not only an effective communicator but also a gifted writer."

And by Dr. W. Randall Lolley, president of Southeastern, that "He

is a superb preacher, a persuasive teacher, a sensitive counselor, and a brilliant administrator. In fact, very few people I know combine in one person all the skills and gifts which are his. He is also a superb writer as evidenced in several of his articles in Baptist literature . . . . He has training in radio and television work, therefore, is a superb communicator in small groups and in large ones. He is a very sensitive, people-centered, issues-oriented person."

So the Flint-Groves mill village's gift to the great Baptist common cause had said his prayers, took a deep breath, and jumped in.

On Sunday night, November 2, 1980, a formal installation service

119

was held at the church. The charge to the pastor was delivered by Dr. Lolley, still Southeastern president. And the charge to the congregation came from Dr. Charles B. Nunn, executive director of the Richmond Baptist Association. With that, Michael, only Monument Heights' third pastor, was off and running — at a gallop, of course.

The Blackwell family in Richmond

To get acquainted, he armed himself with a list that matched the name of every member with the member's birth date. Then for the next 12 months, he called members as their birthdays came around. Usually, he was on the phone for a minute or two, but sometimes it was much longer if he caught someone who had a problem and welcomed a chance to share it. He called everybody. The inactive members were pleased not to have been forgotten.

Planning and stewardship were placed on the front burners. Every special offering goal was exceeded. Budget pledges continued to fall short until a campaign named "Faithfulness" was mounted. A giant thermometer was erected in front of the church to measure progress in a quest for $381,763. In November 1982, for the first time ever, the budget had been fully subscribed, with $4,000 to spare. Members rejoiced by singing the hymn "To God Be the Glory."

Worshippers at Sunday morning service usually numbered around 500. At special times, such as Easter, maybe 600. But Sunday school

attendance was not as good as the church council thought it should be, so it initiated an attendance drive with a goal of 444.

At the suggestion of Michael, never without a promotion angle, it became "Formula 444." (The pastor was attempting to trade on the brand name of a popular cough syrup, Vicks Formula 44.) Then something unexpected happened that made joyful headlines across the country and in some strange way sparked a surge of interest in the Monument Heights drive. After 444 days, the hostages in Iran were released. Much was made of the coincidence that the two numbers were the same. A short time later, Michael stood before his congregation — it was March 1, 1981 — to announce the drive had been concluded and that it had pushed attendance to 576, some 132 beyond its goal. This was more good news. Those in his audience were delighted. They rose up and applauded madly. The 576-mark set in 1981 is yet to be matched.

ROBERT L. CARLTON
Minister of Education/Administration

MICHAEL C. BLAC
Pastor

Vol. 13, No. 48

285-3256 & 282-5.

WE DID

FAITHFULNESS

375000 381000
365000 370000
355000 360000
340000 350000
320000 330000
295000 310000
265000 280000
235000 250000
205000 220000
175000 190000
145000 160000
115000 130000
85000 100000
55000 70000
30000 40000
10000 20000
5000

Stewardship Chairman Al Astle and Dr. Blackwell stand beside the Faith
which shows that Monument Heights, not only pledged its 1983 budget of
"over the top." Total pledges are now $384,745. This is the first ti
history of the church that members have completely subscribed the budge

Michael was again working long hours — pushing programs, starting new ones, writing and rehearsing sermons, doing magazine articles, planning, working on another postgraduate degree, and counseling members of the flock. He averaged working 65 hours a week. As a full-service church, Monument Heights was seldom closed. Various community events were held there.

Much energy went into making the content of his sermons, and the delivery of them, the best possible. "I worked very hard on this."

Bill Childress, for one, thought well of what resulted. "As a speaker, a pastor, just the best, as good as you could find in the pulpit," declares Childress, a home furnishings merchant who was a Monument Heights deacon and head usher during Michael's pastorate. He added quickly, "And such a nice guy. I have the highest respect for him."

Each sermon was published, and copies were made available to the congregation a week after its delivery. That there was an ongoing strong demand for copies surprised and pleased the preacher.

In the wake of a Sunday school revival, Michael initiated a Pastor's Sunday School Class. Those who enrolled ranged in age from 25 to 75. Classes were held in the Pastor's Study at the church.

Another innovation was "Ask the Pastor." This was scheduled on a Wednesday once a quarter. Michael assembled with church members and responded to questions that had been written down and, to encourage frankness, turned in without a signature.

Counseling received a great deal of emphasis, as much as 15 hours a week of the pastor's time. He was available for one-on-one sessions and to meet with married couples. This was something else that helped draw pastor and member close to one another.

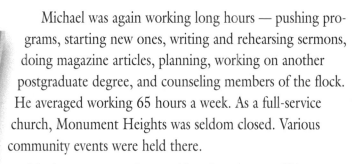

MARK O. CAIN
Minister of Music/Youth
November 28, 1982

Sixteen-year-old Jimmy Cox with Dr. Blackwell as Cox reflects on his duties as Monument Heights Youth Week Pastor.

121

Kaye Carrithers, who had been a deacon and Sunday school teacher, remembered that Michael was a strong counselor, but that he also "was an open and wonderful pastor — and a terrific fund-raiser."

Michael with his family and parents upon receiving his third and final degree (Master of Theology in Christian Ethics) from Southeastern Seminary in 1982.

She added, "the children liked him so much . . . . He remains a dear friend and confidant."

Mary Newsome, once one of the church secretaries, said, "We loved him dearly . . . . I worked alongside him all the time he was at Monument Heights . . . . I'm proud to have known him."

Through intense ministering to them, the energy of young adults between the ages of 25 and 35 was channeled into church drama and music programs.

The pastor and church participated in a first — the pulpit/choir swap in association with an African-American church. A risky but, as turned out, most successful undertaking. Monument Heights served as host on two occasions. Each time, the sanctuary filled up. Michael discovered that preaching at the black church made him feel "high and lifted up." He said, "Blacks have a unique way of 'encouraging' the preacher."

Membership at Monument Heights was open to blacks. Yet, during Michael's time there, only one joined. Blacks seemed to prefer black churches the same as whites preferred white.

Various committees were created and put to work. A promotion entitled "The Great 100 Days" was launched. During this time, members encountered a wave of stimulating activities, a youth seminar and a series of fellowship events being examples. The promotion produced for Michael a keepsake, a gift from Emily Lenz, a T-shirt with bold lettering across the front, "I survived Monument Heights Great 100 Days."

Lenz found Michael validating the expectations of those who had recruited him. She had been a member of the search committee recommending him for the Monument Heights pulpit. "I had the highest admiration for him . . . . A number of our members thought he was the best speaker we ever had . . . . I think his work in radio helped him a lot . . . . He was full of ideas . . . . When he was here, we grew; the church

Professor of Ethics Thomas A. Bland was Blackwell's mentor during his seminary years.

budget was met . . . . He was just a wonderful pastor . . . . He met every criterion I ever had."

Michael addresses the House of Delegates in Richmond, VA.

Through it all, self-improvement was never neglected. Michael enrolled in and graduated from a program offered at Wake Forest University, "The Pastor as Administrator," and he completed all the requirements for and received, in 1982, the research degree

Olin T. Binkley chaired the Search Committee that selected Michael as BCH president.

at Southeastern, the Master of Theology in Christian Ethics. That one was the third of the three on which he had set sights.

Thursdays were his days off, but few were spent on Michael. They went not to golfing, or some such, but nearly every one for the three years in Richmond was donated to the Southern Baptist Convention's Foreign Missions Board (now International Missions Board). The board's offices were seven miles away on the same street as the church. He was persuaded to go and help out there by a member of his who was employed by the board.

He would sit in front of a camera and give voice to a script, thereby helping to produce the board's quarterly 15-minute news video. It was hard work. The board did not own a TelePrompTer, so Michael had to memorize the script.

Also, if the board needed a voice-over while making informational tapes of one kind or another, Michael provided it. Foreign Missions benefited handsomely from what he had mastered while in radio and television.

The preacher's wife, Kathy, worked almost every weekday while in Richmond as a secretary at the office of the Baptist General Association

of Virginia while tending to the two children, 5th and 2nd grades respectively, both enrolled in public schools.

Michael got talked about — in the right places. A committee searching for a new president of the Baptist Children's Homes of North Carolina, largest child care institution in the Southeast, with a national reputation as a place where giant strides in child care had been made, decided that he rated their attention. The committee swung around to him just as he was completing a plan to guide the future growth of Monument Heights, one his congregation would adopt in a vote in May 1983.

BCH needed someone who had been field-tested at the level of

Monument Heights, Richmond, VA

a Monument Heights and in a location as progressive as a Richmond. If still in Carthage, no doubt Michael would have been passed over. It would turn out that he had to leave North Carolina and prove himself in order to return to North Carolina to an elevated position.

A phone call out of the blue in February 1983 is where it started. Calling was the president emeritus of Southeastern seminary, Dr. Olin T. Binkley, who identified himself as chair of the search committee. To the question "would you care to be a candidate for president of the Homes?" Michael, caught completely off-guard, gave a somewhat I'll-get-back-to-you-later reply. Later, he wished he had been more tactful, more composed. But from the time he hung up the phone, he did everything right.

He liked where he was. There was so much he hoped to accomplish. Wouldn't leaving so soon be an affront to his flock? For a long time it had been his conviction that where he would be the happiest in the years ahead and where he could do the most good was in a Baptist pulpit.

Yet, when on the phone with Binkley again, a date for an interview was set. To rule out making any kind of change, Michael had eventually concluded, was not necessarily the most prudent thing to do.

There would be two interviews, both on neutral ground, First Baptist Church of Greensboro, N.C.. Between the first and second, Michael made a point of learning all he could about the children's homes and

William H. "Mace" Brown was chair of BCH Board of Trustees in 1983. Brown was an alum who grew up at Mills Home in Thomasville

what was expected of its president. Running the child care institution would be a ministry, too. Being president would provide opportunities to use all the skills he had acquired, and probably to do far more for the welfare of others than he could as a pastor. He finally made up his mind; he was willing to make a change.

Two members of the search committee, Winfield Blackwell (not related) of Winston-Salem, N.C., and Carroll Wall of Lexington, N.C., visited Monument Heights. They heard Michael preach, had him answer

more questions, and talked to others.

Then, in his second appearance before the full committee, Michael gave a performance he had carefully rehearsed. He impressed members, as he hoped, with the study he had made of the Homes' past and present, and — presumptively, to say the least — with what he felt the institution's future might or could be. At the conclusion of the meeting, one committee member thought Michael knew more about the Homes than he did; Michael thought the job was in the bag.

Indeed, the committee, shelving the dossiers of the other three on their short list of candidates, telephoned the board of trustees the next morning to announce Michael as its recommendation.

While holding a called meeting at BCH's Mills Home in Thomasville, N.C., on May 6, trustees, as expected, voted approval of the committee's choice. Michael, sitting in the next room, was called in. Three days after his 41st birthday, he accepted the congratulations of the trustees, and then, of all things, gave them a pep talk. Together, they would make the future of Baptist Children's Homes bright. The pep talk left them somewhat abashed, but they were impressed – and more pleased than abashed. July 1, 1983, all agreed, would be when he assumed the presidency.

One of the other candidates for president was a member of the administrative staff at the Homes. To Michael's surprise, he took Michael's selection as president gracefully and harbored no ill will. In extending best wishes, he said, "As president, I would have been a Buick. You will be a Cadillac." The two worked well together for years afterward.

(What Michael would soon be driving would be a new Oldsmobile. The trustees would provide that — permitting Michael to dispose of his Ford LTD — along with a place for the Blackwells to live and a starting salary of $42,000 a year for the new president.)

On Mother's Day, May 8, in 1983, at the evening worship, Michael, a red rose pinned to his lapel, stood up, and to those seated in the Monument Heights sanctuary, he read his letter of resignation. The response was predictable, a chorus of muffled gasps. Only one other member of the church knew he planned to leave — Hamilton Q. Fulton, chairman of the board of deacons. For the reading of the letter, Fulton was at Michael's side. When finished, Michael put Fulton in charge of the remainder of the service and slipped out a back door.

The next day, the lead story on the front of the local section of the *Richmond Times-Dispatch* concerned the resignation. The article captured some of the reaction of church members —

a mixture of anger and disappointment that soon gave way to understanding and acceptance.

The paper reported, "Monument Heights Baptist Church may go a month without a pastor since Dr. Michael C. Blackwell caught the congregation off guard by announcing his resignation last night during evening services. He will preach for the last time May 25. His resignation is effective June 30."

Dr. William H. Brown, Baptist Children's Homes trustee chairman and himself a BCH alumnus, spread the word elsewhere. It was a development of wide interest. Some 42 North Carolina newspapers and other periodicals took note of it. Brown was quoted: "Our trustees, in giving approval [to the recommendation of the search committee], evidenced a conviction that Dr. Blackwell will continue to lead this vital ministry in an exemplary manner, in keeping with the wondrous and distinguished heritage

Richmond pastor will take post at Carolina home

Dr. Michael C. Blackwell, pastor of Richmond's Monument Heights Baptist Church, announced last night that he is leaving to become president of a North Carolina children's home.

The 41-year-old pastor will assume the post at the Baptist Children's Homes of North Carolina Inc., a Thomasville-based institution with 285 full-time employees, on July 1.

Dr. Blackwell made the unexpected announcement after Monument Heights' evening service, saying his resignation will be effective June 30 but that he will last preach at the church May 29.

He has served as pastor of that 1,370-member church at Libbie and Monument avenues since October 1980. An interim pastor has yet to be chosen.

The new post "combines everything I've ever dreamed of," he said last night. The home, founded in 1885, "is not just for orphans anymore" because, with a $6.7 million annual budget, it now offers group care, therapeutic camping expeditions, crisis intervention and other services.

The institution is part of the Baptist State Convention and operates from 25 locations in 18 cities throughout North Carolina.

Before coming to Monument Heights, Dr. Blackwell served as an associate pastor of Ridge Road Baptist Church in Raleigh, N.C., and later as pastor of Carthage's First Baptist. A North Carolina native, he earned

Dr. Michael C. Blackwell
Will take new post July 1

similar subjects.

He serves as host of "Missions Update," a bimonthly video presentation of the Foreign Mission Board, and frequently teaches at the Baptist Assemblies at Caswell and Eagle Eyrie in Lynchburg.

Dr. Blackwell will replace Dr. W.R. Wagoner as president of the Baptist children's home. Dr. Wagoner, the home's seventh president, is retiring after 25 years in that post.

of our children's homes and his distinctive predecessors. His unique talents, personality, and commitments will assure that this ministry remains in the vanguard of excellence in child care, in meeting the challenge of resolving the hurts of children and families in need."

The search committee chairman, Dr. Binkley, added: "Dr. Blackwell has a rare combination of theological insight and professional skills. He cares deeply for children and their families. He will render outstanding service as president of Baptist Children's Homes."

When contacted by the *Twin City Sentinel*, in Winston-Salem, for a comment, Michael said, "This position combines everything I ever dreamed of doing. It combines everything I have ever studied for and trained for in areas of executive leadership, management, communications, fund-raising and public relations. I just find it an opportunity that comes along once in a lifetime — to lead an agency that is dedicated to the ideals that the children's homes are dedicated to. And, of course, it is really more than just child care now . . . . It is a massive operation which literally goes from the mountains to the coast."

* * *

The early departure notwithstanding, ties to Richmond ("I count it another great experience for me," Michael says) have remained strong. Friends made there became part of an ever-expanding circle of those Michael had collected along the way at other church assignments. In so many cases, the closeness, the caring that grew from minister/counselor-member relationships, never went away. Monument Heights was no different; it also watched for excuses to call him back. In his most memorable return trips, in 2000 and 2005, he was the featured speaker at celebrations marking the church's 50th and 55th anniversaries.

"In a world where people are
losing sight of respect and love,
we remain hopeful because we
have seen so many lives reclaimed.
We know that ordinary people
of faith and commitment, using
their God-given talents, can turn
the tide."

CHAPTER TWELVE – *A Place for Miracles*

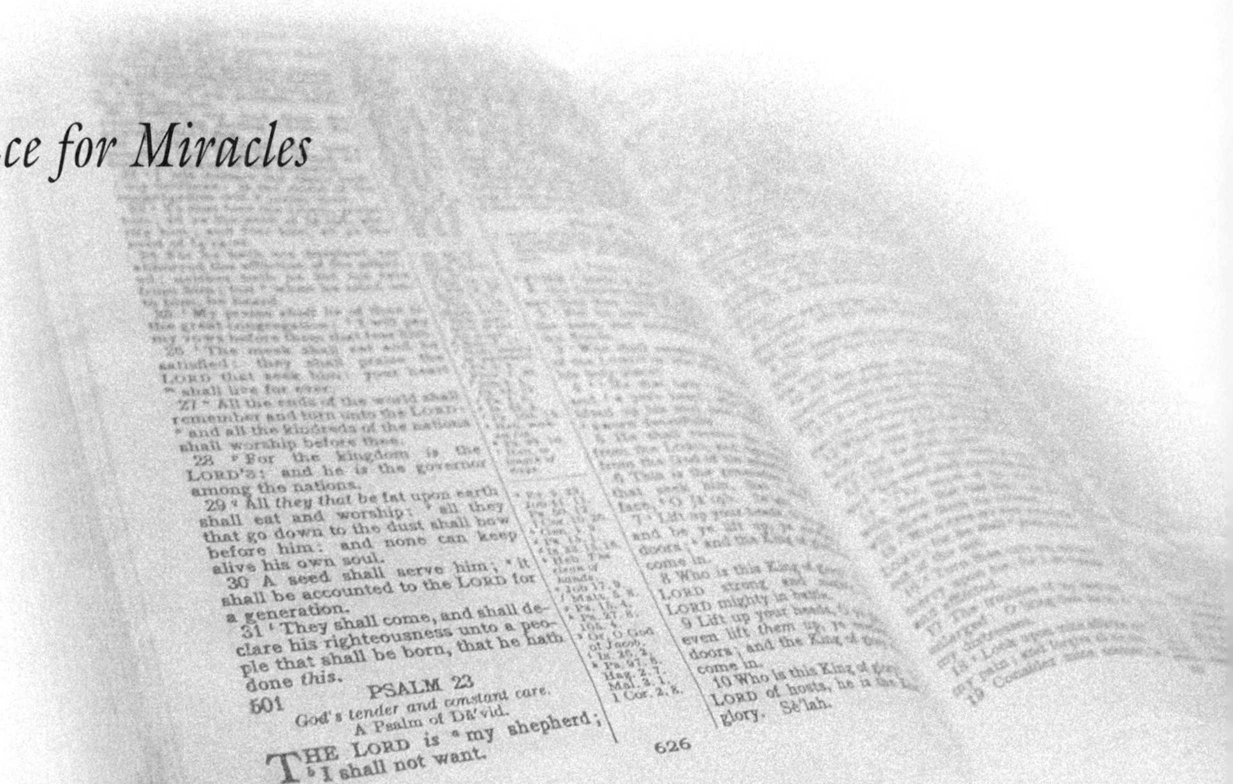

Michael liked to have his outline for his two Sunday sermons finished by Wednesday noon. He would spend Wednesday afternoon putting his final touches on his "prayer meeting" Bible study.

This Wednesday in February 1983 would be different. At 11:00 a.m., he received a phone call.

"This is Olin T. Binkley," the voice said. "I'm chairman of the search committee for a new president of Baptist Children's Homes of North Carolina."

Someone had put Michael's name in the hopper. Michael didn't even know that BCH was looking for a president, "Thank you for your consideration," Michael said. "It is an honor to be considered."

After two interviews, Dr. Binkley called in April to tell Michael he would be BCH's new president.

Michael never looked back. His mind began racing as to what this next chapter in his life would bring.

"To continue the tradition of quality care for the precious children and young people whose lives have been entrusted to Baptist Children's Homes."

That was *No. 1* on a list of goals and intentions drawn up and sworn to by Michael once he had assumed the duties of BCH president.

After his arrival, the first issue of *Charity & Children*, BCH's

Dr. Blackwell poses with Mills Home children in July, 1983.

newspaper, carried an interview with him. The list appeared therein. *C&C* is the historic voice of the children's homes.

Other stated goals were:

– To maintain a harmonious and healthy relationship with the Baptist State Convention of North Carolina.

– To instill a sense of professional excellence and pride among staff members.

– To work with trustees and staff members to produce bold and imaginative plans that will keep BCH in the forefront of child care ministry.

– To be good stewards of our resources and to operate within a balanced budget, seeking to get from each dollar its maximum effectiveness.

– And to joyously celebrate our 100th birthday in 1985 by launching a massive effort to acquaint and reacquaint North Carolina Baptists (and others) with our heritage and our hopes.

There had been seven presidents before Michael, none of whom, so far as is known, began his time in office by announcing a set of goals. Michael would prove to be different in a number of ways.

Most noteworthy of the seven previous presidents would have been John Haymes Mills, a big man, both physically and in the history of child care. Sometimes he is identified as the father of the orphanage movement in North Carolina. With the support of the Masons, he was founder of an orphanage at Oxford, N.C., in 1873, the first in the state. Private child care institutions in America date back to 1717. In that year, one opened at the Ursuline Convent in New Orleans.

CHAR
CHILDR
Dr. Blackwell Ta

by Rick Stegall
Editor

Dr. Michael C. Blackwell arrived at his office early July 1 to begin his administration as the eighth president of the Baptist Children's Homes of North Carolina. It didn't take him long to realize that he was going to be a very busy man.

After a morning of meeting with administrative department leaders, the chairman of the board of trustees and other key leadership people, he had just caught his second wind in time to attend a reception given in his honor. Dr. Blackwell, his wife, Catherine, daughter, Julie, and son, Michael, Jr. met staff members from across the state and members of the board of trustees.

Dr. Blackwell addresses Kennedy Home Alumni group.

The Blackwells attended the annual homecoming festivities at Kennedy Home over the weekend, during which time the new president pledged his help and challenged alumni to continue their role as supporters and active spokespersons for the Homes.

When asked about his feelings concerning his new role Dr. Blackwell stated that many of his feelings concerning BCH's ministry were formed during his 38 years of experience as a North Carolina Baptist. "I grew up in Flintgroves Church in Gastonia with a warm feeling

This country's first Baptist orphanage appeared in 1869 in Kentucky.

When he severed his connections with the orphanage in Oxford, Mills hooked up with a group of Baptists and set out to establish another that the Baptists could call their own. The place they found to put it was midway in the state, in Thomasville, a budding furniture manufacturing center. There, in 1885, they purchased as a site an 80-acre farm three miles west of the heart of the village named for its founder, a venturesome builder by the name of John W. Thomas. Preparations were made immediately to start construction of the first building of the Thomasville Baptist Orphanage.

It grew and changed. Then changed and grew.

But not everything changed. A struggle to find the money to pay the costs began the first day and has never ended. That and the demand for the care offered. From day one, there has been a greater demand than it has been possible to meet.

Services began to be added and diversified, new sites arose across the state, and institutional names were updated. The original Thomasville Baptist Orphanage evolved in other ways, as we see in one of the organization's annual reports, which shows what BCH was moving from and moving to:

– Custodial indentured care, to family-focused services.

– Congregate care, to specialized small living units.

– Long-term custodial care, to individualized goal-based plans.

– On-campus education, to use of public schools and alternative educational resources.

– Individual staff persons with total responsibility, to a teamwork concept.

ns attentively to Sam Wilson,
ensboro and Dr. William H.
stee chairman.

feels "the chief executive
r all the facts, figures, and
y given situation and then be
fferently than anyone else."
he secret to leadership is
secret to refreshment is not
h ideas whose time has come

uation the process of goal
portant in accomplishing
well wishes to continue the
y care for the precious
ople whose lives have been
He states other key early
a harmonious and healthy
Baptist State Convention,
professional excellence and
members, to work with
to produce bold and
will keep BCH in the
re ministry; to be good
es and to operate within
eking to get from each
effectiveness; and to

During his first year, Michael visited the grave site of BCH founder John Haymes Mills. **131**

– Single services, to multi-service programs.

– Rescue of homeless children, to services to families in crisis.

And the name would be changed from the Thomasville Baptist Orphanage to the Baptist Children's Homes of North Carolina.

It has been decades since the practice was to take in orphans (children who had lost one or both parents), feed, shelter, and clothe them, expose them to basic schooling, teach them a trade, then send them on their way. The changeover to the family-in-crisis as the client was not yet under way when Michael showed up. He was the successor to Dr. W.R. Wagoner, who served as president starting in 1958 until his retirement. Others were, after Mills, J.B. Boone, from 1895 to 1905; Dr. Martin Luther Kesler, from 1905 to 1932; Dr. I.G. Greer, from 1932 to 1948; Dr. Zeno Wall, from 1948 to 1950; and W.C. Reed, from 1950 to 1958. Their titles were, first, general manager, then general superintendent, before president was adopted during Wagoner's tenure. Most were, like Mills, known and admired from Manteo to Murphy.

But none, it seems safe to say, upon taking office, experienced anything like the alarming discovery that Michael made. Just at the moment he expected to be enlightened, he found himself in the dark. The fix he was in has been described in some of his writings.

The welcoming committee his first day as new president of BCH,

The orphanage's first three leaders were, left to right, John Haymes Mills, J.B. Boone, and Martin Luther Kesler.

on July 1, 1983, consisted of one person — the president's secretary. (Later in the day, there would be a reception in his honor attended by trustees and key staffers.) Michael had arrived early, was fresh, and was eager to get started. He and the secretary spent a few minutes getting acquainted. He half expected his predecessor, Dr. Wagoner (who had retired at his own request and with the good will of the BCH board), to walk in, congratulate him and wish him well, and then show him the ropes. That didn't happen his first day. And it never did. (Michael would take it upon himself to try to meet Dr. Wagoner, to communicate with him, but each time he tried, he failed to draw a response.)

Once settled at his desk and having steadied himself for the lift-off of his presidency, Michael thought that a proper use of the moment would be to begin making himself familiar with some of the BCH administrative files and records. So he asked the secretary to fetch an armful. Her response was shocking: there were none. On Dr. Wagoner's order, Mills Home maintenance personnel had boxed up documents

Michael's first official visit to Kennedy Home in Kinston was for Homecoming on July 2 – 3, 1983.

133

of many descriptions that had accumulated over 25 years and had trucked them to the ex-president's residence in Thomasville. He looked upon the contents of the boxes as personal property and seemingly had no intention of permitting anybody to have the use of them.

"Imagine," Michael has written, "because there were no files, I had no record, no history, no strategic plan for one-fourth of the institution's entire existence. There was no list of sites, facilities, employees, budgets, or boards. Nor was there any plan for the direction of BCH. I had to find them wherever I could.

"I felt like a new coach of the Atlanta Braves who didn't know

(Left to right) I.G. Greer, Zeno Wall and W.C. Reed provided valuable leadership.

where the locker room is and had to field a team to play the New York Yankees tomorrow. I didn't have a lineup card, didn't even know the names of the players or where to meet the bus.

"Employees [at BCH] were sheepish and afraid to express an opinion. Nobody wanted to do anything. They would tell me anything or deliver whatever I asked for specifically, but nothing else. Everything

I got, I got on my own. I had no help."

Of course, Wagoner, by disappearing with the records, had in mind making a statement. He wanted it fully understood that he adamantly opposed the trustees' choice of someone to succeed him, even though their choice was not someone he knew. But much time would pass before Michael was made privy to exactly what ailed Wagoner.

In various ways and at various times, Wagoner had attempted to handpick his successor. He appeared to be seeking a way to keep a foot in the door at BCH more to his benefit than would be possible through the counseling position he had been offered but rejected.

Usually, he had his way with his board. This time, all his attempts were turned aside. The kind of person he favored as someone to follow him simply did not fit, or perhaps fell short of, the board's criteria.

A final board decision left Wagoner embittered and sorely grieved, and he made certain that how he felt did not go unnoticed.

Clearly, the ex-president knew how to get mad and stay mad.

Then, some five months after his departure, Wagoner received a letter from a BCH attorney informing him that a BCH agent would be calling to reclaim the missing records in Wagoner's possession. Their retrieval took place without incident.

But there was much more than the controversial Wagoner legacy for Michael to dwell on, to confront, to tackle. Just where to start was

134

no easy decision. His patience was tested by the need to step around an obstacle here, an obstacle there, in order to achieve a smooth transition.

One night in his first week, he was still at his office after midnight. Long hours were still being spent on conducting his own orientation. Suddenly, for the first time in his life, he felt lost. A wave of hopelessness washed over him. The new CEO of a statewide organization that served hundreds of children each year and had a 1983 budget of $6 million leaned back in his chair, stared at the ceiling, and asked himself, "What in the world am I doing here?"

W.R. Wagoner

"I knew I was sitting in a nice leather chair in a wood-paneled office," he remembered, "and that it was very dark outside and very empty in the rest of the building and that I had been there 18 hours already, with no end in sight. But after trying to get my arms around

J. Dewey Hobbs gave Michael middle-of-the-night counsel.

the vast network of services, constituencies, employees, board members, budgets, debts and assets, facilities and clients, I realized my arms were too short. And I wondered, 'What have I gotten into?'"

Out of sheer desperation, Michael called friend of many years and fellow minister, J. Dewey Hobbs. "We talked on the telephone for two hours. He was a wise man, a victor in many such battles. Our conversa-

tion gave form and substance to the intangible, dark mists that swarmed over me. He didn't know child care any more than I did that night. But he knew how to direct my thoughts to the task at hand and to the vision that both established the institution 98 years earlier, and that compelled me to invest myself in its next decades of service.

"That long day grown into night [22 hours, 6 a.m. to 4 a. m.] was my epiphany, my turning point. It was not a lot of fun but it was giddily illuminating. I realized I knew nothing about child care, but that was okay. I knew a lot about human relations, families, education, vision, and leadership. Learning about children was the least of it. The processes, procedures, and technicalities were a body of knowledge I knew I could master."

With renewed confidence and vigor, he resumed working long hours to make himself at ease in the driver's seat and to prepare for moving ahead. Of great help

November 11, 1985, marked the 100th birthday of Baptist Children's Homes. The celebration lasted much of the year.

was the research he did when the trustees were thinking of hiring him. He paid attention to planning. The set of goals and intentions emerged. Next to "Celebrate our 100th Birthday" on the list, he noted, "Get busy on this one first."

The centennial took up much of his time for almost two years. The observance began in November 1984 and did not wind down until the following November, or after it had in spectacular fashion fulfilled its purpose, to increase awareness across North Carolina and beyond of BCH and its work, and also to say thanks to all the people who had been of help over the years.

A leading attention-getter was the 40-day marathon relay, "Run for the Children," that stretched from one end of North Carolina to the other, a distance of 1,400 miles. More than a thousand children and adults were participants. They passed from one to the other a baton containing on microfilm the names of all the children ever to receive BCH assistance. Photos of runners, as they passed through 155 towns and cities, appeared in dozens of newspapers and on television newscasts.

A Goldsboro newspaper labeled it "One of the most impressive running endeavors ever held in this state."

(Michael was disappointed that President Jimmy Carter, a Baptist, declined an invitation to run in the marathon's last mile.)

Other centennial highlights:

– A BCH history, "A Hundred Years of Caring," by Alan Keith-Lucas, and a "100 Years of Caring" video.

– A musical, "Praisebook: Music for a Celebration," that was performed in 30 Baptist churches across the state.

– An invitational basketball tournament.

– A time-capsule burying ceremony at Mills Home's Mitchell Museum to mark the beginning of BCH's second century. It is to be opened Thursday, November 11, 2010, the 125th anniversary of BCH.

– Publication of 5,000 copies of a centennial cookbook packed with a thousand recipes.

– The BCH development department raising $109,750

Charity & Children

Baptist Child
Homes Celeb
Centenn

A Hundred Years of Caring
The Story of the Baptist Children's Homes of North Carolina, Inc.

as a Centennial Fulfillment Program.

– A 100th birthday party at Mills Home at which was served a birthday cake that measured 25 by 60 feet.

At about the time of the party, ***The Thomasville Times*** ran an editorial congratulating BCH upon reaching a hundred. It ascribed to its "new" president leadership and vision, someone who was also "a fountain of energy and enthusiasm. Signs of a new spirit surging through the BCH system can be found, which seems to be accompanied by a renewal of commitment to the ideals of John Mills. Just one of the changes here is the return of a neighborliness between Mills Home and Thomasville. It had almost disappeared. Bringing it back is mainly one of Dr. Blackwell's achievements, and it won't be his last."

Massive centennial birthday cake

The celebration climax came on November 12, 1985, in Charlotte at the Baptist State Convention. Children representing each of the BCH units joined Michael on stage there to present a worship/thanksgiving service that inspired a number of messengers (delegates) to declare the service was the highlight of the convention.

Once safely into the second century, Michael turned to coming to grips with the mounting opposition across the country to group care

Thomasville staff gives a centennial wave.

for children, or what mainly BCH had been providing since its start. According to child care authority Alan Keith-Lucas, "The country was. . . in the midst of an anti-institutional wave. A movement begun 10 years before aimed at large public institutions for the insane, retarded, or delinquent was being applied to private and church-related ones." He noted that the 1980 Public Law 96-272, which insisted on "the least restrictive environment" and which governed the federal funds available to public child welfare agencies, marked children's institutions, especially the large ones, the least desirable form of placement, to be used only as a last resort. Large campuses were seen as harmful.

As a result, it was becoming harder for departments of social services to make use of group care for the children for whom they had responsibility.

Michael fumed then and fumes now that group care has been stigmatized. Most times, it is the best of choices, he has argued. He wishes placement agencies would look upon children's homes as "a haven of first refuge, not as the court of last resort. Children's homes are a very important option. Young people shouldn't have to go through courts, mental health facilities, mental hospitals and be one step shy of entering a training school before some one says, 'Well, let's try Baptist.' Children's homes should be a front-line defense in children's issues today."

Without question, planning has helped in large measure to pave the way for steady, systematic growth. In 1983, when Michael moved in, BCH was serving about 1,000 children a year. Ten years later, the number was approximately 1,500, along with the families of many of these. (Much of that increase is attributable to expansions in day care services). Now, two decades later, around 2,000 children, and 4,000 other family members, are receiving BCH help annually.

For residential care, BCH has been accepting children referred by their parents, other family members, church pastors, and psychiatric hospitals, as well as social services departments. The practice of searching for families to adopt children in residence is buried in the past. For a number of years, the objective has been, after intense family counseling, to reunite child and family.

And the effort has met with remarkable success. Most children

Executive vice presidents compose Michael's management group. Left to right, Tim Smith, Jennie Counts, Sam Barefoot, Brenda Gray and C.F. McDowell III.

eventually return home.

"To those under our care," Michael has said, "we teach values and personal qualities that permeate lives and change them, like water and sun and fertilizer permeate a plant and enable it to flower. In a world where people are losing sight of respect and love, we remain hopeful because we have seen so many lives reclaimed. We know that ordinary people of faith and commitment, using their God-given talents, can turn the tide."

It took him a while, but Michael has succeeded in surrounding himself with administrators fully capable of shouldering critical functions of management in a manner that leaves the president feeling confident he has delegated responsibility in the very best interest of BCH — well, yes, that also lets him breathe easier. The President's Management Group is a dynamic combo, by Michael's reckoning. Its members are Tim Smith, executive vice president, programs & services; Jennie Counts, formerly Michael's secretary and executive assistant, now executive vice president, executive administration; Sam Barefoot, treasurer and chief financial officer; C.F. McDowell, III, executive vice president, special ministries; and Brenda Gray, executive vice president, development & communications.

"I'd put them up against any business of any size," Michael asserts. "They're pure gold."

In 1984, Michael tapes the first of many BCH videos.

The one with a working relationship as close to Michael as any of the others, or closer, Jennie Counts, seems to think he's 24-karat too. They go back together to 1987. Her reply to "what's he like?" was: "Dr. Blackwell is an authentic visionary who has the ability of looking into an individual and seeing not just the present but the person's potential for the future . . . warm, caring, sensitive, compassionate . . . demands the very best of his staff . . . generous with his praise for a job well-done . . . . His gift is to motivate, inspire and encourage . . . . It is both a joy and a learning experience to work for him."

There have been lumps and bumps, of course. A special commission appointed by the General Board of the Baptist State Convention did a study of BCH while undertaking to recommend how to apportion the convention's Cooperative Program funds. Michael reacted to the study saying, "We were studied up one side and down the other, and we stood to lose thousands of dollars annually. Fortunately, the board's

executive committee chose not to accept the commission's recommendation because they saw it was really going to decimate us.

"There is no safe stream of income anymore. If I had my way about it, I would like to go back to when 90 percent of our funding came from churches, like it was in 1960."

Trustees have always been supportive of the present administration. Michael has said as long as he has been BCH president, there has not been a single trustee "no" vote.

There are 36 trustees, and they have the last word. The BCH president serves at their pleasure. No major policy or project can be adopted without their approval. They are due much credit for BCH's remarkable progress. BCH is an institution of the Baptist State Convention and its trustees are elected by messengers while the convention is in session. They vote on a slate compiled by a nominating committee. The BCH president can make recommendations to the committee. Those elected serve a four-year term and can serve more than one term, although not consecutively. They must be active members of Baptist State Convention of North Carolina churches.

Agency mascot B.C. Bear is introduced in 1985.

From sensible planning and financial good fortune came many benefits. Michael saw to it that the development department was expanded and ensconced in the former infirmary at Mills Home after it had been remodeled with a gift from the Allred family and then named in honor of both the Allred and the Idol families. It is now the home of the vice president of development and communications, the staff of the redesigned *Charity & Children*, and all members of the development and communications staff.

*Wint Capel produced the centennial edition of **Charity & Children** in 1987.*

Charity & Children, now a monthly tabloid, is one of the oldest newspapers in North Carolina. With as many as 53,000 copies going out each issue to people with a connection to BCH, its friends, and its supporters. John Mills started it and was its first editor, two years after the opening of the orphanage at Thomasville in 1885. There have been other noted editors: Archibald Johnson; John Arch McMillan; Marse Grant, later editor of the Baptist State Convention's *Biblical Recorder*, John Roberts, later editor of the South Carolina Convention's *Baptist Courier*, and lately, Norman Jameson and Jim Edminson. Through its

reports of the BCH story as it unfolds, it seeks support of all kinds for its programs and serves as nothing else can to keep BCH and its president in touch with alumni, Baptist church congregations, benefactors, and potential benefactors, to name a few.

As long as there's a Michael C. Blackwell at BCH, there will be a *Charity & Children*. "I love that paper with all my heart. I can't remember a time when I haven't read it. My warm childhood feelings for Baptist Children's Homes came primarily from what I would see in it."

It comes as no surprise that a college journalism major would have a strong commitment to *Charity & Children*. One of the proudest titles he wears — and the one few people know of — is publisher, *Charity & Children*.

While Michael allows his editor full freedom to write, design, and edit the publication, he reserves for himself final approval of the newspaper's contents.

Michael's monthly column most often relates to family issues, but on occasion, he'll publish what suspiciously looks like a "sermon," adjuring his readers to follow biblical principles toward success and personal fulfillment.

In the paper's special Centennial issue in 1987, Michael wrote:

> *Charity & Children* is here to stay. While few things may be stated so forcefully, I really do believe it — *Charity & Children* will continue to endure. I believe that *Charity & Children* should be a great newspaper, both in content and in appearance. Thus, we will remain updated on the latest publishing technologies. If a paper doesn't secure the reader's attention with an attractive format, it's highly unlikely that the paper will even be opened.

At his core, Michael is a minister with a capital "M." But he also proves what every journalist knows — once "printer's ink" seeps into one's system, it never really dries up.

* * *

Not too long ago, Michael, while rummaging through an office file, came upon a document that recorded the goals and intentions he drew up at the time he took over as BCH president. He removed it and spent a little time reviewing the listings and thinking about the almost quarter century that had rushed past. And he wondered, had he done what he hoped to or promised BCH he would?

"To continue the tradition of quality care" for children and young people was at the top of what he had drawn up. He can point out that, now, not only is the care the best ever, there's more of it. Now the family is included as never before. The relationship with the Baptist State Convention remains harmonious and healthy. "We are humbled by the love and support we receive from Baptists." Pride and excellence have become staff hallmarks, he likes to say. "The staff's excellence quotient is second to none . . . . I have kept the promise to get from each dollar its maximum effectiveness" . . . . And "It's been a joy working with trustees and staff to produce bold and imaginative plans. The results, I feel, are just cause for rejoicing."

That's checking off everything on that 1983 lineup — no x-marks. That could be called batting a thousand.

Every few years, he reprints in one of his ***Charity & Children*** columns a letter he wrote at the time he was to take over as president. It was dated May 16, 1983, and it went out to all the BCH trustees. He found it quite interesting that the contents have remained altogether relevant and just as true. What he reprinted was:

"The years ahead will be filled with challenges that none of us can possibly imagine. Ongoing challenges of budgets and programs and quality care will occupy our creative energies. Innovations and changes will require that we be bold in our thinking, and strong in our doing.

"God has called me to ministry. I cannot think of any finer way to discover the eternal truths of Mark 10: 14-16 than by serving as president of Baptist Children's Homes.

"I am excited about our future as president and trustees.

"God has called.

"We must lead.

"The journey begins."

Michael's focus continues to be the children in care.

Once back in North Carolina and after having become comfortable with handling the reins of the Baptist Children's Homes, he set about deciding whether to venture onto the hustings, whether to declare for public elective office for the first time, a move toward a branching-out he suspected he would find most gratifying.

CHAPTER THIRTEEN – *Getting Political*

The house was quiet. Kathy had given up waiting for Michael and had gone to bed. The lamp in his study was lit dimly, his desk covered with files and papers. The question to accept the challenge to run for office was preoccupying his thoughts and had done so for the better part of the week.

His thoughts went deep, digging into every corner of his mind and heart. He loved politics. But he also loved the ministry to which he had committed himself . . . the ministry of helping hurting children and healing broken families.

The dog's barking drew his attention. Pepper needed to be walked.

PRESSING THE FLESH — Governor Jim Hunt was busy pressing the flesh as he moved around a roomful of campaign workers and supporters at the Sheraton Inn on Friday.

A political adviser might say, "Don't forget to include that he has a commanding presence."

Once, in an essay he wrote, he explained, "Why I am a Democrat." In part, he said, "Because I believe in a party which is willing to cross the moats, scale the walls and strike the wicked in their inner sanctums. Whether it's racism or sexism or ageism, the Democratic Party has struck the match and taken the heat because it dared to afflict the comfortable as well as comfort the afflicted."

When looking for the embodiment of that kind of shining idealism, Michael would turn to Jim Hunt, who owned the governorship of North Carolina for a long, long time, much longer than anybody else — two four-year terms, then two more, or 16 years. During his stay in Carthage, Michael did low-key campaigning for him at a time he was running for governor for the first time, in 1976. He never again became that visible as a campaigner, for Hunt or anybody else, yet it was well known within the core of the party that he was a valuable source of private endorsement of candidates, and that he made generous use of it. (He left campaign financing to others.)

Once back in North Carolina and after having become comfortable with handling the reins of the Baptist Children's Homes, he set about

Thinking about becoming politically active would fire Michael's imagination. Since reaching voting age, he had been an avowed Democrat who enthusiastically backed the Democratic party's candidates and upheld the party's principles. He was the son of a "yellow dog Democrat" and an idolizer of John Fitzgerald Kennedy. Maybe he ought to make a run at winning public office. It was his good fortune to have most of the attributes of candidates who were successes: a reputation for helping others, no skeletons in the closet, a bushel basket full of credentials.

deciding whether to venture onto the hustings, whether to declare for public elective office for the first time, a move toward a branching-out he suspected he would find most gratifying. Serving in the state Senate or House of Representatives, as a starter, had a fair amount of appeal.

Few of those with whom he came in contact were aware of his marriage to the Democrats. Most thought of him as apolitical. Kermit Cloniger encouraged him to be a House candidate, which was flattering, but Cloniger was "Mr. Republican" in Thomasville, BCH headquarters, and wanted Michael's name on the GOP slate.

What he needed was a "go for it" from the Democratic faction rulers, who, it turned out, were quite willing to provide it, including the county's No. 1 Democrat, Sheriff "Jaybird" McCrary, sometimes ranked the most powerful individual in the county.

Wayne McDevitt was a BCH trustee and Gov. Jim Hunt's Chief of Staff.

Yet Michael did not find the same degree of encouragement when he divulged to a few of the Baptist Children's Homes trustees he sort of had a hankering to test the political waters. Those in which he confided feared that support of the institution would suffer if its personifier was publicly taking sides when sticky political issues boiled up. They opined, best not to.

There was this worry as well: The effects of gerrymandering had become increasingly a factor. A Democratic candidate was finding it harder than ever to collect enough votes to win in either the Senate or House district in which Michael was a resident.

So after a bit more ruminating, Michael laid aside whatever his political ambitions might have amounted to at that time — for the moment.

Then, by the early 1990s, that itch was back, strong as before. In the interim, he had carefully avoided doing anything publicly to appear to be politically partisan, but his mixing with ranking Democratic party operatives had been increasing steadily, and

WHY I AM A DEMOCRAT

I am a Democrat because I believe in the principles of the ratic Party: Courage, Compassion, and Change.

I became a Democrat by choice. It was 1963; I was a 21-year ollege student. John Kennedy was President; Terry Sanford overnor.

grew up in Democratic environs. My major influencers were ats. I came of age politically under Democrats. President ly came to Chapel Hill my Sophomore year. His speech fired husiasm and idealism.

became a Democrat nearly 30 years ago. I remain a Demo-ecause it is compatible with my life's purpose of serving . I do this in several ways. As a professional needy children

147

soon he again was asking whether he should get involved in government at some level as holder of public office. Maybe he needed a complete change. Maybe the yearnings persisting would be best accommodated if instead of serving his fellow man through a private institution, he channeled his energies into public service. Maybe he should set his

sights on a goal not exposed to the vagaries of gerrymandering.

To hasten his decision, he applied for and was accepted for enrollment in one of the classes of the nonprofit, nonpartisan, privately funded North Carolina Institute of Political Leadership, formerly affiliated with the University of North Carolina at Wilmington but now headquartered in Raleigh. Its purpose was to prepare North Carolinians for public office or, if office-holders, to help them do better. Usually, about half of those who apply are selected to become students. A class consists of 20 students who meet for 10 alternate weekends either in the spring or the fall. Michael became a member of the Institute's fall 1992 class.

Walt DeVries knows Michael well. He was the Institute's founder and only executive director until June 30, 2004. First he knew Michael as student, then even better once Michael was elected the organization's chairman of the board in 1997. Michael was chairman — leader of the leaders, so to speak — until 2004. DeVries said he has "pumped new life into the Institute."

It is a connection that has helped Michael firm up relations with more of the state's political movers and shakers.

And there could be no doubt a connection with the governor had been made. It also was in 1998 that Hunt, to help mark Michael's 15th

anniversary as Baptist Children's Homes president, conferred upon him "The Order of the Long Leaf Pine." Only Tar Heel governors can honor a person in that way, a special way of paying recognition to Tar Heels who have served the state with distinction.

DeVries was surprised that his chairman had not already become a candidate. At the time Michael signed up as an Institute student, DeVries had the impression he was cranking up to make a run for either the state Senate or state House. There's no doubt, DeVries added, "he's well-qualified," and that he would find plenty of support if and when he were to file for some office. His qualifications are extensive. In the view of DeVries, any state government administration would welcome Michael's availability to head up some agency or program.

For good measure, Michael took another leadership course. This time it was instruction offered by Leadership North Carolina, described

First Lady Carolyn Hunt kicks off the statewide Smart Start initiative at BCH's weekday education center in Thomasville.

as an innovative program designed to help the state's potential leaders learn more about North Carolina's social and economic problems and opportunities. It professes to serve all citizens of the state, a nonprofit, nonpartisan organization governed by a board of directors (Gov. Hunt was chairman) who reflected prevailing leadership in government, business, education, and the nonprofit sector. Michael was in a class of 50 who graduated in May 1998, after which he was made a member of the board's executive committee.

Wayne McDevitt affords assurance that Michael was acquainted with but also well regarded by Jim Hunt and his lieutenants. Now a senior vice president in the University of North Carolina general administration, McDevitt is a former chairman of the Democratic party in North Carolina and for several years was Hunt's chief of staff. "Michael's name elevated several times" when consideration was being given to filling high-level positions, McDevitt said. Michael was contacted, for instance, when McDevitt associates needed "squeaky-clean" appointees for director of the Governor's Office of Citizen Affairs, and again as chairman of the state Alcoholic Beverage Control board.

Gov. Jim Martin increased state funding for children's homes throughout North Carolina.

"When we needed qualified people, we'd find Mickey's name on the tip of our tongues."

How near he came to becoming either head of Citizen Affairs or the ABC board is hard to measure. He felt he could have become one or the other if he had been more certain that he wanted it and had made himself the strongest contender in his power. The Hunt people never said outright, about one or

Michael says he is always thoughtful about how the political process can improve the lives of children and families.

the other, "It's yours if you want it." Firm offers of political plums normally are withheld from all but the most eager and most able. Administration managers play it close to the vest. They want their appointees to be known as their first choices, and for appointees to be convinced they are. McDevitt words it carefully: "Mickey was a great team member . . . . We all wore the same jerseys . . . If he wanted to change positions, well, that didn't happen, for whatever reason."

Charlotte Observer writer Jack Betts put Michael close to the Hunt administration in Betts' column that appeared in July 1999. An *Observer* associate editor who at the time was based in Raleigh, where he covered state politics, Betts was filling a column with his choices of "my heroes of democracy in the statewide community." He described Michael, one of four he chose to write about, as "a down-to-earth Baptist minister who has managed to bridge church and state affairs better than anyone I've known . . . . [His influence] is felt in state politics and government as well as in the church and nonprofit world. He has been an informal adviser to Gov. Jim Hunt, was a leading candidate for the presidency of the N.C. Department of Community Colleges, has been chairman of the N.C. Institute of Political Leadership and is a member of the board of directors of Leadership North Carolina, two statewide organizations that train future leaders of this state."

But, yes, Michael has stayed put, without serious misgivings. However, he stays in touch. He responded with great pleasure and gratitude when invited by Gov. Hunt to join the state board of the North Carolina Partnership for Children (also known

as "Smart Start"). His term began in 1998 and is yet to end. He describes this program as "near to my heart." BCH headquarters was the venue for the governor's wife, Carolyn Hunt, to give the program its send-off in October 1994. It has kept expanding until now it reaches into each of the state's one hundred counties with its mission to make it possible for every child

You've got your heroes, I've go

RALEIGH — Former Duke University President Keith Brodie came up with the term in 1990 when he urged citizens to become involved with their world and to make a difference. Speaking at a high school commencement ceremony that June, he urged graduates to "find opportuni- . . . democracy: to refuse . . . stems, to help

Jack Betts

ble weapons of prejudice and cruelty."

For the past four years, The Observer on July 4 has recognized heroes of democracy from the region around Charlotte. They have included some well-known, high-profile folks, but all have been people who by their example have been sterling citizens who made this part of the country a fine place to live, work and raise families. You can read about The Observer's 1999 Heroes of Democracy on the next two pages. In this column, you'll read about some folks who qualify as heroes of democ- . . . community

lawyer who may be the nearest thing we have in the late 20th century to a founding father. He has played a major role in the brainstorming, creation, funding and operation of some vital nonprofit institutions that have made a remarkable difference in North Carolina.

You may remember Hancock's service as a state senator from Durham, a place that has produced a long list of prominent lawmakers. Hancock was a good one, but I think his place in North Carolina history is for his leading role in creating such organizations as the N. Center for Public Policy Research, a . . . old private, nonp . . .

BETTS *from 1C*

Bob Spearman.

But Hancock, a Charlotte native, has taken part in a host of foundings, including the N.C. Electronic Town Hall and the Public School Forum of North Carolina (Hancock recently stepped down as chairman of its board of directors). He helped set up a host of other organizations that have been strong advocates for better government, better schools and a better place to live.

And then there's Michael Blackwell, a down-to-earth Baptist minister who has managed to bridge church and state affairs better than anyone I've known, including the magnificent stainless-steel-spined Marse Grant. Blackwell once worked as a journalist for Big WAYS radio in Charlotte, but he felt a higher call. He went to seminary and became pastor for some big churches. He also felt the call to minister to the young, and for more than 15 years he has been president . . .

ng heroes of democracy

GERRY HANCOCK

MICHAEL BLACKWELL

formal adviser to G . . .

to arrive at school healthy and ready to succeed. He chaired the search committee that found current president Karen Ponder .

How Michael has been of help impressed Ashley Thrift, Smart Start state chairman. Thrift likes "his strong commitment and focus on matters affecting children, and it carries over in everything he does."

In June 2002, Leadership North Carolina presented to Michael its L. Richardson Preyer Alumni Award, named for a Greensboro, N.C., citizen who had been both an outstanding congressman and federal district court judge. How Michael had helped find an executive director for Leadership had impressed the awards committee. The awards citation stated in part, "Beginning in the spring of 2001, Dr. Blackwell served as chairman of the search committee for Leadership North Carolina in seeking to find a new executive director for this organization. More than two hundred candidates were considered. Dr. Blackwell led the search committee through a well-organized and detailed process. His diligence, substantial commitment of time, and exceptional leadership resulted in Leadership North Carolina finding its new executive director."

Preyer was one of the founders of

Leadership North Carolina.

In claiming the award named for Preyer, Michael became the first Leadership North Carolina graduate to win both of the organization's primary honors. The other, the Stanley Frank Class Award to the graduate whose leadership influence has been felt statewide, he received at graduation in 1998.

A North Carolina Baptist, of course, and a particular brand of one at that. While a seminary student, he settled on a set of persuasions that landed him among the denomination's conservatives. The progressive wing of the conservatives, in fact.

CHAPTER FOURTEEN – *Incurably Baptist*

During a quick visit to Gastonia, Michael had one last stop before his return to Thomasville. His car pulled into the driveway of the home of the man Blackwell fondly calls "Preacher."

Love and Edna Dixon were expecting him and were sitting comfortably on their porch dressed for company. As he walked toward them, they waved and greeted him with smiles.

"Not many 60-year-old men have the privilege of visiting their childhood pastor," Michael spoke, looking into the eyes of the 94-year-old man. "Preacher Dixon baptized me on April 16, 1950, two weeks shy of my eighth birthday."

Michael remembers Love Dixon parking his Hudson Hornet on the dirt street in front of his family's home. He spent an hour sitting with Dixon on the front seat of the massive automobile.

That day, Love opened his Bible and shared with the boy how he could know Jesus. The very next Sunday during the worship service, "Mickey" came forward and accepted Christ as his personal savior.

After their visit, Michael stood and thanked the couple for their warm reception. But before he left, he leaned toward Dixon almost whispering and asked, "How've I done?" Referring to a life that has led him to be the president of one of the most beloved institutions in North Carolina Baptist life. His "preacher" replied, "You've done real fine . . . real fine."

Michael is a Baptist born and a Baptist bred — and a practicing, card-carrying Baptist ever since. He has never given serious thought to being anything but.

Love and Edna Dixon were married 76 years before her death in December 2004.

His good friend Dr. Randall Lolley once said of him, "Michael is incurably a Baptist . . . . He makes people want to be a Baptist . . . . He is extraordinarily Baptist . . . . He is profoundly Baptist, pro- foundly Christian . . . . He lives out the name Baptist."

A North Carolina Baptist, of course, and a particular brand of one at that. While a seminary student, he settled on a set of persuasions that landed him among the denomination's conservatives. The progres- sive wing of the conservatives, in fact. And he has never moved much, this way or that, even as the fundamentalists of the Southern Baptist Convention (SBC) steadily gained in numbers and as their influence increased.

Within the SBC, largest of all the Protestant denominations with 42,000 autonomous churches made up of 18 million members, there can be found plenty of theological disagreement. It is universally accept- ed, however, that Jesus is Lord and Savior. And, historically, Baptists believe in the Priesthood of the Believer, that there is no middleman between God and the believer — that each person is his or her own priest. Therefore, the interpretation of the Holy Bible is left up to the individual.

The fundamentalists take what they find in the Bible literally (the belief in biblical inerrancy). The moderates say the Bible is open to interpretation. And therein lies most of the disagreement.

As a seminary student, Michael became familiar with, an admirer of, and was influenced by Carlyle Marney, something of a pariah among Southern Baptist preachers. Marney's ethical thought was the subject of Michael's master of theology thesis. Marney became a harsh critic of the fundamentalists long before they had won the high ground. This is a taste of his acerbic criticism as quoted in a 1964 newspaper article:

"A social revolution is going on, but we Baptists who are on God's right hand had precious little to do with it except when run over from the rear . . . . There are hundreds of colleges and dozens of seminaries and scores of Baptist organizations, which provide little kingdoms which

Carlyle Marney

little men just love to run. They won't give up their thrones for unity's sake . . . . The Southern Baptist Convention is a Jesus cult dressed like Buster Brown and Little Lord Fauntleroy with a Bowie knife handy to cut the throats of any who disagree with a regional point of view."

So Marney firmly believed back then what many moderate Baptists now contend — the fundamentalist movement is more about power and control than about what the Bible says or doesn't say.

Burning issues today for Southern Baptists are homosexuality and whether women should be allowed to serve Baptist churches as pastors.

It is not easy to find Baptists who uphold gay rights. They accept the homosexual, but condemn his or her behavior. Some moderates and

Michael, preparing to preach in Sao Paulo, Brazil. The three-year partnership between Baptist Children's Homes and Sao Paulo was both gratifying and humbling to him.

Baptist State Convention President Jerry Periera joins in worship as thousands of individually signed prayer links form a massive chain of prayer. Broyhill alum Roberta Rosenbalm Brunck leads in singing.

the less conservative say let the local church decide what to do about the homosexual issue, if anything.

For the far right of the SBC, it's "no" to women in the pulpit. Men are the authority in the church and their households. Women should be content with submissive roles. The moderates, on the other hand, approve of the ordination of women.

Some 5,000 people witnessed BCH's 1995 convention presentation in Winston-Salem.

The Baptist Faith and Message, the SBC's doctrinal statement, was revised in the year 2000 to forbid women to serve as pastors and to assert that the Bible teaches that wives should "submit graciously" to their husbands. A new controversy swirled up when the SBC's 5,000 foreign missionaries were told to affirm the revision in writing. Some 150 balked and risked expulsion. A former president of the SBC foreign mission board chafing under the order said the beliefs of missionaries have not changed, "only the rules have." R. Keith Parks added, "It has never been clearer that the fundamentalist leaders have changed the very nature of the Southern Baptist Convention."

Requiring an affirmation was likened to forcing a creed on the missionaries, whom some perceive to be the glue that binds all the independent congregations together.

If there is to be any reforming, in all likelihood it will be slow in coming, and then most likely only because of a changing culture — because of external influences. Reform is not likely to originate within.

The SBC did not repent of its tolerance of segregation practices until quite late in the 20th Century (in 1995 it apologized for its racist roots and past defense of slavery), long after North Carolina's Baptist State Convention had taken a stand in support of civil rights. Not that Baptist churches have become integrated. Like they say, Sunday at 11 a.m. is still the most segregated hour of the week, in all kinds of churches in all parts of the country. The doors of the white churches being open has not caused the blacks to turn away from what for some is the focal point of the African-American community, the black church.

Other less divisive issues get the attention of Baptist assemblies from time to time, of course. A resolution condemning abortion pops up once in a while. Like many others, Baptists occasionally wring their hands over the skyrocketing divorce rate. Some congregations also struggle with baptism requirements. However, most Baptist churches remain sticklers for full immersion for first-time believers.

Michael with Billy Graham during the 2005 groundbreaking for the Billy Graham Library in Charlotte.

Speaking to a sanctuary full of senior adults at Kennedy Home Baptist Church.

The world-renowned evangelist and Southern Baptist middle-of-the-roader, Dr. Billy Graham, has strayed occasionally toward the far right, but never far enough to cost him Michael's admiration. When Michael was only age 5, in 1947, his father took him to Charlotte to hear Graham, holding only his second of hundreds of crusades. In time, Michael would hear him often, and his respect for him would grow. It has been Michael's privilege to speak with Graham several times face-to-face.

But only until assuming the position of BCH president in 1983 was Michael a practicing Baptist progressive conservative. Since then, he has been a practicing progressive conservative in remission. That's because of the nature of his job. What he thinks and feels about Baptist controversies and issues, and what he might want to do about them, he keeps to himself. Otherwise, BCH would suffer. The chief spokesman for BCH avoids alienating supporters of BCH and forfeiting their gifts to the institution he represents by refusing to take sides.

It has been necessary to avoid partisanship and issue stands in religious matters for much the same reasons he has been a virtual closet Democrat since aligning with BCH.

Well, yes, he has put the heat on North Carolina Baptists a few times, from pulpits and through newspaper articles, but only to promote unity, to reduce discord, or to practice "shared leadership" at state conventions.

Just Call Me Mickey

As their chief executive, he has cautioned his staff members: "Never utter words that would position our institution in either the moderate or conservative camp."

Dixon Free of Lincolnton, speaking as the Baptist State Convention's general board president, once said, "The ministry of BCH transcends political and theological lines. Their staff and children speak in the smallest rural church as well as the largest urban church. They are widely embraced."

That's the way Michael wants it to stay.

There are about 4,000 Baptist churches in North Carolina. Over the years, he has propounded the BCH cause at hundreds of them. So far, when

Now is time for Baptists to reconcile

● The good work of Baptists is endangered by the divisions between moderates and conservatives.

BY MICHAEL C. BLACKWELL

When North Carolina Baptists meet in annual session next week in Winston-Salem, they will discuss a concept that is unique among state religious bodies.

It's called "Shared Leadership." Simply put, if the amendment passes (and that's a big if), moderates and conservatives would alternate one-year terms as convention president.

The plan is an effort to end years of political bickering, posturing and outright campaigning for the convention's top elected position.

I believe the plan is biblical, attainable and workable. But whether the other two-thirds of the messengers (the number required for a constitutional change) agree with me Nov. 16 is another matter altogether. Right now, garnering a two-thirds vote seems dim.

Many laity, however, will come to Winston-Salem undecided, and many moderates and conservatives who oppose the plan may still have a change of heart. I hope so.

Why? Because now is the time for reconciliation among Baptists in North Carolina. Nov. 16, 1999, will be Baptists' best (and perhaps last) chance to get it right. If messengers approve the Shared Leadership Plan, it will be "the Baptist shot heard 'round the world." That much I can guarantee. If we don't muster the two-thirds vote, the thud of despair will be felt for years to come.

When Hurricane Floyd left much of eastern North Carolina under water, thousands of Baptist volunteers streamed in. Nobody cared whether they gathered at a conservative or moderate church or whether the hungry people were moderate or conservative — or even Baptist.

The good work of the Baptist State Convention is endangered by denominational floodwaters that spring from longstanding and unfortunate levels of distrust. Sadly, there are many who would rather drown than pull the plug on contentiousness and let the sun of our common causes burn away the dark clouds of our pride.

In earlier storms, the statewide ministries of N.C. Southern Baptists offered hope to those who needed it. Can Baptists not agree to walk and work together to comfort the sick, clothe the naked, visit the prisoner, shelter the homeless, protect the vulnerable and, foremost, share the love and the good news Gospel with our world?

Goodness knows there are enough problems to go around. Drugs abused. Abused children. Children having babies. Babies left in Dumpsters. Dumpsters covered with gang signs. Signs of the times. Times are hard. Hard-core pornography.

Blackwell

he approaches any congregation, church leaders greet him warmly, with "Here comes the man who's trying to help hurting children and heal broken families," not as someone weighted down with the baggage of controversy. Michael has said, "I am probably the only denominational CEO who is able to go into churches in North Carolina of all theological stripes and receive a hearty welcome."

* * *

Once when asked to "list some basic theological affirmations that motivate your ministry," Michael responded:

God is God.

Jesus Christ is the Son of God.

The Bible is the Word of God.

The Holy Spirit is God's gift
to the church.

Prayer is essential.

Worship is necessary.

The church is indestructible.

The power of evil is insidious.

The spiritual journey never ends.

Incurably Baptist!

There is a pad at his bedside on which to set down those thoughts worth saving that hit him in the middle of the night and might not be remembered after the sun comes up.

CHAPTER FIFTEEN – *Soulful Words*

In the stillness of the early morning as the clock ticked toward two o'clock, a seemingly loud noise woke Michael from a restless sleep. He had tossed and turned all night, struggling with the question, "How can I motivate the BCH family to focus on the one important task of providing quality service to the children and families for whom we care?"

Sitting bolt upright, he experienced an epiphany. "QSTQR!" he thought. "That's it. Quality service through quality relationships." This seemingly simple idea would become the rallying cry that defined a yearlong emphasis for Baptist Children's Homes.

Being a self-confessed workaholic who doesn't play golf, refinish furniture, or engage in cross-country skiing doesn't seem to bother Michael.

"My mind is always engaged," Michael once wrote a friend. "I love the world of ideas, especially when I come up with an original idea of my own. And that's not as easy as it may sound."

For him, what is more appealing than having an idea is implementing an idea. To do that, "I call upon every talent at my disposal." And none has had more impact than his ability to communicate through the written and spoken word.

Just Call Me Mickey

To describe Michael as a gifted communicator is to get it only partly right. He has been, conspicuously, a busy gifted communicator. At an early age, he discovered his facility in speaking and writing and since then has passed up few opportunities to stand up and say something, or sit down and write something. More times than not he stood up for or wrote in behalf of improving the human condition.

Take writing. He has been a newspaper reporter who thought and typed rapidly and a columnist, has penned two dissertations and hundreds of sermons, has been a prolific source of magazine articles, an editor of church bulletins, and a producer of copy for brochures, manuals, and annual reports, and has written miles of letters.

Plus, he has been a book author.

Of four books, in fact. The first of which was **New Millennium Families: How You Can Soar Above the Coming Flood of Change**, published in 2000 in hardback by Parkway Publishers of Boone, N.C.

BCH trustee William Friday is a strong advocate for Cameron Boys Camp. Friday is pictured with camper Tim and Michael.

It came out not long after back-to-back hurricanes, Dennis and Floyd, caused eastern North Carolina creeks and rivers to overflow and wash away not only crops, animals, churches, and human life, but one entire community. Michael wrote in the book's prologue: "Floods surround us. They threaten to undo us. Nowhere is the coming flood of change more ominous than in the basic unit of society: the family. The purpose of the book is to offer a roadmap of encouragement and hope to families facing their own personal floods, and to say, 'You can soar above whatever flood that comes your way.' Soaring demands work, commitment, trust, and discipline, but it can turn a flood of disaster into a rainbow of hope."

Insight is found as well in the book's foreword, written by a friend who also sprang from the good soil of Gaston County, William Friday, president emeritus of the University of North Carolina. He wrote in part: "As a fellow North Carolinian — he from Gastonia and I from Dallas — I have seen firsthand as a trustee [of Baptist Children's Homes of North Carolina] the good things Michael and the Homes do for children and families. It is a Christ-like, God-honoring work. Michael is a prophet, and my friend of 40 years . . . . From the longtime vantage point as head of the largest child care organization in the state, and from a heart dedicated to helping hurting children

162

*Michael signs copies of his book **New Millennium Families**.*

and healing broken families, he has pondered the state of the American family. Like the Old Testament prophets, he weeps over the destruction and ruin of what God intended the family to be. Like them, he calls for a return to basic actions — what once upon a time would have been called common sense — fully aware of modern social and economic realities. Like them, he is ultimately optimistic for the future of the family . . . .

"He calls us, as husbands and wives, parents and children, friends and mentors to do what is right and do it consistently. He calls for us to soar above the flood of change marking the 21st Century and shows us how to get wind beneath our wings. Specific suggestions on how to invest time with your children, how to get along with your spouse and your mother-in-law, how the church needs to support divorced parents, even how to pick out a quality day care and how to simplify your life — it's all [there]."

One of a number who read the book and then sent their praise of it to the author was James B. Hunt Jr., still governor of North Carolina at the time. He felt fortunate to have read a copy, and added, "I applaud your high standards of excellence in your work to improve lives of children."

Two years after *New Millennium Families* appeared, along came his second book, *A Place for Miracles*. Again, the publisher's imprint was Parkway, with the date 2002. Copies were produced in both hardback and paperback.

Where miracles take place is, of course, the Baptist Children's Homes.

In this second book, Michael mixes history, autobiography, inspiration, and vision. The part about history details the changes from the old self-contained orphanage to the child-centered but family-focused home of today. Through interviews with older alumni and recent residents, the author emphasizes that, while the methods and scope of Baptist Children's Homes are different, the "basics" have remained the same.

"The Baptist Children's Homes' mission," Michael wrote, "has taught us everything is possible, and it is up to us to foster the good, the right, and the caring side of children . . . . *A Place for Miracles* tells what we have learned about sowing seeds for miracles . . . . In favorable conditions, the life and spirit of a child blossoms."

"If your heart is open," he adds, "the Spirit will invade and sow miracles in your life."

Both *New Millennium Families* and *A Place for Miracles* picked

Upside
Down
Leadership

*A Dozen Big Ideas
To Turn Your Nonprofit Organization
Right Side Up*

12

MICHAEL C. BLACKWELL

up first-place ribbons as entries in Wilmer C. Fields Awards Competition for new books, an activity sponsored by the Baptist Communicators Association. One won in 2001, the other in 2002. (In the same competition for 1999, an article by Michael entitled "Carlyle Marney as Ethicist" was awarded a blue ribbon. It competed in the Interpretive Reporting division. Marney was the subject of Michael's Master of Theology thesis.)

Parkway can be classified a regional publisher. Its book press runs had not exceeded 1,000 copies. But some 5,000 copies of *New Millennium Families* were printed and a like number of *A Place for Miracles*. Both author and publisher were pleased and relieved by the remarkable eventuality in each case — sold-out. The Broyhill Family Foundation of Lenoir, N.C., helped to cover publishing costs. Michael, in turn, donated all the royalties he received to worthy causes.

It is not the prospect of royalties that drives him; it's some kind of need to write that has to be fulfilled. To be able to hold in his hand a book bearing his name as author has been a special thrill. He has compared completing his first one to the elation he experienced when he made his radio debut in 1956, received his first newspaper byline in 1962, or his first day as a television reporter and anchor in 1967.

His third book, on leadership, was published in March 2003. A compelling title, *UpsideDown Leadership: A Dozen Big Ideas to Turn Your Organization Right Side Up*, it is a valuable tool in the leadership toolbox for anyone who finds himself or herself in charge but aren't sure which way to go. One premise of the book, The Big Idea #11, is that leadership is the art of influencing others to work willingly for your goals. Michael uses his own experiences to drive home important fundamental rules of leadership: your

Michael greets friends as he signs copies of Riches Beyond Measure at the 2004 Baptist State Convention.

organization needs a face – yours; you must use the tools available to help you uncover the leader within you; even springs run dry if not replenished; and your staff will embrace change when you help them understand what's in it for them. ***UpsideDown Leadership*** not only makes his leadership philosophy transparent to help leaders excel, but also provides a view of the man who has put his institution on solid ground providing services to thousands of children and their families. In 2004 came "my spiritual book" entitled ***Riches Beyond Measure*** (Creation House Press). The subtitle pinpoints its purpose: ***Creating A Life Worth Living.*** Twelve steps lead the reader to a more fulfilling life, including, "accept yourself," "love abundantly," "do good deeds," and "find passionate pursuits."

Michael is due credit for the arrangements under which the widely known authority on residential child care, the late Alan Keith-Lucas of the faculty at the University of North Carolina at Chapel Hill, produced the book, ***A Hundred Years of Caring: The Story of the Baptist Children's Homes of North Carolina, 1885-1985***, and then a sequel, ***Intent to Serve: The Continuing Saga of Baptist Children's Homes of North Carolina, 1983-1995***.

*The publisher of **Charity & Children** admires the centennial issue.*

Michael was responsible for publication, in 1987, of a glossy 56-page, extensively illustrated, centennial issue of ***Charity & Children***. Much of the pictorial content came from photos housed in the Mitchell Museum. He has lent strong support to the development of the museum that occupies the former Mitchell Cottage on the campus of Mills Home. The house is now on the National Register of Historic Places.

Teaching, motivating, encouraging, and inspiring the staff are indispensable parts of Blackwell's presidency.

While *Charity & Children* now has a different format and is a monthly publication instead of a weekly, it continues to spread the story of the Baptist Children's Homes far and wide and is still essential to the institution's successful operation.

One page at the front of each issue is set aside for Michael's use, in the role of Baptist Children's Homes president. He has been filling that space for more than 20 years with personal commentary on everything imaginable. It is his second stint as newspaper columnist. When in Carthage, he wrote "Coping" for the weekly *Moore County News* for almost three years.

Between 1979 and 1982, he did book reviews for *The Christian Century*, an ecumenical weekly published in Chicago, Illinois.

A chapter by him, "Transmitting Your Values to Your Child," appears in *Stage Coach*, a 60-page paperback setting forth coaching tips for 10 rough life stages that was written and edited by the Baptist Children's Homes staff.

A collection of sermons he has written appeared in *Pulpit Digest*, a bimonthly by Pulpit Publishing Co. of Jackson, Mississippi.

How he viewed with alarm the rise in divorces was expressed in his essay in the *News & Observer* of Raleigh, N.C., headlined "The Monster that Menaces Kids." Articles by him also have appeared in the Greensboro (N.C.) *News & Record* (in defense of residential child care); the Winston-Salem (N.C.) *Journal-Sentinel* (helping the child by helping the family); and the High Point (N.C.) *Enterprise* (children living in poverty).

His articles have been printed in *Caring*, a private, nonprofit quarterly published by the National Association of Homes and Services for Children, and his "The Administrator — Setting the Pattern" can be found in a manual by the Sunday School Board of the Southern

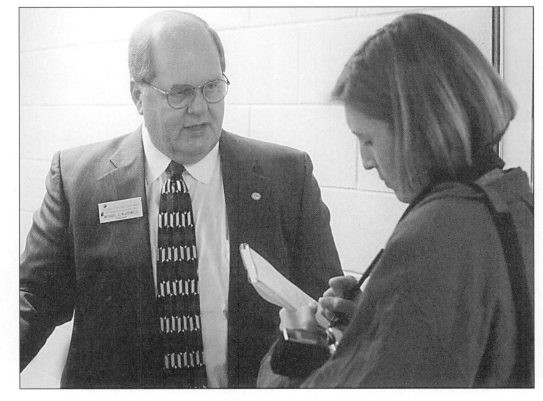

Michael has also been a valuable resource for state news outlets on topics related to children and families.

Baptist Convention entitled *Basic Small Church Administration*. (The Sunday School Board presently is named Lifeway Christian Resources.)

That board is a cornucopia of publications. While at Carthage and in Richmond, Michael did pieces, usually when assigned to, for at least 17 of those publications. They include:

Encounter, Come Alive, Youth Alive, Baptist Youth, Event (For Youth)

Youth Leadership, Care for Leaders, Becoming for Leaders, Collage (Leaders Resources)

Living With Preschooler, Preschool Bible Teacher, Guide C (For Preschool Teachers)

Church Administration, The Deacon, Proclaim, Search (For Pastors, Staff and Leaders)

The winter 1979 issue of that last one, *Search*, carried a feature of Michael's: "Becoming an Effective Leader–Openness." Apparently, it was the most widely read of anything of his in the Sunday School Board's outpouring, and certainly the piece that generated the most positive reaction. In writing it, Michael embraces this definition of openness in leadership: "Out of one's own commitment being able to be empathic about views of others and to entertain other ideas critically." Then he sets out to convince the reader that such openness imbues leadership with strength and character.

A calamity or disastrous turn of events might invade his conscience and drive him in the direction of his computer. Before the sun had set September 11, 2001, the day of the terrorist attacks in the United States, he, as someone who for 30 years had observed how violent acts can affect families, had written and delivered to newspapers an article in which he offered guidance to parents whose children had been

The captain of the BCH ship addresses the crew in 2000.

frightened, intimidated, or bewildered by the wide exposure given the horrible destruction of buildings and lives. Also on that dreadful date, he responded to invitations from no fewer than four television stations to go on the air and give counsel to parents.

The value and usefulness of his videos are not neglected. One 1995 video captures him infusing Baptist Children's Homes employees and trustees with energy and enthusiasm at his daylong "Terrific" seminar. Inspirational remarks to "The Family Gatherings" in 2000 and 2005, daylong celebrations for as many as 600 staffers and children, are preserved on tape. He widely distributes copies of the 1996 and 2005 videos of North Carolina Public Television's "North Carolina People," in which the host, William Friday, takes his viewers on a tour of the Homes' Cameron Boys Camp ('96) and probes Michael's personal views on ministry and service ('05). Friday says his own involvement at Cameron was "one of the most rewarding experiences of my life."

Annually, Michael puts a Thanksgiving Offering appeal on tape and distributes copies to Baptist churches around the state. Requests are still received for copies of his Baptist Children's Homes videos of the convention presentations that electrified messengers at Baptist State Convention sessions in 1995, 2000 and 2005. He keeps available the taping of seasonal audio and video presentations, as well as some of his sermons and motivational

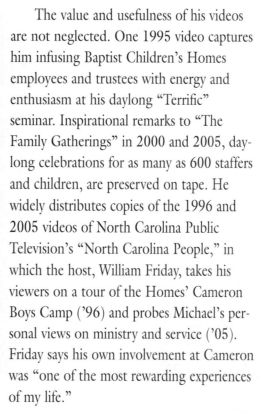

speeches.

Sadly, he said goodbye to a beloved companion in 1987 — the electric typewriter he had used for 20 years to type all his correspondence, sermons, articles for magazines, and seminary papers. It had grown both worn-out and obsolete. Michael stepped hesitantly into

Videotaping "North Carolina People with William Friday" from Cameron Boys Camp in 1996.

the age of computers. Immediately, he became enamored of them and is one of their dependents. They are by far the best yet, he said he soon discovered, as an instrument for the writer to use, for doing research, for editing. Now, one sits ready to be used by him at his office, another at his residence. In addition, a reliable companion is his hand-held PDA (personal data assistant), which stores data, records his voice, and allows remote access to e-mail.

But pen and yellow pad remain indispensable. As a rule, he fills pad pages with notes before taking a seat at a computer to work on a column for *Charity & Children* or some magazine or newspaper piece. There is a pad at his bedside on which to set down those thoughts worth saving that hit him in the middle of the night and might not be remembered after the sun comes up. He keeps note cards handy wherever he goes. One of these can help him preserve an idea that pops up when least expected, or a way of saying or describing something that he might like to make use of later, perhaps in one of those books yet to be published.

"It's a pleasure to meet employees, to thank them for the good job they do. Anybody who knows me well knows I am a nurturer and an encourager."

— Kathy Blackwell

Chapter Sixteen – *Close to His Heart*

I It was a struggle for his wife, Kathy, to cut away completely from her Presbyterian upbringing in order to embrace her husband's faith — while lovingly embracing him.

As she puts it, "I had a hard time changing over to being a true Baptist."

But love can make a difference.

"When we started dating," or while Michael was still with Big WAYS, "the possibility that he'd go into the ministry was never discussed. Then by the time he 'felt the call' and appeared to be headed for another career, I was so in love with him it didn't matter to me."

Although what did matter was whether to get baptized a second time and for the second time to be by immersion. "As a baby, I had been baptized in the Presbyterian church. I didn't think it was necessary for me to be immersed. You know, I can be really stubborn. We had many long, hard discussions about it."

The Blackwells had been married only two weeks when the newly licensed minister put his wife "under."

Her feelings were somewhat different afterward. "It was very special, for him and for me, because I was the first person he baptized. As I look back on it, it was a good beginning for us."

The parents of the Blackwells are deceased. Both Kathy and Michael retain good feelings about how they related to them. No matter how fast-paced the lives both lived, they stuck with two rules: don't put off writing or calling, and never neglect a reason to visit. The approach of a birthday to celebrate or a holiday to observe signaled a family gathering was imminent. Kathy admired her in-laws, Viola and Clitus, and Michael literally adored his, Jack and Mildred Kanipe.

The couple's two children were in and out of the laps of their grandparents. The many occasions they were together were happy, memorable times.

The children have now grown up and moved away. Currently, both are residents of Black Mountain, N.C.. Their daughter, Julie, is married and has a daughter of her own. And a lot of visiting is going on once more. If not in Thomasville, the new grandparents are likely to be

MISS KANIPE

Miss Kanipe To Wed Michael C. Blackwell

The parents of Miss Mary Catherine Kanipe, Mr. and Mrs. Jack Edgar Kanipe, of 4941 Tewkesbury Road, announce her engagement to Mr. Michael Clitus Blackwell, of Gastonia. Their wedding will be an event of August 12, 8 p.m. in the First Associate Reformed Presbyterian Church, Charlotte, with the Rev. W. Nale Falls, the bride-elect's pastor, officiating at the wedding. He will be assisted by the Rev. Hoyle Allard, the minister of the bridegroom-elect.

The bride's only attendant will be her sister, Mrs. Robert Dayton Denham of Emory, Va. Miss Kanipe, known to her friends as Kathy, is a graduate of North Mecklenburg High School and is also a graduate of Brevard Col-

in Black Mountain. Michael has promised himself he will be a doting grandfather. It is his practice now to drive to Black Mountain about once a month, mainly to stay abreast of how his grandbaby is growing into a little girl, but also — and this is almost as important to him – to provide a refreshing break from weighty professional responsibilities.

The Blackwell daughter, Julie Renée, born August 14, 1970, in Raleigh, graduated from Thomasville High School in 1988.

Grandma and Grandpa Blackwell with a young Julie and Michael in Carthage.

She earned a B.A. in history at the University of North Carolina at Greensboro, then became a licensed massage therapist after training at Body Therapy Institute in Siler City, N.C.. Now she is employed in her own massage therapy business in Black Mountain.

Julie's husband is Aaron Curtis of Searsport, Maine. She kept her maiden name, which was totally acceptable to her mom and dad. Their daughter, Gabriella Blackwell

Jack and Mildred Kanipe celebrate 50 years of marriage in 1989.

Curtis, was born in Asheville on July 15, 2000.

The son of Kathy and Michael, Michael Clitus Blackwell Jr, was

born March 13, 1973, at Rex Hospital in Raleigh like his sister. He graduated from East Davidson High School, just outside Thomasville, in 1991, and also attended UNC-G, where he received a B.A. in media studies. He, too, goes by "Michael." He is not as much an extrovert as his dad, but he has his dad's voice. While not yet settled in a career, his sights are set on a position in communications.

Michael baptized Julie in Carthage and Michael Jr. in Richmond.

Kathy and Michael know love and caring for one another thrive on visitation within the family circle. They intend to continue to practice it and encourage it.

Kathy taught until July 2003. She became a part-time instructor in the literacy program at Davidson County Community College, less than 10 miles from home, in 1988. Her thinking was, "Now it's my time to be something other than a stay-at-home-mom." A decision to enroll in the evening program at High Point University was made several years later, and in 1997, after three years of night classes, she received from HPU a B.S. in psychology. This additional schooling caused her to be elevated to lead literacy instructor at DCCC.

Purvis the cat was a part of the family for 18 years.

Until her retirement from that position, she worked a five-day 9 a.m.- 1 p.m. schedule at the community college.

She has not found a need to be deeply involved in more than teaching and homemaking. Being a behind-the-scenes person is more to her liking. She can be happy standing in the wings while her husband takes

Return visits to Gastonia were times of special memories.

center stage.

"I am a very private person," she says. "I have almost always taken the supportive role, especially at BCH. Michael does not need me as an employee or to be upfront in his work. I keep a low profile, and that works for both of us. I'm quite comfortable assisting in hosting meetings and traveling with him to various churches and BCH functions. It's a pleasure to meet employees, to thank them for the good job they do. Anybody who knows me well knows I am a nurturer and an encourager."

Still, take a bow, he says to her: "She's such an asset, particularly in public relations. It's a delight to be with her. She goes with me as much as possible. She relates particularly well to female spouses of trustees and female trustees."

173

A week-long cruise along Alaska's Inside Passage provided breathtaking views of hundreds of glaciers.

Kathy felt a void when the two children finished growing up and left home, but "I'm delighted they're on their own. I have always wanted them to find their own way and be happy and productive adults. We were blessed with Julie and Michael, and we're proud of them. They're both very different, true individuals, and that's the way it should be."

Today, filling the void is their first and only grandchild, Julie's daughter, Gabriella, "someone I simply adore and want to spend as much time with as possible. She is truly the light of my life at this time in my life."

She explains, "I tried to give our children unconditional love, and I admit, I was too lenient. They both had me wrapped around their fingers. They still do. There's nothing I wouldn't do for my children." Michael parented Julie and Michael Jr. with lots of love and object lessons rather than assuming the role of the enforcer.

And now it's the grandbaby. "There's nothing we wouldn't do

for her, too. Michael has been a wonderful father, always active in the family and just a fun dad. Now he's a fantastic grandfather, spends a lot of time with Gabriella, likes nothing better than playing with her. She has called him 'Boppy' since learning to talk. I am 'Granma.' I could never see myself being called that, but whatever she calls me is just fine with me."

Kathy worries about today's youth. There was never a time when it was more difficult for parents to persuade their offspring to adopt good values and high standards. "Television, movies, and advertising can be such bad influences. Peer pres-

Kathy is an asset to Michael as he serves as BCH's president.

sure can be an obstacle. Fortunately, it's the parents who influence the child the most, and they do it by how they live their own lives.

"Acceptance, tolerance, and structure are what young people need today. It's hard for a parent to accept many things their youngsters may try as they grow up. But communicating and setting levels of expectation makes a lot of sense to me. Most young people will eventually appreciate how they were reared if they are reared by loving parents in a safe environment."

Now that she's retired, Kathy is not likely to neglect her favorite pastimes, such as watching "reality TV," turning on her computer and "surfing the Net," and — she's an avid reader — browsing among the shelves of books at the library. One thing she will not be doing is writing a book. "One writer in the family is enough."

Not only does she like staying at home, "I have reached a point in my life at which I am happy with what I have and appreciate what I have. Material possessions have never meant a lot to me. What we have I really do appreciate. I am a real down-to-earth person, and think folks that try to be something they are not are real phonies."

But a night out once in a while is nice. "We do love the theater. We have always enjoyed live stage performances. Our second date was to see *Music Man* at Ovens Auditorium in Charlotte. Bert Parks was the lead. We have never forgotten his performance."

She longs for the day Michael will retire. Until he does, she wishes he wouldn't work as hard. "He always has taken pride in his work and loves to help others and see positive changes in his work. He has a heavy workload, and I know it is part of his job, but I would like for him to have more fun and slow down. I hope that's what the retirement years will be for us. I can't wait."

She dreams that one day she and Michael will own two condos, one at Black Mountain, where their children presently live, and one at a North Carolina beach, preferably Holden Beach. She imagines what fun it would be to go condo-hoping several times a year. "Holden is

Michael says of his granddaughter, Gabriella Blackwell Curtis: "She brought me new hope, new light, new joy."

a great place to get away from it all."

If in retirement Michael were to succumb to the urge to run for public office, he can count on the unqualified support of his wife. "He has a lot to offer the state of North Carolina. With his outgoing personality and honesty, he would be an excellent candidate on any level. We have talked about it many times. We both enjoy politics. We are pretty

Michael Jr. gets a surprise high school graduation kiss (1991) from his proud father. Like his sister, Michael Jr. makes his home in Black Mountain, N.C..

even in our political beliefs. My parents were Democrats, and I always have been a Democrat. Except, I tend to vote for the person today. I consider myself a moderate — neither far left nor far right."

Everything and everybody changes. "Over the years I have changed. He has changed, too," Kathy says. "Still, he is the same dear man I married. Someone with a great sense of humor. We laugh a lot. I think that has helped us keep our lives in perspective. Through thick and thin, we have stood by one another. During our 38 years of marriage, our love for one another has only deepened."

Then she says, "I would sum up Michael C. Blackwell this way: he is a generous, kind, hard-working person. He wants to see the best in people and help bring out the best in them. He has a love for children that sometimes will move him to tears. He has a very sensitive side when it comes to his family. I cannot imagine not having him in my life, and I thank God for him and for the life that we have been privi-

leged to live."

Kathy's parents died in the summer of 1998. Mildred Kanipe, a registered nurse, died first, then only a few weeks later, Jack. Mildred died unexpectedly at home in Charlotte, maybe of a heart attack or stroke. The true cause was never

The last picture of father and son at Thanksgiving 1987.

ascertained. Jack, who had been a salesman most of his life, mostly as an awning salesman, died at the Presbyterian Hospital in Charlotte after a lingering illness. The ashes of both were interred side by side in a country cemetery in Caldwell County, near Lenoir, N.C.. Michael had the honor of conducting a joint committal service. ("It was the hardest thing I've ever done in all my life.") Coming from Virginia to take part were Kathy's sister, Rachel, and from Colorado, her brother, Stephen.

For Michael, his parents' deaths were the other way around. His father went first. Michael once wrote, "My father is more of an influence on me than any other person. I admire him as a person. He is a man of strong character and integrity. His advice is always sound."

Clitus died at age 78 on January 16, 1988, at Gaston Memorial Hospital in Gastonia. He died a cigarette-smoker's death. His undoing: emphysema. He had been a chain-smoker for most of his life.

Flower Cards

For The Funeral Of

Mr. Clitus S. Blackwell

WARD FUNERAL SERVICE INC.
220 South Broad Street

177

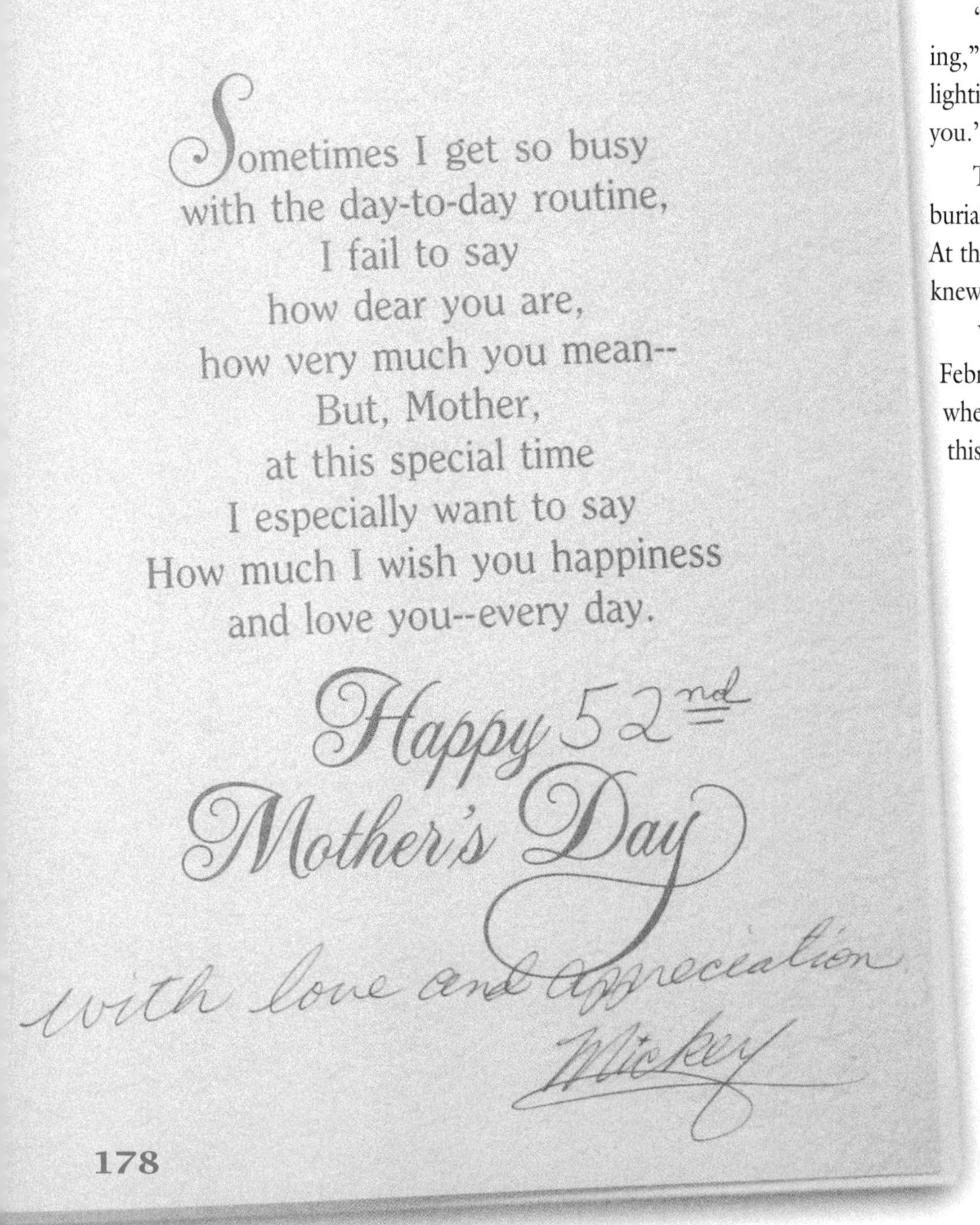

Sometimes I get so busy
with the day-to-day routine,
I fail to say
how dear you are,
how very much you mean--
But, Mother,
at this special time
I especially want to say
How much I wish you happiness
and love you--every day.

Happy 52nd Mother's Day

with love and appreciation

Mickey

"When it comes to soapboxes, mine is to campaign against smoking," Michael, who has never used tobacco, confesses. "I see somebody lighting up, and sometimes I can't resist saying, 'You know, that can kill you.'"

The funeral for Clitus, a Mason, was at Flint-Groves Church and burial was in the Masonic section of Gaston Memorial Park in Gastonia. At the time of death, he and Viola had been married 51 years. Michael knew it as a solid marriage.

Viola lived another eight years. She died of kidney failure on February 8, 1996, at the Baptist Retirement Home in Asheville, where she had been a resident since 1993. Her passing was described this way by her son, in his book *New Millennium Families:*

An early morning call [February 7, from the retirement home] alerted me that Mother's kidneys were shutting down. When the nurse handed her the phone, we shared an emotional and very loving conversation, telling each other that we loved one another very much.

As my wife, Catherine, and I made the trip from Thomasville to Asheville, Mother issued the nurses one of her famous directives: "I want you to wash my hair and put on my makeup. I will then see Mickey and will get ready to die tonight."

The nurses could hardly believe what they heard. "But, Mrs. Blackwell," they protested, "it will be painful for you to have your hair washed. You gained 20 pounds from fluid build-up last night, and it will be very difficult to do what you ask."

Of course, Mother won out. When we arrived after the three-hour drive, she could barely speak but she sat up in bed with her silver hair, freshly washed

Viola at the Baptist Retirement Home in Asheville.

and set, shining.

I told her how beautiful she looked, especially her hair. She smiled, called Kathy over to whisper a few unintelligible words, and soon eased into unconsciousness. For several hours I held her hand, stroking her arm and patting her hand.

As those final, silent minutes passed, God granted me the opportunity to relive the complex interactions between a mother and a son. Understanding ebbed and flowed between my fingers and her skin. We celebrated, grieved, explained, and affirmed without words. It was a holy time as two of God's children wrapped up their earthly relationship.

Then, after several hours, she suddenly pulled away from my grasp. Our final conversation was over. It was time for her to break both my physical hold on her hand and the spiritual hold this world had on her body.

There was no "death rattle," just the slow ebbing of a determined life which "passed to the other side" shortly after midnight. Mother's last wish was her final gift to me and one that remains fresh and precious to this very minute: "I want to wash my hair, see Mickey, and then die."

His mother's funeral also was at Flint-Groves, a service for which the church was filled with mourners and sympathizers. Burial was alongside her husband. She was laid to eternal rest on her birthday. She would have been 83 years old. Most all her life she had found ways to make her birthdays special. This last one was, too.

"I am naturally an outgoing person. I can tire working a crowd. But when I stand up before an audience, they don't know it. I find the energy, sound the notes, and make music."

CHAPTER SEVENTEEN – *A Destiny to Claim*

Michael advocates attending church as a family. He has written, "Togetherness in God's house will bring togetherness in other areas of life. A family that shares the insights of the gospel at church will be able to live them when they are away from church."

"So go to preaching — and sing a few of the old-timey hymns" is his advice. And "for a rollicking, soul-cleansing good time, take part in a lively, foot-stomping hymn-sing. Hymn singing is good for what ails you." Michael has never tired of helping to belt out those he first got to know while a member of the Flint-Groves Church choir. His strong, rich baritone has yet to lead him into performing solos, but it has been known to light the way when while standing in the pulpit he says, "Please rise and join me in singing Hymn No. 232."

Michael continues to put in appearances at the church in which he grew up, sometimes on happy occasions, sometimes sad. He and Kathy have their memberships, however, at First Baptist Church in High Point, N.C., a 20-minute drive from their residence, where "we enjoy

traditional worship . . . . We prefer our own spiritual world, that is, one apart from professional concerns." But Michael nonetheless finds ways to support the Baptist church on the campus at Mills Home that has a long, rich history.

Any list of his favorite hymns would include: "Come, Thou Fount of Every Blessing," "Joyful, Joyful, We Adore Thee," "A Mighty Fortress Is Our God," "Morning Has Broken," "Holy, Holy, Holy," "Crown Him With Many Crowns,"

Mills Home Baptist Church

"All Hail the Power of Jesus' Name," "Jesus Loves Me," "Come Thou Almighty King," "God of Grace and God of Glory," and "Great Is Thy Faithfulness." As any churchgoing Baptist might agree, a most hummable lot.

His favorite Bible verse? Philippians 4:13: "I can do all things through Christ which strengthen me." Kathy knew it was, and had it engraved on the back of a wristwatch she gave him as a wedding present.

Charities to which he is partial are Leadership North Carolina and the Institute of Political Leadership.

Practically any Sunday now, he will be in church, maybe seated in a pew, but just as often in the pulpit as the speaker once the 11 a.m.

service is under way. He now makes about 75 speaking appearances a year – and at times, six in one week. Attired in signature dark blue suit, white shirt, and a no-nonsense necktie, he'll rise to his feet, grip the sanctuary lectern, summon his gift for public speaking, and then begin working his way into the conscience of his listeners. Usually after a little Bible-thumping, he will pitch a plea for support of Baptist Children's Homes. "Michael, the BCH pitchman," as he is sometimes known.

Michael is known as a graceful and fluid speaker.

"Usually, an organization needs a face," Michael has said. "I am not Baptist Children's Homes, but I have worked hard to become the face of Baptist Children's Homes, so that whenever people see this face, hear

"The face" is a familiar sight in North Carolina Baptist circles.

this voice, they think Baptist Children's Homes and how we help hurting children . . . heal broken families."

A public-speaking tip of his goes like this: "Get to speaking engage-

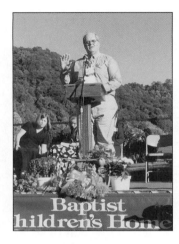

A mountain rally

ments early to get a sense of the crowd. I want to become a familiar face before the face utters a word. Even if I've spoken to that church congregation or civic club a dozen times before, I do not assume everyone knows me.

"When you're there early, you can work the crowd. Learn some names you can throw out during your address. It's an important way of connecting." He adds, "I am naturally an outgoing person. I can tire work-ing a crowd. But when I stand up before an audience, they don't know it. I find the energy, sound the notes, and make music. I'll rest in the car on the way home. In fact, I may collapse in the car and take five minutes of recuperation time even before I turn the key. But when I'm 'on,' I find the energy to be the face of Baptist Children's Homes."

A boon to his performing is his innate faculty for remembering. His recall is impressive. He can still recite perfectly something he memorized while in high school, the prologue to Chaucer's **Canterbury Tales** — the Middle English version:

> ***Whan that Aprill with his shoures soote***

> *The droghte of March hath perced to the roote,*
> *And bathed every veyne in swich licour,*
> *Of which vertu engendred is the flour,*
> *Whan Zephirus eek with his sweete breeth*
> *Inspired hath in every holt and heeth*
> *The tendre croppes, and the yonge sonne*
> *Hath in the ram his halfe cours yronne*

One of his five annual speaking engagements is at Memorial United Methodist Church in Thomasville. He teaches the Sunday school lesson at the church's R.L. Pope Bible Class, the most famous church class in Thomasville, on the first Sunday in December. The first time was soon after his arrival in Thomasville in 1983. He has been doing it ever since, which has made it possible for him to become acquainted with

Come, Thou Fount of Every Blessing

Robert Robinson

Traditional American Melody

1. Come, Thou fount of ev-ery bless-ing, Tune my heart to sing Thy grace.
2. Here I raise my Eb-e-ne-zer, Hith-er by Thy help I come.
3. Oh, to grace how great a debt-or Dai-ly I'm con-strained to be!

Streams of mer-cy, nev-er ceas-ing, Call for songs of loud
And I hope, by Thy good plea-sure, Safe-ly to
Let thy grace, Lord, like a fet-ter, Bind

183

Holding the handwritten journal of John Mills, Michael assumes the persona of BCH's founder.

some of Thomasville's most distinguished citizens.

Under also a tradition of long standing, the BCH president is

Speaking at the City of Thomasville's 200th birthday celebration.

the speaker at the Thanksgiving Eve service at First Baptist Church in Greensboro. Michael was the speaker in 1983, the year he became president, and has made an appearance there each year since then. Traditionally as well, after that engagement, he and Kathy drop in at Yum-Yum, Greensboro's venerable ice cream oasis, for a big cone of chocolate or strawberry.

He is in demand as a baccalaureate service speaker. One invitation, and one he accepted, was from Georgetown College in Georgetown, Kentucky. The invitation came from the president of the college, William H. Crouch, Jr., once a member of Michael's staff. He served as director of development for four years.

In giving a high school commencement speech in 1988, Michael

put the emphasis on the challenge of learning. He stressed that learning goes on forever. "Education is about beginnings, not endings." Then, in the wind-up, as his gaze swept the sea of caps and gowns, he said, "So don't just stand there — grow on!"

Because he is a member of the board of the state's Partnership for Children, or Smart Start, he gets three or four requests a year to speak at Smart Start functions across the state. He was the keynote speaker at one of the annual statewide Smart Start conferences in Raleigh.

He became a Rotarian again soon after locating in Thomasville. One meeting of the club was made remarkable by him appearing as speaker of the day in dress and makeup as John H. Mills, founder in 1885 of what became BCH, a person whose stature and voice resembled those of Michael's. His speech was a dramatic monologue, as Mills might have spoken before some assembly of the brethren. In his hand while speaking was Mills' journal. Because, in preparing himself, Michael had visited Mills' grave and also God's Acre, the Mills Home cemetery, he found it possible to mention names of Mills' contemporaries while using the present tense.

Volunteer recognition day at Odum Home in Pembroke.

A singular honor was being chosen featured speaker for the Founder's Day service, an October 2002 highlight of Thomasville's observance of its sesquicentennial. To a crowd in Cushwa Stadium, on a beautiful fall afternoon, he paid his respects to the irrepressible spirit of John H. Thomas, founder of Thomasville, and his compatriots.

Just Call Me Mickey

They were, he said, possessed of the spirit of the American Dream, an uncompromising force that helped to achieve and now to sustain this nation's world pre-eminence. He called on today's American family to

Michael with Evelyn Alexander, BCH's first female Trustee chair, and her husband, Ben.

draw on it "to find happiness in its diversity, health in its traditions and promise in its future." He concluded with, in this, the 21st Century, "We have a life to preserve, a future to secure and a destiny to claim."

Michael works at making himself a part of Thomasville. Wachovia Bank, in recognition of BCH's economic importance and the hometown presence that Michael has acquired, put him on its Thomasville board of directors.

Once upon reaching the checkout counter at the grocery, Michael exchanged words of greeting with the cashier, a woman who was probably somebody's grandmother. There was a lapse of only a few seconds before she said, "I don't know who you are, but with that voice you've got to be either a radio announcer or a preacher." Michael's reply: "I'm both."

It is granted by all who know him, it seems, and Michael as well, that his voice is his most distinguishing characteristic, an asset of inestimable worth and a hand-me-down from his father. It is a finely textured, mellifluent baritone, ordinarily crisp and clear as a bell, but he can make it do all kinds of things: sound stentorian if addressing thousands of messengers at a Baptist convention, be

soft and warm if relating a touching story, or be sunny and cheerful. Usually harmonic and fluid, it has a built-in friendliness. It can be reassuring, yet will suddenly go boom or swing into a Baptist-revival cadence capable of tempting pews full of the young and old to tap their toes and clap. It is most useful when there is a need to "put on the rousements." In a small, walled-in space, such as his office, it has an odd but engaging wrap-around quality, an in-stereo effect.

"People say I have a personality trait," Michael has observed, that makes it possible for him to reach and to disarm people of almost any age, when with one or two or an audience of hundreds, to cause them to be ready to accept him as someone to trust, to believe in. What it is, some have concluded, is charisma. A reporter labeled him a spellbinder. "God has blessed me with certain native abilities," he has remarked, "and I have sought constantly to use them for maximum effectiveness."

■ Nuclear waste strategy faces hurdles. **B8**

Man is tireless advocate for kids

● Michael Blackwell would rather not talk about himself, but others have plenty to say about him.

BY NANCY H. MCLAUGHLIN
Staff Writer

THOMASVILLE — He'll have you crying one minute and reaching for your wallet the next.

It's his mission — not out of greed but out of need.

And that's for the good of the hundreds of orphaned, neglected and abused children who are counting on his success, in N.C. Baptist Children's Homes residence halls throughout the state.

Michael Blackwell, the children's home president, knocks on a lot of doors.

He's in Raleigh, meeting with legislators. He travels the state on Sundays, visiting churches.

He's making appointments with the business and religious communities, inquiring about grants or possible tax-deductible donations.

"What I see in him more than anything is a strong commitment and focus on matters affecting children, and it carries over in everything he does," said Ashley Thrift, chairman of the N.C. Partnership for Children, which oversees the statewide Smart Start program. "He creates enthusiasm, he gains respect."

The ordained minister speaks eloquently and with passion about those children in his care.

Some are orphans. In many cases, a court has found their homes dangerous or unsuitable for them.

In others, their parent or parents simply do not want them there. The Baptist Children's Homes, founded in 1885, served more than 1,500 children and their families last year.

In his office, chock full of awards and com-

Michael huddled with children at Broyhill Home in Clyde.

Broyhill family that has been an outstanding benefactor of BCH for many years. "He's brought professionalism to the management of [BCH]," he says, "and the charisma necessary to raise the funds to make it grow."

There are a few voice lessons in his past, but he is essentially a self-taught public speaker. "Practice makes perfect" is a dictum he endorses. Nearly every day, he tries in some manner to be more effective, perhaps by tweaking his delivery, his hand gestures, or possibly his body language (ever striving to be able to "transport one to the very steps of the throne and fill one's soul with true believing"). He makes videos of himself practice-speaking, and then, while screening them or those made of him during some public appearance, watches for where and how to make changes. "I'm looking for ways to make words dance." But he also works on pausing: "Silence during a sermon or speech can grip an audience as words never could."

He has been described as "The kind of fellow you'd want to preach your funeral." Photos show BCH kids clinging to him. They do that because "I work hard to be a man youngsters can throw their arms around." He often tells audiences he has found a treatment for feeling blue: "I go and visit among the children. A hug from one of them will always lift my spirits."

Someone who knows him well is Paul Broyhill of Lenoir, N.C., a member of the

Nobody has to push Michael. He pushes himself. His walk is almost a trot. At bedtime, he is pleased with himself if the hours he put in have been long, challenging and worthwhile. A lot of

Paul, Faye and Satie Broyhill at the dedication of Noel Home and Care House in Lenoir.

phone calls, conferences, answering and sending emails and letters, counseling a troubled staff member, reading three newspapers, and driving a long distance to make a speech or plead for a donation — these can be some of the makings of a satisfying day. ("That's how I'm hard-wired.")

Michael at the USS Arizona Memorial at Pearl Harbor.

He sets himself apart from the day-to-day operation of the BCH units. "There are resident directors and area directors," Michael says. "You've got to let them do their jobs. There are also social workers and the houseparents. I often tell people I could more easily be president than a houseparent."

Once he described himself as "an enabler and lover of people, a good listener, a sensitive listener, somebody who doesn't have all the answers but is willing to enter the struggle to find some solutions. I see myself as a problem solver, as having abilities in discernment, in leadership, in compassion.

"For me, BCH is a way of life. As such, my employment becomes an offering to God to seek to fulfill his purpose through work . . . . All I have ever trained and prepared for has coalesced in this position [of president]. That's why I feel good about what I'm doing. I'm energized by my work."

Back in 1993, when an interviewer asked him to reveal something about himself that would surprise his friends, he confessed, "I like cats. That is a real secret, because we've had this ole stray cat for 15 years now and I have feigned my dislike for her all these years. But my family knows how devoted I am to her. I picked up this stray in Carthage in 1978. Named her Purvis. She just celebrated her 15th birthday, and is healthy as a horse."

Purvis' nine lives did not run out for a quite a long time, until she was 18 — and Michael cried like a baby.

Sometimes a question is posed by visitors to his office, "What's with the toys?" they see lying about. They were Michael's when he was a child, including his baby-hood stuffed bear named "Teddy." Youngsters who visit play with them.

Kathy and Michael on a sabbatical in York, England.

Surgical repair of his Achilles tendon forced him to give up jogging and to get his exercise from a treadmill at his residence. (More extensive repairs, to foot, ankle, and tendon, took place on May 20, 2003.) "A deep regret," Michael says, "is that I have not yet learned how to relax easily. Or worry less." More times than not, his first thought after breakfast is,

"Now where am I going to get the $55,000 it takes to run BCH today?" He has found that to completely clear his mind of cares and concerns, he needs to flee the country. He has engineered escapes five times so far — to Scotland, England, Brazil, Canada, and, even though a part of the United States, Hawaii. Each proved to be elixir for mind, body, and soul.

He has passed up becoming a golfer or adopting a hobby. When there's time for taking it easy, reading a book or watching a movie works just fine. He says that biographies and other non-fiction works appeal to him. He likes books on leadership and health/wellness. His Internet connection permits him to read articles on sports, entertainment, and politics, as well as human interest stories, in the state's major daily newspapers. Magazines as well are part of what he reads. He also takes in some of the comedy on television.

Once Michael was asked, "What would you really like to do that you haven't done?" His answer revealed a strong taste for a popular television network show that parodies people and events in the news. Michael said it would be great fun to be the one to open the show, by saying, "Live from New York, it's Saturday night!" the trademark introduction of television's "Saturday Night Live."

Good health has been one of his blessings, even though a tendency to be overweight has plagued him. Someone with whom he has shared good times is "my best friend," Tim Norman, director of congregational relationships, Baptist Theological Seminary at Richmond. Norman speaks of what the two of them have in common: "mirth and girth."

Good health was a requisite of a strenuous weekend he experienced in November of 1993. With 12 others involved as he was, in a leadership development program, he got himself into one predicament after another in the wilds of western North Carolina — at the Nantahala Outdoor Center. Perhaps no one was more surprised than they that all

Michael tackles the rapids on North Carolina's Nantahala River.

189

*Campbell University President
Jerry Wallace*

of them passed every test of courage to which they were subjected during the three-day ordeal. The sternest tests for Michael were mountainside rappelling and an eight-mile solo trip on a raft through the whitewater rapids of the Nantahala River.

He came away from the program, offered privately by the Farr Leadership Associates of Greensboro, N.C., convinced that the leadership leaders were right: "Fear is nothing more than False Evidence Appearing Real." Yes, "The greatest limitations we face are those we impose upon ourselves."

In 2005, Michael had another taxing physical experience. To become a Senior Fellow of the American Leadership Forum, a requirement was a grueling five-day Outward Bound adventure in the mountains of North Carolina.

Meanwhile he continued to collect honors and awards. In January 2000, the *Biblical Recorder*, voice of the Baptist State Convention of North Carolina, named him one of the "Top Tar Heel Baptists of the 20th Century." Thirty were named by the journal from among 300 nominated. An honoree had to be "a native of North Carolina or have spent at least 10 years in active Baptist work as a resident of the Tar Heel State."

When syndicated columnist D.G. Martin called for names to be included on his list of North Carolina "public intellectuals, or the people who form public opinion, not follow it," Wayne T. Adams Jr., member of the Baptist church in Carthage, nominated Michael.

In 1987-88, Michael was president of the North Carolina Child Care Association and in 1991-92, president of the Child Care Executives of Southern Baptists.

At Campbell University in 1999 to deliver the keynote address at Campbell's Education Convocation, Campbell President Norman A. Wiggins presented him with one of the university's highest awards, the Presidential Medallion, which

190

Campbell Univers

*on the recommendation of the Faculty,
the Board of Trustees has conferred upon*

Michael Clitus Blackwell

the degree of

Doctor of Humane Letters

Honoris Causa

is reserved for individuals whose personal lives and professional accomplishments mirror the character and commitment of the university's first three presidents.

It was back to Campbell in December 2003, this time to give a commencement address, but also to receive yet another doctorate, the Honorary Doctor of Humane Letters degree. The accompanying citation, read by the new president Jerry Wallace, included: "His lifetime humanitarian efforts reflect an individual whose commitment to service, especially to children, is virtually unparalleled."

Also in 1999, the North Carolina Parent-Teacher Association presented him with a lifetime membership, in recognition of outstanding contribution to children and young people and their education, health, and welfare.

He was president of the Southeastern Baptist Theological Seminary alumni association for the year 1985.

Ten labor-intensive years into his presidency, Michael was asked by his trustees what they could do special as a reward. They granted, and sponsored, his wish, a sabbatical leave. Their gift permitted him to establish himself as a fellow in the spring term of the Center for Continuing Education at the Episcopal Theological Seminary

Campbell University Divinity School Dean Mike Cogdill hoods Michael as he receives the Doctor of Humane Letters degree.

in Virginia at Alexandria.

"What you do there," Michael has noted, "is to get in touch with yourself, to get in touch with God, and to experience deep rest. This structured, restricted time helped me and others to get in touch with nature and listen to God when most of our lives are spent in offices and cars listening to ideas, complaints, issues, and problems."

The director of the center, Dr. Richard A. Busch, according to the letter he wrote BCH trustees at the end of the six-week term, concluded that Michael, a participant in the total, multifaceted life of the center's program, "is a person of deep and lively faith. This is evidenced in part by his very special commitment to children. Michael is a multi-gifted person and born organizer. High on his list of priorities are efficiency, orderliness, careful planning, and reasoning. Schedules and goals tend to be important to him, and he runs his part of the world with facts and situations well thought out and with operations well conceived. He is hearty, enjoys talk, and has a sparkling sense of humor. He possesses deep personal loyalties."

What's more, Busch said, "At times, Michael can be overpowering

Michael after worship in Oxford, England, with Pastor Alan Duke.

and hold out unrealistic expectations in regard to the work of associates. He is aware of this tendency and is seeking to address it in a creative manner."

All in all, a pretty good report card.

Michael gave high marks in return. For the first time, he could enjoy and profit from provision made for just sitting, reflecting, meditating. He said he had slipped out of and away from his professional identity. He felt "out on my own," a new, a calming feeling.

There were 14 men and two women in the class, all in church-related careers. Some barely survived a three-day "silent retreat," a time when no one was to speak a word.

As result of the physical, mental, and spiritual self-evaluation that took place, Michael drew up a plan to make greater use of meditation, to work on his diet and to exercise more. "I wanted a holistic approach to health. That time away gave me the impetus and the tools to research and establish the approach that works best for me, that keeps me refreshed, invigorated, excited, and energized for my work. Refreshment is the key to this work."

There was room for a bit more refreshment. The sabbatical

was for 18 weeks, so he squeezed in a month at Oxford University in Oxford, England. He boned up on Baptist history. Wife Kathy went along. He was part student and part tourist, having a wonderful time.

The time spent in both Alexandria and Oxford added up, according to Michael, to "another pivotal point in my ministry." He had come to realize "in a very deep way how supported I am, by God, by trustees, by my management group and staff, the Baptist State Convention, and by all the churches who assist in [BCH's] work. As a result, I achieve more, trust more, and make decisions quicker. I am not alone, and I don't have to be anyone but myself."

Nothing is more memorable about the time at Episcopal Theological Seminary than the "silent retreat." It was a revelation that some people simply are unable to bear being silent. Some ministers in Michael's class found it impossible to forgo talking and in other ways making a noise. Michael, on the other hand, discovered "it was in stone silence that I best experienced the presence of God. It was so powerful and intense that I could only stand that kind of intensity for a short period of time. It was like being on the Mount of Transfiguration, and like those in the New Testament, I didn't want to come down."

During the three-day silent retreat, Michael paused to acknowledge "my God-given gifts . . . . We each are given gifts in this life . . . . By encouraging self-awareness and with the help of friends and co-workers, we come to understand what our gifts are. Mine include:

– An openness to follow God's will.

– The ability to get things done.

– A strong people-orientation with the ability to inspire trust and confidence of disparate groups.

– Self-confidence and self-awareness.

– Self-motivation.

– A willingness to learn.

Friends join Kathy and Michael Jr. at the 15th anniversary celebration for BCH's president.

– An ability to lead a diverse and complex statewide organization.

– The ability to have a vision and communicate it precisely and repeatedly.

– To interpret this vision to others who can achieve it by working together.

– The ability to bring unity out of diversity and consensus out of chaos.

– Strong listening skills.

– A love of Jesus, a strong faith and habit of prayer.

– A respect for the dignity of the individual.

– And a passion to make Christ known through every means available.

Every once in a while, something would happen that would move

Michael to want to rise up and renew his vows, those he made when he first became BCH president. One of the times particularly memorable to him was on September 14, 1998, at the Colonial Country Club in Thomasville. Around 200 friends,

associates, and co-workers, a few from some distance, some from high places, had gathered there to roast and toast Michael as a way to mark his 15th year at BCH.

Trustee chair Sybil Stewart leads a Litany of Commitment.

He knew in advance that a dinner was to be held in observance of this anniversary, but much of what took place at the clubhouse was not anything he expected. For him not to be overjoyed would have been impossible. Praise came in waves; the roasting was never more than lukewarm.

It was during this affair that he received the Order of the Long-Leaf Pine. A Gov. Jim Hunt surrogate, Wayne McDevitt, made the presentation.

Thomasville Mayor Don Truell presented him with a copy of a Mayor's Proclamation that designated the day after the celebration "Michael C. Blackwell Day" in Thomasville, home office of BCH, Thomasville's oldest continuously operating "business."

Sybil Stewart, 1998 trustee chairman, doffed her bonnet to Michael as a ground-

State of North Carolina

James B. Hunt, Jr.
Governor

Reposing special confidence in the integrity, learning and zeal of

Dr. Michael C. Blackwell

I do by these presents confer
The Order of the Long Leaf Pine

With the rank of Ambassador Extraordinary privileged
to enjoy fully all rights granted to members of this exalted order, among which
is the special privilege to propose the following North Carolina
Toast in select company anywhere in the free world:

Here's to the land
of the long leaf pine,
The summer land
where the sun doth shine,

194

breaker, someone whose vision deserves credit for a long list of "firsts" for BCH, who "had the skills, perseverance and stamina to build where his vision lay . . . . As a leader he makes a difference in lives."

William Friday, a BCH trustee, called Michael "a longtime and dear friend," and said "I want to congratulate [him and] thank him for being such a splendid example for all the children in his care." He saw the honoree as "a marvelous example of James' admonition to not be just hearers of the Word, but doers as well."

Another trustee, Dorothy Allred, told about watching Michael grow up in Gastonia. She is the widow of Hoyle Allred, one of Michael's pastors when he was active in Gastonia's Flint-Groves Baptist Church, and one-time Baptist State Convention vice president. Michael and Hoyle were much alike, she said. "Hoyle could spot the best people, get them on his team, give them a vision, and step back to become their encourager, and the first to pass out accolades when success came."

Randall Lolley, former president of Southeastern Baptist Theological Seminary, admired Michael's Baptist convictions. "His . . . is not narrow or exclusive or parochial. It is visionary and contagious and nurturing."

It went on and on. The entertaining emcee was Ty Boyd, widely admired public speaker personality. It was he who helped Michael,

BCH Trustees stand in affirmation of support for President Blackwell.

a student in Chapel Hill, get a radio job. They became good friends. Boyd said to his audience, "There's a saying that no man stands taller than when he stoops to help a child, and Mickey is the perfect example."

With the end drawing near, everybody stood, joined hands, and in unison recited a covenant of affirmation that bound one and all "by common mission to helping hurting children . . . healing broken families."

Immediately thereafter, Michael rose up to deliver one of his renewals, a personal affirmation: "I pledge to you tonight, as big John Mills did in 1885, I'm going to let my mission and vision and passion burn for Baptist Children's Homes of North Carolina until, as John Mills said, 'it bores a hole in my skull.' Thank God for [these last] 15 years . . . . But the best is yet to be!"

* * *

One of Cleve Wilkie's regular columns in *Charity & Children* hailed Michael's attainment of the 15-year milestone. Wilkie, who grew up at Mills Home and for many years was both an outstanding Baptist minister and fabulous golfer, had this to say, in part, not forgetting to reveal his well-known penchant for humor:

"I think he [Michael] deserves a word or two from me — whether he welcomes or wants it or not, for out of warm friendship and deep admiration I feel obligated to say my say on Mickey — and I informally just call him 'Mickey,' for I'm old enough to be his great-grandfather and ugly enough to be his old maid aunt. He doesn't strut his doctorate status in my presence. In fact, he doesn't do it in anyone's presence.

"And that's the gist of what I want to extol about him — his genuine down-to-earthiness, despite his place and status among the high and important. He moves and works in high circles, but in actions, relationships, and words, he remains just plain 'Mickey' — down on your level, in your language, and in your lifestyle . . . . I have never felt uncomfortable or ill at ease in his presence, despite what I am in relation to what he is — and who he is! Why, he even said once, 'Wilkie, I admire you.' Goodness, the feeling is mutual!

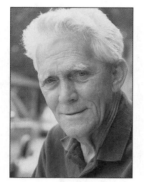

Cleve Wilkie

"I've known all the leaders of the Children's Homes but the first two, Mills and Boone, but I've walked with, talked with, and worked with Kesler, Greer, Reed, Wall and Wagoner — tall, tall men, indeed, in child care work, but as Mickey takes his place in this illustrious list, he doesn't stand in the shadow of any of them, but rises and soars to the same height and level — true greatness in child care work."

"That part of my job I really like. Just meeting these people and seeing their interest develop is extremely gratifying. When you have someone agree to give a gift that you've been a part of cultivating, now that's a great feeling."

CHAPTER EIGHTEEN – *The Joy Geologist*

BCH's development staff stood around the conference table. Michael entered the room. The group shared small talk and poured cups of coffee. Taking their seats, Blackwell's fundraising team looked toward the agency's president.

Michael leaned forward in his chair, saying, "You are our 'friend-raisers.' You have one of the greatest jobs and one of the most important." Encouraging the small group to be fervent in their task he added, "Our children's well-being depends upon us."

The New Testament says we are not to grow weary in well-doing. Some would find that a daunting commandment.

Michael has said many times as BCH president, he leads in the raising of millions of dollars every year to help needy children and families. "It is by far my job's most wearisome task," he says, "one that takes up much of my energy and close to a third of my time. Yet, strange as it may seem, the task gives me pleasure."

Just Call Me Mickey

Most people dread or dodge having to go out with hat in hand, no matter how worthy the cause: the United Way, Girl Scout cookie sales, church budget pledges. Not Michael.

Michael with members of BCH's development staff

"I've gotten to the point where it's a joy and sheer privilege to ask for money for BCH. I enjoy the friend-raising that leads to fund-raising. That part of my job I really like. Just meeting these people and seeing their interest develop is extremely gratifying. When you have someone agree to give a gift that you've been a part of cultivating, now that's a great feeling."

Not surprisingly, Michael and BCH have found they do best

Sharon Allred Decker and Angus Mercer attend a Charlotte campaign victory lunch.

with their asking if they wage highly organized, finely tuned, statewide financial campaigns. Michael has put together two of these since becoming BCH president in 1983. Both were hugely rewarding. Gifts were as small as one dollar, the largest an astonishing $3.5 million. The two raked in a total of $21.4 million, plus worlds of valuable publicity. The stage is being set for a third.

The first drive, once the BCH development and communications departments' staffs had been extensively strengthened and geared up, was "Give a child a chance!" from 1989 to 1991. With BCH trustee James D. Goldston, III of Raleigh as chairman, it produced $11.2 million. The North Carolina Child Care Association was moved to make Goldston its "Trustee of the Year."

The Fleshman-Pratt Foundation presents a $1 million gift.

Afterward, BCH children were enlisted in "Operation Thank You." With their handwritten letters, they expressed gratitude to every single campaign donor.

The title of the second drive was a reference to the dark road so many BCH children travel before reaching help. It was named "Light Their Way" and co-chaired by Angus Mercer of Charlotte and Jacque Pennell of Winston-Salem. The campaign ran from 1995 to 1997. Its goal was $10 million. The amount raised — $10.1 million. BCH trustees led the way. They helped make regional campaigns top their

Jim Goldston chaired the "Give a Child a Chance" campaign.

goals, but also oversubscribed their own goal of $1.5 million. The BCH staff topped its target of $100,000.

And there are dozens of individuals, families, and organizations that share their dollars with BCH before, during, and after drives and times in between.

An outstanding example of these is the Broyhill family of Lenoir, N.C.. Its friendship with BCH goes back more than 70 years, to when I.G. Greer was at the head of BCH. J.E. Broyhill admired Greer and was willing to give support to his ministry once Broyhill founded what became the world-famous Broyhill Furniture Industries of Lenoir.

Then there was Willard Parker of Hertford County, N.C., somewhat a recluse after retiring from the postal service. He lived a frugal life, sometimes sleeping outside in an abandoned taxi. By skimping he managed to save a lot, more than anybody imagined. He made his own soap, and instead of subscribing to a newspaper, he borrowed his neighbor's.

By some means, he got to know about BCH and its work. There can be no doubt he thought well of both. After his death, BCH received a check from his

Since the 1930s, the Broyhill family of Lenoir, N.C., has been staunch BCH supporters.

estate. It was for $1 million, BCH's first million-dollar gift. There was another from the estate later on, for an additional $225,000.

Thomas H. Davis of Winston-Salem, N.C., someone who profited handsomely from the sale of a business he founded, Piedmont Aviation, is another example. He wondered aloud if even more could be done. "What can we do to challenge our best and brightest?"

The answer BCH came up with was the "Thomas H. Davis Runway for Success." This was an arrangement funded by Davis's generosity that in the summer of 1993 exposed 20 or so high-achieving BCH children to "Lessons of Leadership." Teaching the lesson

The family of Willard Parker presented a $1 million gift.

light Their way

A campaign of hope for hurting children and broken families

201

Thomas A. Davis, founder of Piedmont Aviation and BCH's Runway for Success.

and providing the inspiration, at a seminar the children attended, was none other than Thomas H. Davis himself. The seminar became an annual event.

An attorney in Wilkesboro, N.C., Clyde Hayes, made a momentous decision after touring Broyhill Home and learning how young people were being helped there. Hayes, who never had children of his own, decided to help North Carolina's largest family. When he died in 1998 at age 86, he left BCH $4 million, the largest gift in BCH history. Beneficiaries of that include BCH's new ministry to developmentally disabled adults.

BCH has told its story to foundations, too, and a number of them have been regular, steady, generous supporters of its mission. Foremost is The Duke Endowment, which dates back to 1926. Annually, it mails checks to institutions in North and South Carolina — not only child care institutions but also to rural Methodist churches, hospitals, and colleges and universities.

Then there are the 4,000 Baptist churches scattered over North Carolina, the big and the small, the veritable backbone

of financial support, not just today, but ever since BCH's beginning in 1885. Not a great deal has changed. Regularly representatives of BCH fan out and make known to the churches the needs that exist at BCH, and just as regularly, the churches respond. A speaker's bureau at BCH now solicits opportunities for speaking and preaching. Michael and members of his staff make appearances at nearly 800 churches every year.

As recently as 1960, church gifts funded 90 percent of BCH's annual budget. But lately the increase in services BCH renders has been greater than the

Spring 1998   Volume 11 ▪▪ Number 2

Development digest

QUARTERLY REPORT TO THOSE WHO INVEST IN LIVES AT
BAPTIST CHILDREN'S HOMES OF NORTH CAROLINA

Hayes Estate Yields BCH Record $2 Million Gift

Clyde Hayes

Baptist Children's Homes of North Carolina has received its largest gift ever, a $2 million bequest from prominent Wilkes County attorney Clyde Hayes, who died January 5, 1998.

Hayes' gift will memorialize himself, his wife, Ella Mae Hayes, and his parents, Ida Huffman Hayes and C.C. Hayes. Hayes was a lifelong Wilkes County resident.

"Although Clyde and Ella Mae Hayes had no children of their own, their gift will have an incredible impact on generations of children who lo to Baptist Children's Homes for help and healing," said BCH President Michael C. Blackwell. BCH serves more than 1,500 children each year at facilities statewide, with a $13 million annual budget.

The sale of several additional parcels will increase the final total, bu BCH already has received a $2 million check, now invested pending dec sions by BCH trustees for its use.

Part of a prominent family, Hayes earned a law degree at Wake Fore College (now University). His brother, Kyle, ran for governor in 1956. courthouse in downtown Wilkesboro is named for his uncle, Johnson instrumental in starting Bapt

increase in what the churches provide. They are now furnishing over one-fourth of the annual budget and do that through the Baptist State Convention's Cooperative Program and designated offerings.

BCH's special Thanksgiving Offering is also collected each November. It has been a widely shared ritual at the churches at least since 1910. A little booklet issued that year speaks of the offering as the child care institution's "lifeline of support."

Michael has soapboxed, pleaded, and prayed at nearly all the annual Baptist State Conventions since becoming BCH president in 1983. At almost all of his appearances, Michael has sought to impress on the Convention BCH's importance to the children and families who receive care as well as to North Carolina Baptists themselves.

Michael expresses his gratitude to North Carolina Baptists for attaining BCH's first million dollar Thanksgiving Offering in 2000.

for the welfare and comfort of 'his kids.' If you have a million dollars, you'd better not get in a conversation with Mickey — he'll have you donating the whole caboodle to his latest project at the Homes, plus having you make a $500,000 pledge to his next one! He gets to you — and from you. He's an expert. As long as he is at the helm, things will go forward for the betterment.

"I honestly believe, if absolutely necessary, with no other alternative, that for the sake of his needy children he would be willing to emulate famous Lady Godiva and ride bare on the back of a mule down Main Street in Thomasville in broad daylight.

"And to make it worse, unlike the long-tressed lady rider, Mickey doesn't have enough hair to cover anything!"

* * *

Michael helps collect a Mile of Pennies at Robersonville Baptist Church.

The late Cleve Wilkie, a Mills Home alumnus and syndicated newspaper columnist, once wrote that Michael's consuming passion is concern for the children: "He'll go to any lengths and suffer to any extreme

The Lord was looking after those under the care of BCH when a retired hog farmer of Peachland, N.C., John Duncan, a bachelor, made friends with unemployed architect Bob Lotz of Polkton, another North Carolina hamlet, and in time named Lotz the executor of his estate.

As reported in ***Charity & Children***, not long after the two had become closely acquainted, they sat down with an attorney to establish what disposition to make, after Duncan's death, of his worldly goods, which consisted mainly of the house in which he lived.

 In one period, he and Lotz had lived under the same roof for almost a year.

Lotz didn't know what to expect. He had already rejected Duncan's offer to make him his sole heir. He could not have been more surprised, or pleased, to hear his friend inform the attorney that he wanted everything he'd leave behind to go for the good of the youngsters at the Baptist Children's Homes. No explanation was forthcoming, but it may have been because Duncan's mother had been a faithful Baptist.

Duncan died March 5, 1992, at the age of 81. Lotz set out to do his duty as executor.

There would be cash someplace, but Lotz knew not where. Certainly not in a bank account, or stocks or bonds. Duncan had guarded against there being a record that he had accumulated any money. He feared the federal government would discover what he had and quit sending his monthly Social Security check.

"He'd keep $50 and $100 bills in the center pocket on the bib of his overalls, but he'd stash away any more he had," Lotz said. "I didn't know where." He told Lotz he was going to hide the rest, and he didn't care whether it was ever found.

If there was money anywhere, Lotz was pretty certain it would be in Duncan's house, or not far from it, so he began searching, a few hours one week, a few another. That went on for 13 months. Any further search would require Lotz to tear the house apart and dig up the yard.

First, the treasure hunt produced $2,080 from under a potato bin. Then there was $1,580 that Lotz found in a medicine tube placed in a Wheaties box nesting in grass clippings left from mowing the lawn, $7,000 in plastic and paper bags tucked into a pump house cinder block, $1,800 in a peanut butter jar that had been inserted in a building column and $700 in a Prince Albert can lying on one of the house's rafters.

Bob Lotz keeps promise, helps children

Diligent Estate Executor Finds Bu

John Duncan didn't trust the bank or the government.

A few years ago, when Duncan couldn't get his friend, Bob Lotz, to take the $8,000 he had accumulated in his humble house in Peachland, N.C., he declared he would bury the money and he didn't care if it ever was found.

Duncan, who never married, died March 5, 1992, leaving all his posessions to BCH. Lotz, estate executor, spent 13 months looking for

no one would see him and think he was stealing.

He looked in the attic and in foundation bricks. He looked inside the columns at the front porch.

After three days, he found $2,080 beneath the potato bin.

Two or three days each week he searched. Anywhere a fresh nail on trim hinted recent work, the trim came off. If a patch of dirt looked freshly turned, he turned it again. He moved a ton of firewood and dug beneath the pile.

On his very next excursion, into the woodshed, Lotz noticed, laying against the foundation, a plastic medicine tube and a Wheaties package containing $1,580. Lotz had been blowing more grass on top of the spot every time he mowed.

Right after that, Lotz attacked the pump house for a

"I fought for every and did the estate up

Much of the searching was done in the middle of the night with a flashlight. Lotz didn't want anybody to see him poking around and think he was trying to steal something. He used a friend-neighbor of Duncan's to help keep an accounting of what was being discovered. His last and final "find" was stuffed into a little can that once held snuff. Inside was one dime and 20 pennies.

He had ferreted out a total of $13,206.45. This was sent to BCH. Then BCH arranged for the sale of Duncan's house, which went for $15,000.

As its president, Michael expressed the deep appreciation of BCH, not only for the generosity of John Duncan, but also for the extraordinary diligence and persistence of Bob Lotz.

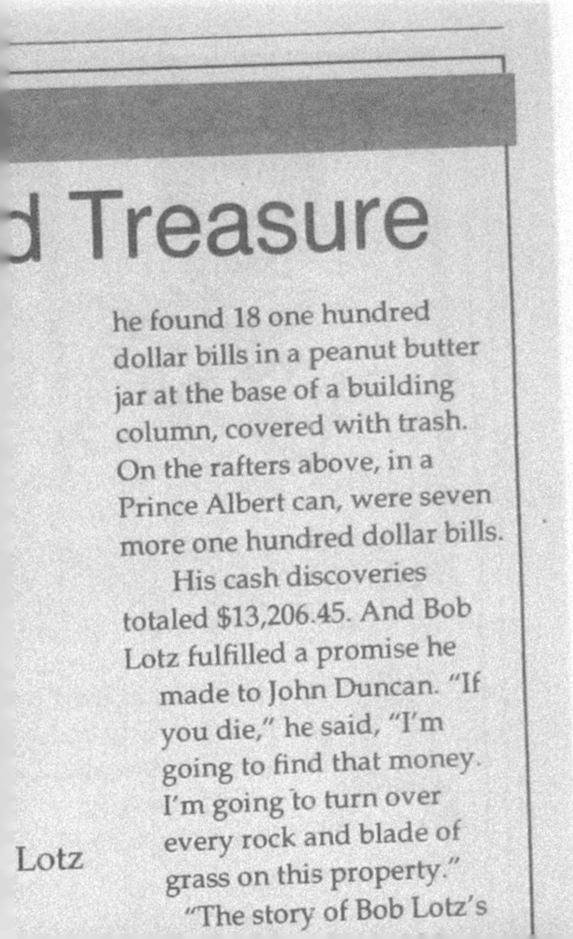

d **Treasure**

he found 18 one hundred dollar bills in a peanut butter jar at the base of a building column, covered with trash. On the rafters above, in a Prince Albert can, were seven more one hundred dollar bills.

His cash discoveries totaled $13,206.45. And Bob Lotz fulfilled a promise he made to John Duncan. "If you die," he said, "I'm going to find that money. I'm going to turn over every rock and blade of grass on this property."

"The story of Bob Lotz's

Lotz

Michael knows his staff and trustees well enough that in a crowded meeting room, "I can call any one of them to the front and talk about them, name their children, where they live, their likes and dislikes. That's managing relationships."

CHAPTER NINETEEN – *Natural Leader*

M More than 600 BCH children and staff members had come together for The Family Gathering. This first-ever event bringing all employees and children from BCH facilities around the state was held at Mills Home in Thomasville June 28, 2000. After the excitement of a day of hot dogs, hamburgers, and games, everyone gathered at the campus church auditorium. Following an enthusiastic introduction, Michael took the stage.

Addressing the group, Michael said, "Today, on this historic occasion, I challenge you to see life as an adventure, as opportunity, as something to celebrate."

As leader, Michael has worked hard at finding ways to earn his staff's respect and trust. "I expect only one thing from them . . . their best," he said. "Once I have the authority of leadership and give my best, then I can demand theirs."

To catch the eye of a child, Michael has often said, brings "refreshment of heart and renewal of spirit."

It has been a remarkable stretch of personal progress. Michael has evolved during the last six decades from simply an out-going person to a leader. And now he is a leader who produces treatises on leadership.

In high school and at the university, he was a conspicuous student. He was an all-out participant in all kinds of extracurricular activities. He was often on stage, on the air, one of the first on the scene as a reporter or broadcaster, and in print. His name and photo were in the papers many times.

Postgraduation found him in North Carolina's largest city, Charlotte. There, while with an upstart radio station, he quickly became a news celebrity.

Then he reversed his field and enrolled at a seminary, where he took scholarship seriously and emerged as the student who inspired his professors to invite him back, after his own graduation, to inspire other students.

From the pulpit and pastor's study of two churches – one small, one large – he used innovative means and hard work to lead them to more growth and greater security. Neither wanted to turn him loose.

And he relished being a Baptist preacher. Still, when a ministry in child care beckoned, he jumped the traces. The Baptist Children's Homes of North Carolina desperately needed a leader with energy and vision. He was packed with both.

History made: All BCH residents and staffers together in Thomasville for Family Gathering I, June 28, 2000.

In 1992, Michael hit the half-century mark. By then he had nine years as BCH president under his belt. One of his surprise birthday presents was a binder presented by the administrative staff at BCH. The letters, the testimonials inside were two inches thick. People from all over lauded him for his work at BCH and extended birthday best wishes. Many of the letters had one thing in common: thirty-two used the word "leader" or "leadership" when the writer was making a reference to or thanking him for how he had been performing as BCH president.

Some could not have failed to make Michael happy on his birthday. The courtly Winfield Blackwell (no relation), for many years BCH attorney, was eloquent: "When he enters a room or approaches you, everyone feels an electric charge of warmth and friendship. He was born to lead others in the rightful path, and to give generously of himself to

Jennie Counts has worked with Dr. Blackwell for 20 years.

children and others in need." Leon Talley, executive director of the Illinois Baptist Children's Homes, also went pretty far: "You have provided leadership not only for North Carolina but nationally." The one from Betsy Wall Medford, a BCH board member added, "a leader your trustees are proud to call president." And so it went.

Mayor Don Truell, when declaring "Michael C. Blackwell Day" in Thomasville in 1998, asserted, "He's a good leader for our times."

Few people would disagree that the man had gotten himself a reputation.

His branching out to write about leadership, among other topics, began as early as the 1970s, while he was an associate pastor in Raleigh. For 15 years starting in 1971, he wrote articles for the publications of the Sunday School Board of the Southern Baptist Convention.

He practiced being a leader, wrote about being a leader, and never stopped studying how to lead better. A favorite saying of his is "School is never out for the pro."

His collection of certificates of attendance, diplomas, and awards from courses and seminars in management and leadership is so broad it could plaster a wall in his large office. Connections with four leadership training programs are active and growing stronger. One is the American Leadership Forum. The other three are the Center for Creative Leadership, Leadership North Carolina, and the N.C. Institute for Political Leadership.

By now, as to be expected, he has arrived at a number of quite firm notions and convictions about leadership and has not been averse to organizing them and writing about them. He shared his thinking on these subjects in his book *A Place for Miracles* and in a form that became a part of his published *UpsideDown Leadership: A Dozen Big Ideas to Turn Your Nonprofit Organization Right Side Up*, his third book,

G IDEA

dry if not replenished.

210

Chapter Three

KEEP THE LEADER REFRESHED

There's no juice in a steamrolled tomato. You need to get up every day with a purpose. A lot of people don't consciously aspire to great leadership; they just want to make a living and live a life of purpose. People who do their best at whatever they do are leaders in their part of the world.

I have loved every job I've ever held. I loved being a cashier, serving with a smile. I loved dipping and gave big scoops. I loved having elboy, spinning platters and

published in the Spring of 2003. Catchy chapter titles include "Your organizational mirror should reflect your face" and "There's no juice in a steamrolled tomato."

"Leadership," by Michael's definition, "is the art of influencing others to work willingly for your goals." What's more, "Leadership is relationship management. Leaders are not born, although natural abilities should not be discounted. Leaders are not made, although motivated individuals can be taught skills and new modalities. Rather, leaders are self-made, and the best leaders are those who lead by example. Leadership is a challenge because it involves change. Leadership is dynamic, not static; flexible, not rigid; inclusive, not exclusive. Leadership requires vision, resolve, courage, compassion, and sometimes steel-willed determination. Leadership is prophetic and redemptive, soothing and blistering, majestic and humble. Leadership comforts the afflicted and afflicts the comfortable."

"Willingly" is the key when it comes to getting others to work toward a set of goals. "You can badger others to do a job. You can demand, threaten, and intimidate to get the job done. But a person convinced against his will remains unconvinced still. You must work

Michael and children celebrate BCH's 115th birthday on November 11, 2000.

to build commitment. The only way to be a leader and motivator is to build it.

"Which means," Michael explains, "not being aloof, but being in the trenches where your soldiers can see your head and heart. At my organization, Baptist Children's Homes, I carry the torch, and seek other torchbearers. I make enthusiasm a contagious part of all we do. Trust enthusiasm to overcome many forms of opposition."

A few years back, he dreamed up a concept he later would name Quality Service Through Quality Relationships (QSTQR). He felt it would answer a pressing need, that in order for BCH to serve children and families across the state the best possible, BCH employees needed to know and appreciate both each other and the vast array of BCH constituents. "I wanted something that everybody in the system could be involved in because everyone in the system would be affected. To improve service by improving relationships and bring an awareness to the staff that we need to change the culture in the way we do business.

"My enthusiasm sparked employee fire that soon smoked me. They got very creative. This BCH cottage prepared lunch for that cottage. Teams made cross-stitched QSTQR logo banners, quilts, and decora-

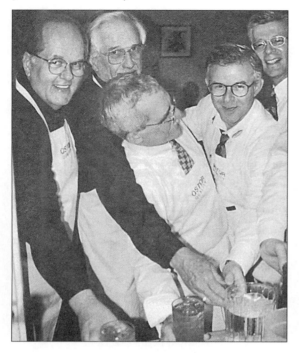

Senior staff members wearing QSTQR aprons.

tions. Others made lunch for child care workers, or delivered a goodie basket to another building, or sent greenhouse plants from the farm to other sites. Many staff members made personal visits to trustees and referral sources. The staffers and the children under their care made more visits to more state Baptist churches to inform them better of the program of services at BCH and how indispensable the program was. We did all we could to cause those congregations to wrap their arms around our ministry."

In time, Michael's fondest hope became reality. "We reached my ultimate goal, to celebrate our ministry and our mission on the threshold of the new millennium in the most rewarding way it was possible to do. That is to say, for the annual offering we would be receiving from North Carolina Baptist churches to top, for the first time ever, the million-dollar mark."

Leading today, he maintains, requires remaining flexible while managing complex relationships. "I expect a lot from my staff, and because they know I care about them, they respond with their best. Once when a key staff member was at the end of her rope after working especially hard, I ignored the employee manual and gave her an extra week of vacation. Exercising flexibility, I call it. It was a good decision. She was thankful, grew more loyal, and worked even harder after that."

Michael knows his staff and trustees well enough that in a crowded meeting room, "I can call any one of them to the front and talk about them, name their children, where they live, their likes and dislikes. That's managing relationships."

"All around," Michael submits, "is proof that leaders are self-made. I find it in Bill Friday, my hero. He grew up in a broken family in tiny Dallas, N.C., used a scholarship to go to college, served in the Navy, and after a stint as a university administrator, became, at age 36, president of one of the nation's finest educational institutions, the University of North

QSTQ
Quality Service Through Quality

EASTER 1

Celebr

THE MILLE

THE MI

THE MIN

THANKSGIVING

Baptist Children's Homes of North
Michael C. Blackwell, president
Thomasville, N.C. 27361-0338
336-474-1222

Carolina. As holder of that office, he was one of North Carolina's most influential leaders. He is retired but his influence has never waned.

"At BCH, we try to provide an environment in which staff members can develop their strengths and rise to their potential, where a sense of mission can prosper. We all want to feel we are contributing. I want each staff member to end each day feeling he or she has done something of value."

It has been said, "Vision is foresight, with insight, based on hindsight." Michael says, "Vision is the mantra of the 21st century."

Michael has recorded these other thoughts and views:

"My leadership philosophy was developed over more than three decades of leading organizations into a brighter, stronger future."

"Like my former pastor, Hoyle Allred, I believe leadership is about relationships, mutual respect, valuing one another, teamwork, and fun. In enjoying such relationships, I hope I am inspiring others to develop better relationship skills, while passing along the capacity for love, respect, and caring all across the BCH system."

"To me, leadership, especially in a Christian organization, means spiritual leadership. It is up to me to hold the vision, enthusiasm, and sense of ministry for the entire institution. Spiritual matter is bigger than any one person. It's way beyond me. If I can allow the blessing that's on my BCH ministry to flow through me and bless everyone, they can share the blessing of God. I'm a conduit, a flow-through teabag for blessings. I am leader, guide, and friend."

"A great part of leadership is inspiring your organiza-tion to claim as its own the vision of the president. And I see a part of that inspiration to be helping my marvelous BCH staff draw strength from our remarkable heritage. I want them to do the best possible job in the present, and look with me to the future, planning and taking responsibility for what will come."

"I realize I cannot motivate those under me. Individuals motivate themselves. Motivation is inherent. I can inspire them, which I guess is a form of motivation, but I can't motivate them if they don't want to be motivated."

"Someone said sincerity is the key to success, and once you've learned to fake that, you've got it made. I don't know about that. All

BCH staffers Kristin Liles and Brian Johnson met while working at Cameron Boys Camp and are now married.

I know is, there is no faking genuine caring. Employees look for it in their leader. When you care, you'll earn the authority of leadership."

"The most important leadership function is to have a dream,

Children

October 1999

(Photo by Bryan)

Scrub orphan Daniel Portera with squirrel.

but before evacuation, Kennedy Home had its own water park. Above, Glenn strolls the campus.

Floods Force Pre-Dawn Kennedy Home Evacuation

Flowing Caravan Takes Boys To Thomasville, Girls To Pembroke

Stories By Craig Bird
Associate Editor

Floyd. Flood. Flight.

That three-word progression describes—in a nutshell—the panorama of the pre-dawn evacuation of Kennedy Home. A 3 a.m. phone from the Federal Emergency Management Agency strongly advised residents to abandon the Kinston facility to rising waters of New Creek and Neuse River.

By 5 a.m. a caravan of vans and cars plowed through the floods, carrying approximately 100 children and staff members to safety. The boys headed to Mills Home in Thomasville, the girls to Odum Home in Pembroke.

Speaking of a nutshell: non-humans also benefited from the escape. Unwilling to abandon three newborn squirrels he had rescued the day before, Donald quietly included them with the boxes of personal items the boys packed into the vans.

"I heard them crying while I was walking through the water," the 16-year-old explained. "I was in Raleigh last year when Hurricane Fran hit. I found some orphaned squirrels then too but I couldn't save them. This time when I heard the crying, I knew exactly what it was."

The squeals came from one of the approximately 20 huge trees leveled by the 100 mile per hour winds that pounded Kinston Wednesday night, Sept. 15 and the subsequent floods. Though he had seen several highly agitated water moccasins and clusters of "brown water spiders" and

red ants flushed from their shelters by the deluge, Donald waded into the limbs and leaves. There, already half submerged and soon to be completely underwater, the three squirrels clung precariously to safety, life and each other.

"There was no way I was going to let them drown," Donald stated. "And when we had to leave, there was no way I was going to leave them behind to starve."

By unspoken consensus the trio became both mascots and symbols of the evacuation. Boys took turns coaxing them to take milk from a medicine dropper and holding them, usually wrapped protectively in their shirts or a towel, while they slept.

"I didn't even realize we had squirrels with us until we unloaded at Mills Home," Linda Haynsworth, lead administrator for

(Please see 'Evacuation–' on Page 5)

Kinston Facilities Absorb Major Damage

Five miles east of Kinston there is little that passed that way. But

camped in Cedar Dell, surging at times into the heat ducts and pulling them down. Four feet of water submerged the gym, floor on the basketball

a vision that is in some way ennobling, to communicate it precisely and repeatedly, and to interpret this vision to others who can achieve it by working together. You must constantly and enthusiastically reiterate the vision. You must have the conviction to see that the original vision is not unnecessarily changed by the whims of fashion or tarnished by the immediate problems of the day. At the same time, the vision also needs constant and new expression."

A secret to long-term, effective leadership is refreshment, and the secret to refreshment is not to get boxed in with ideas whose time has come and gone. Smith-Corona, after having asserted, "We make typewriters and we'll stick to that," was swept away by an avalanche of personal computers.

* * *

So there is Michael the tireless BCH president, leader and chief fund-raiser, but, as if that wasn't enough to occupy him fully, there is also Michael the energetic BCH manager and inspirer of the 350 in the BCH work force.

That's a big job and a lot of people, but he is invigorated by the challenge to devise a way to master it and then see to it that it proves to be advantageous for BCH. The chance that he would shrink from this responsibility does not appear to exist.

One of those times Michael could be found in the trenches with employees was in the wake of a hurricane that savaged the eastern part of North Carolina. This tempest, by the name of Floyd, was the most damaging, the most costly natural disaster the state has ever experienced. The flooding it created claimed lives and destroyed properties over nearly a fourth of the state in September 1999.

Kennedy Home girls were transported to BCH's Odum Home in Pembroke. The boys were taken to Mills Home in Thomasville. A few brave souls from the work staff stayed behind to do what was possible to minimize damage. They were joined before long by groups and individuals from other BCH sites. And before the sun went down again, the repair of the Kennedy facilities, a huge undertaking, was well under way.

Michael says he finds the energy to serve as BCH's president by spending time with those BCH serves.

Michael has spoken of having been uplifted by how BCH employees pitched in to put Kennedy Home on its feet again. There was never a time when QSTQR (Quality Service Through Quality Relationships) was more in evidence. "Our staff members emptied their pockets to help their fellow workers in Kinston. Closets and cupboards were emptied to provide clothes and household items for those who were left with nothing.

"Words of encouragement and prayers for peace and safety were offered in great profusion. An undergirding spirit of support was experienced and felt by those directly impacted by the flood."

Most of Michael's assistance was to make certain a swift and sure recovery had begun, and to provide counseling to victims whenever it seemed of benefit. Also, he rolled up his sleeves and helped one staff member free his residence, on the Kennedy Home campus, of the mud and other mess left behind once the high waters had receded.

Having done the best he could to alleviate emotional damage to people, he arranged for a record to be made of the harm to the personal property of those residing on the Kennedy Home campus. This information was submitted to The Duke Endowment of Charlotte, which

215

had set up a Hurricane Floyd relief fund. Duke, in turn, wrote checks to compensate for the losses. Check amounts ranged from $500 to $5,000.

Less than a month later, Michael was honoring a promise to fill the pulpit at Oakmont Baptist Church in Greenville, N.C., one of the places hit hard by the storm and only 25 miles from Kennedy Home. While he was speaking, it began to rain heavily. The congregation could hear it. He was made painfully aware once again of the hurricane heartaches many of those sitting in front of him had endured. Some were glancing upward, apprehensively, wearily. Was more rampaging water on the way? Michael struggled to complete the delivery of a message in which he made a place for stressing the need to be hopeful and trusting.

Skies cleared later in the day, but only after weeks and weeks had passed would North Carolina's Down-Easterners once again be looking to the heavens for blessings, rather than looking anxiously above for signs of a return of weather-borne miseries.

So it seems symbolic in the grand tour of his life — from his modest beginnings in Gastonia to his current position of prestige and responsibility — that he is likely to say, "Just call me Mickey."

Chapter Twenty – *Still Rockin'*

Sitting on the ground, Michael contemplates the Spirit of God.

"The breeze blew across my face, and I felt God's presence," Michael remembered. Looking around the group, Michael could see the same euphoria in the eyes of the others. It was a time to be remembered for years to come.

In 1972, Michael experienced one of two epiphanies of his lifetime at Caswell, a Baptist retreat on the North Carolina coast that would undergird him for the rest of his ministry.

"I, as well as those with me, so strongly felt the presence of God that it seemed we could feel him in the gentle breeze coming off the ocean. It was a most peaceful feeling that came over all of us, that God was reassuring us of his presence. We were not to fear anything in the future. Or, if we did, we were to hark back to that moment when God's presence was so strong."

On July 1, 2003, Michael had been president and chief executive officer of the Baptist Children's Homes of North Carolina for 20 years. He had held those positions, had worn those titles, had been the face, often the personification, of the child and family care institution longer than most of the other individuals — those giants in the field of helping needy children and families who had preceded him. In the long history of BCH, there had been only seven others.

Reaching Career Milepost No. 20 can be made, of course, an occasion to pause and reflect, to size up what had gone before, to ponder what might come. The 61-year-old Michael made it just that, and it proved a time, when looking back, he could rejoice about how much had been accomplished and about how far upward he had traveled. On the other hand, when it came to confronting the tomorrows, he found it, clearly, a time to do some get-down-on-bended-knee, honest-to-God praying. For the moment, where he had been looked far better than where he was going.

Surveying property for Joy Cove Ministries, Boone

DDM Davis House ribbon cutting, Winston-Salem

BCH had grown and expanded readily under his guidance, making secure its claim to being the biggest and best of its kind in the southeast. Growth had been aggressive. More children were benefiting from BCH services. Places had been made to care for more adults with developmental disabilities. Some accommodations had been replaced, modernized, and newly constructed. The size of the staff and the amount of the budgets had been increased. Many of the special gifts had been record-setters, the same as the periodic financial campaigns. Michael had never tired of exercising his extraordinary fundraising skills, the major explanation for the Homes' coffer's good health. He had challenged his trustees time and again. During the 20 years, not once had they say no.

Elmore Cottage dedication, Odum Home

Blackwell Cottage dedication, Mills Home

At the end of those two decades, because of his successes at BCH, his frequent public addresses, his widely published writings, and his far-flung extracurricular activities, he was one of North Carolina's best-known and most influential Baptists. He managed to be so while remaining nonpolitical, a noncombatant. The reputation he had built should have made him extremely proud, just as it had earned the esteem of some of those of stature in the areas in which Michael was most active.

He had not failed to impress Dr. Elizabeth Locke and Rhett N. Mabry. She is past president of The Duke Endowment of Charlotte, one of the nation's foremost foundations. He is director of the Endowment's Child Care Division. They agree, "Dr. Blackwell is indeed a leader in his field and has established an organization that will no doubt thrive well into the future. He has been particularly effective in mobilizing his base to strengthen [BCH's] financial position. It is without question that Baptist Children's Homes is one of the premier residential providers in North Carolina. Obviously, much of it can be attributed to Dr. Blackwell's leadership."

Acquiring the first DDM home, Winston-Salem

Dedication of Lindsay Education Center, Odum Home

The Endowment has given money to BCH annually since 1926, the year it was founded. There exists a "longstanding partnership," one of several with homes in North and South Carolina "that we have enjoyed," Mabry says.

M. Austin Connors Jr., another Michael-watcher, is complimentary of the BCH president's vision. He sees and recognizes "that while children might need to come into residential care for a limited period of time, it was the entire family that was the true client." So now, first attention is paid to the needs of the child, then to those of the family, in the hope the reunion that is likely to follow and will be lasting under the most favorable circumstances possible. If BCH doesn't undertake to make this happen, it may not get done. Public funds usually are not available.

Dedication of Blackwell Cottage, Kennedy Home

Johnson Cottage groundbreaking, Mills Home

With a sweeping look across the state as executive director of Children and Family Services Association–North Carolina, with offices in Raleigh, Connors finds that Michael is identified the closest with the growth, stability, and strength of BCH, but he is also widely recognized as "the tireless spokesperson for children and families, beginning with the Baptist

In mid-2005, Blackwell still makes sure his schedule includes time with children.

denomination and extending throughout North Carolina and beyond."

Connors praises the BCH head's ability "to communicate the message of broken families and children to an ever-expanding audience in North Carolina . . . a passionate voice for the cause of children and their families . . . and a master at fund-raising . . . . Dr. Blackwell has generated the necessary financial resources that have allowed BCH to expand, grow, and build in ways not seen elsewhere in the state. In addition to allowing BCH to have some of the finest facilities available for children, his successful funding efforts have allowed BCH to serve children who had needs but not the public or personal resources necessary for addressing those needs. The availability of funds has allowed BCH a measure of independence that is the envy of others. BCH can chart its own course and not always be subject to short-term trends and directions that come into the child welfare field from time to time."

An echo from Dr. Tony W. Cartledge, editor/president of the Baptist State Convention's **Biblical Recorder**, another someone with eyes and ears trained on events and happenings of social and religious significance in North Carolina: "He is a fund-raiser par excellence, and an effective administrator, along with being a tireless advocate for chil-

dren. . . . The ministries of his BCH have grown to encompass new types of care and categories of people cared for, embracing change when needed and innovating when other models did not exit." And even more telling, perhaps: "People who have worked for him for many years continue to hold him in high regard."

History repeats itself: June 14, 2005, 600 BCH residents and staffers meet for Family Gathering II.

Most discerning of all might have been the findings of Bill Boatwright at a time he took the measure of the man. "Michael," concludes Boatwright, retired director of public relations for the Baptist State Convention of North Carolina, "enjoys an almost unprecedented breadth of support from North Carolina Baptists, an unusual occurrence given the denomination's past 25-year struggles and conflicts. His influence among Baptists goes well beyond his role as president of Baptist Children's Homes. Perhaps no Baptist leader is afforded the opportunity to speak in more churches across the state, from the small village congregations to the megachurches of urban and suburban communities. His constant appeal for cooperation transcends Baptist differences."

He speaks out for many, adds Boatwright, a Michael acquaintance since 1971. "While eloquently garnering support for Baptist child care ministries, he likewise represents the entire denomination's missions, education and benevolent ministries. In a word, he is an excellent spokesman for all North Carolina Baptist causes. And, in a time desperately searching for solid broad-based leadership, Michael Blackwell has few peers."

With such ringing accolades a matter of record, his physician might have advised Michael to calm down and rest on his laurels for a spell, enjoy contemplating what had been achieved, and do what he had often encouraged others to do — pause for refreshment.

Unfortunately, in his case, that was an impossibility. The prolonged slowdown in the national economy had combined with other hardships to produce, at Michael's 20th-year milepost, the worst financial crisis at BCH in 20 years. Giving to charities and nonprofits across the country had spiraled painfully downward. (*The Chronicle of Philanthropy's* annual survey found that donations to the 400 largest charities dropped 1.2 percent in 2001. This after donations had increased an average of 12 percent every year for five straight years.) Stock market reversals had curtailed endowment revenues; insurance costs were climbing; unemployment shot up while personal incomes were going down. The value of BCH's own endowment funds dropped nearly 40-percent during this time. The institution was one of many victims of shortfalls in the Baptist State Convention's Cooperative Missions giving. Its allocation was reduced by $100,000 for the 2002-03 year.

Michael recovering in 2003 from the first of three unanticipated surgeries.

All this time, BCH's cost for providing quality services was on the rise. Overall operating costs had been climbing by more than 11 percent a year.

The 2,106 children being cared for was a record number. A majority were private placements receiving service at a minimal charge, if not at no cost at all because of personal economic conditions. Concurrently, income from the Departments of Social Services had plummeted. They pay BCH for taking over the care of children under their jurisdiction. In 1993, the number was 50 percent of BCH's census. In 2003, it was only 17 percent, a new low. The resulting sharp drop in income from DSS came to $1.3 million annually.

Indeed, earnest praying was in order, not rest. Postponing the start of a search for a way to contend with this mounting adversity was scarcely an option.

One of Michael's prayers was, "Lord, please let me see us through this thing despite my being one-legged." Less than two months before arriving at his 20th anniversary as president, he had elected to undergo surgery (May 20, 2003) for a second time, to repair the Achilles tendon in his right ankle and relieve the nagging pain in his heel caused by an embedded and diseased bone spur. He went home from the hospital with an airbag splint that reached from high on his thigh to his big toe. At home he remained, and getting from one room to another was difficult. But nothing was allowed to prevent the designing of a quick and comprehensive response to the crisis still running hot.

The housebound president made his home the center for strategic planning. A series of meetings were held there. Members of the President's Management Group assembled. They assumed the role of Budget Allocation Committee and set out to find how best to adjust to what Michael stated had been "an overwhelming decline in income."

Once having reviewed how the $18 million budget for 2002-03 had been pared some $1.9 million, Michael and committee persons ultimately concluded, with heavy hearts, that revenue anticipated for the ensuing fiscal year dictated much deeper cuts than those for the year about to end. They designed a plan to reduce a needed $18 million by a total of $4 million, or more than 20 percent, effective with the start of the 2003-04 fiscal year in October. Characterized as "the least disruptive solutions," the plan was promptly approved by BCH trustees, then announced and explained first to the BCH staff and then the public.

Care that BCH children were getting was not to be disturbed, but 60 of the existing 430 beds would temporarily not be utilized. Five cottages at various campuses would close. While no child would be told to leave, the number served during the fiscal year ahead would be about a hundred fewer than the year before. The deadline for job cuts would be before the start of the new fiscal year. Some 69 staff positions were to be abolished, although because of reassignments and leaving vacancies unfilled only about 20 employees on the statewide staff of 350 would lose their jobs, including social workers, child care workers, supervisors, and secretaries. Granting raises was postponed. The Intensive Family Preservation Service, an attempt to keep parents and children together by counseling with them in their homes, was eliminated. Taking away one of the four 10-boy groups at Cameron Boys Camp was pending, and closing the Baptist Maternity

BAPTIST CHILDREN'S HOMES OF NORTH CAROLINA, INC.

Michael C. Blackwell
President

BCH Administration
P.O. Box 338
Thomasville, NC 27361
P. 336.474.1222
F. 336.474.7776
www.bchfamily.org

une 26, 2003

ear Friends and Supporters,

It is important to me that you are among the first to know that Baptist Children's Homes is king necessary actions to respond to serious financial challenges. In response to an overwhelming cline in income and a projected budget deficit of $4 million for fiscal 2003-2004, BCH will make ts to the 2003-2004 budget (effective October 1, 2003). These cuts will result in the closing of e or more cottages on each of BCH's four campuses, the possible reduction of one group at meron Boys Camp, the closing of Baptist Maternity Home in Asheville, the elimination of the ncy's Intensive Family Preservation Services, and a reduction of 68 1/2 budgeted positions. e to positions currently vacant and the reassignment of some staff, the actual net loss of positions 1. This is a regrettable, but necessary step at this time, made more difficult because the lives of individuals will be affected.

This is the second round of budget reductions BCH has enacted this year, but the first sigcant reduction in staff and programs.

For nearly two years, Baptist Children's Homes of North Carolina has faced ever-growing ncial hardships. At a time of dynamic expansion for BCH and increased potential to reach people

225

Michael, in 2005, with Outward Bound group at Devil's Cellar, near the summit of Table Rock Mountain in western North Carolina.

Home in Asheville was ordered. The maternity home had been serving about 20 pregnant girls each year.

 BCH unrestricted reserves were tapped again.

 Coming out of it all unscathed was the quality of service. Michael stressed, "We will continue to give love and our best care to the children and families who come through our doors. We will continue as always to offer hope, help, and healing."

 He was confident the best decisions had been rendered. Time would soon tell. Meanwhile, he was hounded by regrets that so many good employees were losing their jobs. Nothing during his 20 years had been as dire as the financial crunch that had been encountered, and nothing about the crunch was any worse than having to dismiss good workers.

 Never had there been a sterner test of his proclivity to lead, his training to be a leader, his experience as a leader.

Within an e-mail on late developments that went to key trustees, Michael stated, "My senior management staffers have gone way beyond the call of duty to study and then deal with the crisis. For some of us, it has consumed our thoughts 24/7 for many days. Even as I have been recuperating from surgery, I have had staff members at my house almost daily, and have been using the phone and e-mail constantly in seeking solutions. I don't think I have ever prayed more fervently about a situation than I have this one."

 ". . . I am still committed to the task of 'helping hurting children . . . healing broken families.' I am confident despite the pain of these adjustments that BCH will emerge stronger than ever. The vision will not be dimmed."

 On August 1, his cast came off. To celebrate, he and Kathy left on a seven-day vacation. Doctor's orders, no doubt. On his return he would

CELEBRA

Twenty Years o

Dr. Michael C

learn, in addition to the progress of the cutback plan, the outcome of appeals for special contributions from friends of BCH who had been contacted in the hope they would help save some of the programs placed on death row. Baptist churches across the state also heard the plea. One faithful supporter had already put up a challenge gift that would lead to saving the 10-boy group at Cameron Boys Camp slated for elimination.

On September 16, 2003, for the first time since ankle surgery, Michael appeared decked out top-to-toe in his traditional dark suit, white shirt, no-nonsense necktie habiliment. A sign, to be sure, of a return to busy business-as-usual.

The coming-out took place at the semi-annual session on the campus of Mills Home of the BCH board of trustees. This assembly would be special. Trustees gave it a name, "Celebrating 20 Years of Ministry," of Michael's ministry. He had been kept in the dark as to exactly what turn the celebrating might take. Whatever it was to be was scheduled to provide an uplifting conclusion to a meeting dominated by concerns for BCH's financial position. His only expectation was that it would be, as he had insisted, nothing more, if anything, than some sort of bare-bone testimony to what all agreed was his dynamic 20-year reign, or nothing resembling the extravagance of the affair that marked his 15th year. Five years earlier, how to make ends meet had not been a preoccupation.

Once trustees and guests were settled after a recess, fancy brochures were distributed bearing quotations from trustee Chairman James D. Goldston, III, as well as one by Michael himself, conveying a thought or two on leadership, plus a recap of how he had served BCH from 1983-2003. Goldston, as presiding officer, then called on Michael and Kathy to occupy seats of honor so they could witness close-up a succession of salutes to what his leadership had yielded. Young and old dished out the praise, some in word, some in song. A video caught him in action at various BCH events and assemblies.

When it came to her turn, Jennie Counts, a top associate for most of her 16 years at BCH, added levity to her commendations by "name-dropping." There are a number of Michael appellations, she noted. Sometimes he is called "Big Daddy," at others, "the big kahuna," but always to grandchild Gabriella, he's "Boppy."

At the heart of what she had to say was, "[Michael] loves children. Children bring the light into his eyes and the spring into his step. On the darkest days and the saddest of occasions, his demeanor can change in a moment in the presence of a child. That, my friends, is what keeps him going. That is what makes this work worthwhile for him and what causes tears to come to his eyes when a child is in distress. That is what makes him press on to the far reaches of the state to tell the BCH story and to enlist one more dollar and one more friend to ease the plight of hurting children and families." With that she presented to the boss man a memory book loaded with plaudits and letters of praise and appreciation provided by trustees and several others, including North Carolina Gov. Mike Easley and Thomasville Mayor Hubert Leonard.

Other speakers explained why they admire Michael and his work. Evelyn Alexander spoke of Michael's years at Ridge Road Baptist, and Bill Walton spoke of those at Carthage.

It all concluded with comments by Goldston and a presentation of gifts. One was a check in a sealed envelope for Michael from the trustees to spend at and for his pleasure. With that gesture and others, trustees could scarcely conceal that they feel BCH is most fortunate

Faith & Finances

Abounding love and a keen business sense
guide Michael Blackwell's work for the Lord

228

T HE corporation headed by Dr. Michael Blackwell is Thomasville's oldest continuously operating business, but its products can't be found on any store shelves.

BY JERRY BLACKWELDER

product is changing lives."

This year the institution is expecting to

"In business the man or woman at the top has to engender trust among employees in order to accomplish anything," says Blackwell, a Gastonia native and former Baptist pastor.

to have the benefit of Michael's services, and would use most any means to keep the still energetic 61-year-old from leaving for other endeavors. Goldston said, "I thank God for having His man at BCH for 20 years." Indeed, the chairman avowed, it has been a tremendous blessing.

One additional gift was money, too, in an amount that caught most present by surprise. Not for Michael, but a gift for a most needy cause, the BCH general fund. The board members had decided, once aware of the president's veto of a Michael bash, the best way to honor him and his extraordinary ministry at this crucial point in the history of BCH finances was to try to restore some of the cuts in the BCH budget. Those present heard Brenda Gray, BCH executive vice president of development and communications, announce their trying had produced an astonishing $331,174.93. The Trustee Challenge Gift campaign had snowballed nicely after each

President Blackwell leads 600 children and staff members – the entire BCH family – into Mills Home Church on June 14, 2005, at Family Gathering II. The look on his face reflects the depth of humility, gratitude, commitment, pride, and love that children say they feel when they are with him.

of three trustees had come up with a $50,000 challenge. All in all, it was a Godsend for a hurting budget struggling to enable the president's ministry to maintain a high level of help for hurting children, for broken families.

The next day, Michael was back on the front lines. There was much he hoped to accomplish before being awarded his 25-year pin. Reports

A 2005 family portrait: (l to r) Kathy, Michael, Julie, Michael Jr., Gabriella, Aaron

on the special drive for funds to shore up the budget created jubilation. No one had expected the SOS for funds to cause giving in 2003 to increase by 25 percent, a shocker in the hard-hit world of nonprofits.

But even greater energy was being funneled into preparations for making the 2003 Thanksgiving Offering, with a goal of $1,225,000, the blessing so desperately needed.

Some of the spring was back in Michael's step. He had healed nicely from ankle surgery. Still, it was taking more effort than usual to go at full tilt. Something wasn't quite right physically. Something was sapping his energy. He kept wishing he knew just what, or why.

From a sound night's sleep, at 4:30 a.m., he was awakened by searing pain in his abdomen. A short time after his arrival at the Thomasville hospital, doctors had solved the mystery. He needed a gallbladder operation — immediately. Quick action by the medical professionals probably saved his life. His gallbladder was horribly diseased — and, it would turn out, brimming with gallstones. Gangrene had set in. In his surgeon's view, another five days without aggressive medical care and the organ probably would have burst, thereby reducing Michael's chances of drawing another breath to almost zero.

His very first case of needing emergency surgery at a hospital had proved to be a really scary close call.

Where he had been, indeed, was much better than where he happened to have been going of late. A sudden, major health problem piled atop BCH's financial distress formed a burden he had never dreamed he'd have to bear.

The gallbladder was excised October 3 through small abdominal incisions. The prognosis: a rapid recovery. He was discharged October 7, hoping never to return, and with absolutely no warning of the u-turn ahead. Twenty-four hours later, a recurrence of debilitating pain. This time he had been lowered to his knees by what turned out to be an incarcerated hernia. Once in the hospital again, on October 12, a medical team went to work on a hole in his abdominal wall the size of a baseball. No small surgical incisions this time. To make needed repairs, his surgeon had to "open him up."

Hospital discharge came on October 17. No more than a week

later, he was feeling pert again. Two weeks after that, he had returned to his office, in high spirits, re-energized, ready to go — just like it used to be. Prayers for the return of his good health had been answered.

Then, when January 2004 rolled around, it fell to him to step forward and reveal whether the latest annual Thanksgiving offering, now and more crucial than ever, had measured up, or whether it had fallen short. Yes, he rejoiced, the goal of $1.225 million had been met. That and slightly more. The final tally was $1,298,073 or $73,073 more than anybody dreamed could be raised. A combination of an exhaustive solicitation effort by BCH personnel and the compassion of nearly 4,000 Baptist congregations in North Carolina had achieved success-plus once again, but this time it was during an economic slowdown when appeals by non-profits everywhere were disappointing far more often than not. Thanksgiving Offering victories were also realized in 2004 and 2005.

Michael was back behind the microphone for BCH Employee Pride Day.

Gabriella – the Baby Grand – celebrates her first Christmas in 2000.

While changes in the BCH financial picture continued to lift spirits and ease the money jitters, Michael and staff began assigning some of their time and energy to what to do about the future. They soon concluded that another comprehensive strategic plan was due. One decision they made was that, unlike with the others, Michael, proven master at leading, would personally take over the lead of this one, one to be more comprehensive, more far-reaching than any before. He was willing and eager to, as he put it, "ride the lead horse." It was decided as well to employ a planning consultant. This would be Jack Ferner, a professor at the prestigious Babcock Graduate School of Management at Wake Forest University. The first planning session was put on the calendar for February 2004. After almost a year of preparation, the new plan — GuidingStar: Illuminating the Lives of Children and Families — was unveiled in January 2005, and several years would be devoted to producing the desired results. A few parts of the plan would extend to November 11, 2010, or to BCH's 125th anniversary.

As almost always, Michael was both optimistic and enthusiastic.

231

Just Call Me Mickey

"BCH is already a first-class institution. I think by carrying out this new plan we can become a world-class institution." He relished the expectations that the months just ahead would be for him and BCH a period of shoring up and expanding. He would be shooting for the highest profile yet in both the Baptist world and the donor world when, in search of new beneficence, that world-class status and reputation could become a reality.

Michael and BCH personnel celebrated because more cuts in the 2003-04 budget could be restored, that they would be able to reach out further than expected to help those in need. The same held true for the 2005 and 2006 budget.

The GuidingStar Strategic Planning Team, 2005

In a way, it was the best of times for the individual born of trying times in a textile mill village. He and his wife of 38 years were still in love, happy their children were doing well, and that they had a grandchild to spoil. He had a comfortable home in a place he liked to live. He felt right with the Lord. His work was still challenging but enjoyable and fulfilling. He still could supply the energy and imagination it demanded.

It made him proud that he was the chief executive officer of one of the finest child and family care institutions in the world. Planning for the future had been given proper attention. The nation's economy seemed to be on the rebound, heralding happy hunting for him when seeking financial security for needy children and families. Best of all, perhaps, he was completely healthy again. Nothing hurt.

When reflecting, he found he felt at peace with where he had been, what he had accomplished, and where he was going. "I'm just so fortunate. I simply have a good feeling about who and what I am." He would glance heavenward to offer up his gratitude: "To borrow from Paul's message to the Corinthians, blessed be God, even the Father of our Lord Jesus Christ, the Father of mercies, and the God of all comfort."

Over the years and in the many places he has served, Michael Clitus Blackwell has been addressed in several ways: Mickey, the kid in Gastonia and budding DJ; C. Michael Blackwell, the star reporter; Michael Blackwell in graduate school. But folks insisted on calling him Mickey anyway. It was the Rev. Dr. Michael Blackwell, officially, as a pastor, but "Mickey" prevailed with those who knew him personally.

Michael C. Blackwell, from Mill Village to Mills Home. Still Rockin'!!

He was Dr. Michael C. Blackwell when he first came to BCH, and no one there knew him by any other name. But some folks there got wind of "Mickey," and somehow they felt comfortable with it or thought that it gave them the more familiar connection with him they already felt. So it seems symbolic in the grand tour of his life — from his modest beginnings in Gastonia to his current position of prestige and responsibility — that he is most likely to say, "Just call me Mickey."

The journey continues with an address before the Baptist State Convention of North Carolina on November 15, 2005.

ABOUT THE AUTHOR

— Wint Capel —

After graduating in journalism at the University of North Carolina in Chapel Hill and service with the U. S. Army during World War II, Wint Capel, native of Greensboro, N.C., became a newspaperman. He was made editor when the Thomasville (N.C.) *Times* was established as a morning daily, and held that position until retiring 30 years later with the title of Editor Emeritus. He has written three Thomasville histories and other biographies, including that of the first dean of the UNC School of Journalism, O. J. Coffin, and a record-setting Major League Baseball pitcher, a Baptist Children's Homes' product, Johnny Allen of the New York Yankees and Cleveland Indians. Capel died in 2005 shortly after completing the manuscript of this book.

COORDINATING EDITOR

— Jim Edminson —

Jim Edminson directs all communications for Baptist Children's Homes of North Carolina, and he is the editor of the institution's historic monthly publication *Charity & Children*. He enjoys traveling and meeting North Carolina Baptists and other friends of children, taking every opportunity to tell the Home's story. His regular *Charity & Children* column "Homeword" moves and inspires readers with personal anecdotes about home life that is reminiscent and heart warming. He is an expert in the field of communications and is an award-winning designer. Edminson attended Louisiana State University where he earned a BFA. He is married, has four children, and lives in Thomasville, N.C..

INDEX